Family Time

Time is NOT money! If anything, it is MORE important than money. The time we have to care for one another, especially for our children and our elderly, is more precious to us than anything else in the world. Yet, we have more experience accounting for money than we do for time.

In this volume, leading experts in analysis of time-use from across the globe explore the interface between time-use and family policy. They show how social institutions limit the choices that individuals can make about how to divide their time between paid and unpaid work. They challenge conventional surveys that offer simplistic measures of time spent in childcare or elder care. They summarize empirical evidence concerning trends in time devoted to the care of family members and debate ways of assigning a monetary value to this time.

This important book is well researched, well thought through, and well written. It will be highly regarded amongst those interested in the sociology and economics of the family, as well as those with a general interest in gender studies.

Nancy Folbre is Professor of Economics at the University of Massachusetts at Amherst, and staff economist with the Center for Popular Economics. Amongst other books she has written is *Who Pays for the Kids* also published by Routledge.

Michael Bittman is Senior Research Fellow at the University of New South Wales, Australia, Chair of the United Nations Expert Group on Time-Use Surveys and co-author (with Jocelyn Pixley) of *The Double Life of the Family*.

Routledge IAFFE Advances in Feminist Economics

IAFFE aims to increase the visibility and range of economic research on gender; facilitate communication among scholars, policymakers, and activists concerned with women's wellbeing and empowerment; promote discussions among policy-makers about interventions which serve women's needs; educate economists, policymakers, and the general public about feminist perspectives on economic issues; foster feminist evaluations of economics as a discipline; expose the gen-der blindness characteristic of much social science and the ways in which this impoverishes all research even research that does not explicitly concern women's issues; help expand opportunities for women, especially women from underrepresented groups, within economics; and, encourage the inclusion of fem-inist perspectives in the teaching of economics. The IAFFE book series pursues the aims of the organization by providing a forum in which scholars have space to develop their ideas at length and in detail. The series exemplifies the value of feminist research and the high standard of IAFFE sponsored scholarship.

Family Time

The social organization of care

Edited by
Nancy Folbre and Michael Bittman

Routledge
Taylor & Francis Group

LONDON AND NEW YORK

First published 2004
by Routledge
11 New Fetter Lane, London EC4P 4EE

Simultaneously published in the USA and Canada
by Routledge
29 West 35th Street, New York, NY 10001

Routledge is an imprint of the Taylor & Francis Group

© 2004 Nancy Folbre and Michael Bittman for selection and editorial matter;
individual contributors for their contributions

Typeset in Goudy by
Newgen Imaging Systems (P) Ltd, Chennai, India
Printed and bound in Great Britain by
TJ International Ltd, Padstow, Cornwall

British Library Cataloguing in Publication Data
A catalogue record for this book is available from the British Library

Library of Congress Cataloging in Publication Data
A catalog record for this book has been requested

ISBN 0–415–31009–1 (hbk)
ISBN 0–415–31010–5 (pbk)

Contents

Figures

Tables

Contributors

Michael Bittman is a Senior Research Fellow at the Social Policy Research Centre of the University of New South Wales, Sydney, Australia.

Michelle J. Budig is Assistant Professor of Sociology at the University of Massachusetts at Amherst.

Lyn Craig is a Postgraduate Student at the Social Policy Research Centre of the University of New South Wales, Sydney, Australia.

Janet E. Fast is a Professor in the Department of Human Ecology at the University of Alberta in Canada.

Kimberly Fisher is Chief Research Officer, Institute for Social and Economic Research, University of Essex, United Kingdom, and also works with the Social Policy Research Centre of the University of New South Wales, Sydney, Australia.

Nancy Folbre is Professor of Economics at the University of Massachusetts at Amherst.

Anne H. Gauthier holds the Canada Research Chair in Comparative Public Policy, Department of Sociology, University of Calgary.

Duncan Ironmonger is Director of the Households Research Unit of the Department of Economics at the University of Melbourne.

Joseph T. Marchand is a Graduate Student in the Center for Policy Research at the Maxwell School, Syracuse University.

Shelley Pacholok is a Ph.D. candidate in Sociology at Ohio State University.

Timothy M. Smeeding is Director of the Luxembourg Income Study and the Center for Policy Research at the Maxwell School, Syracuse University.

Cathy Thomson is a Research Fellow at the Social Policy Research Centre at the University of New South Wales, Sydney, Australia.

Judy Wajcman is Professor of Sociology in the Research School of Social Sciences at the Australian National University, and a Visiting Centennial Professor in the Gender Institute and Sociology at the London School of Economics.

Douglas A. Wolf is Gerald B. Cramer Professor of Aging Studies at the Center for Policy Research at the Maxwell School, Syracuse University.

Acknowledgments

We gratefully acknowledge the financial support of the MacArthur Research Network on the Family and the Economy, and the support, enthusiasm, comments, and criticisms of participants: Jeanne Brooks-Gunn, Lindsay Chase-Lansdale, Cecilia Conrad, Greg Duncan, Kathryn Edin, Paula England, Irv Garfinkel, Sara McLanahan, Ronald Mincy, Robert Pollak, Timothy Smeeding, and Robert Willis. Bruce Bradbury, Jenny Chalmers, Frank Jones, Melanie Oppenheimer, and Jan Warburton, all made editorial suggestions which improved specific chapters, while Claire Atkinson and James Rice assisted with data preparation and analysis. Special thanks are due to Denise Thompson for improving the readability of much of the manuscript. Joanne Spitz provided invaluable assistance, and our editors at Routledge/Taylor & Francis offered patient encouragement.

Introduction

Michael Bittman and Nancy Folbre

How do families juggle the competing demands of paid employment and care for one another? The ways that people spend their time are surely as important as the ways they spend their money. Opportunities for close personal and emotional interaction are key to the quality of life and the development of human capabilities. Yet, modern accounting systems devote far more attention to money than to time. National statistical agencies have only recently begun to collect systematic time-use diaries that allow for accurate cross-sectional and longitudinal comparisons. The growing availability of these important data intensifies the need to develop strong conceptual frameworks for understanding the ways people allocate their time.

In this volume, we bring together critical analyses of the social organization of time devoted to the care of family members, especially young children and the elderly. Gary Becker and many economists influenced by the Chicago school of neoclassical economic theory express confidence that individuals make efficient decisions regarding time allocation that lead to socially desirable results. We are less optimistic, pointing to ways that the structure of social institutions and altruistic commitments can lead to inefficient and unfair outcomes. Public policies that have evolved without much consideration of their consequences for family life impose significant constraints on individual choices.

The work of caring for dependents creates positive spillovers for society as a whole, creating and maintaining the next generation of workers and citizens. Yet, the individuals who pay the highest costs in terms of both time and money derive few of the pecuniary benefits. Both capitalist firms and public enterprises tend to take the larger supply of human and social capital as a given. They reward and promote individuals who devote themselves to paid work, focusing on outcomes easily measured in the metric of the market. As a result, employees who make substantial time commitments to family or community work generally pay a large social and economic penalty.

The disjuncture between individual and social benefits is intensified by the coordination problems that arise when workers are subject to fierce, "winner-takes-all" conditions in the labor market. Individuals who might prefer to work shorter hours or to take time out of paid employment while their children are young or their parents are in poor health fear displacement by coworkers unencumbered by family responsibilities. In the past, both discriminatory laws and traditional gender norms enforced restrictions on women's participation in paid employment, imposing what might be termed patriarchal constraints on competition.

Thankfully, these constraints have now been loosened. But overconfidence in individual choice has made it difficult to develop new forms of social coordination. It is easier to reduce one's own care time than persuade someone else to take it on. Women have increased the time they devote to paid work far more dramatically than men have increased the amount of time they devote to family care. New professional opportunities for single women are counterbalanced by increases in the relative cost of fulfilling family responsibilities.

The evolution of the welfare state reflects major historical changes in the relationship between the family and the economy. Yet, public policies have failed to keep pace with economic and demographic change. Many citizens of the advanced industrial countries are pushing for programs that could make it easier for families to mediate the conflicting demands of paid and unpaid work. More generous public provision of childcare and paid family leave, as well as improved pay and benefits for part-time employment, could help workers find a better balance.

Many tax policies subsidize traditional breadwinner/caregiver households, but a growing social movement partly inspired by feminist ideals challenges the traditional gender division of labor. Policies encouraging shared responsibility for care as well as shared responsibility for earning income could promote greater equality between men and women and increase the amount of time devoted to family and community responsibilities.

Reliable time-use data has only recently become available in many countries, and many empirical patterns remain unclear. Are people working longer hours than they used to, or shorter ones? Are parents devoting more time to their children, or less? Are fathers taking on more responsibilities for family care, or not? Experts disagree over the extent to which individuals face problems adjusting to shifting demands on their time. These substantive disagreements help explain the importance of a number of methodological issues concerning definitions of work and measures of time-use. A better understanding of these issues can contribute to the development of better social policy.

The chapters in this volume focus on family time, the empirical dimensions of unpaid work devoted to the care of family members. The first part provides an overview of the issues. In "A theory of the misallocation of time," Nancy Folbre addresses issues of individual choice and institutional constraint, and outlines an alternative to traditional economic analysis of time allocation. In "Family time and public policy in the United States," Timothy Smeeding and Joseph Marchand summarize empirical research on time devoted to the care of children, the elderly, the disabled, and to community and volunteer work in the United States. They describe what we know – and do not know – about the causes and consequences of time allocation decisions. Emphasizing the need for more policy relevant research, they conclude with a discussion of priorities for future survey design and data collection.

   The second part confronts the difficulties of accurately defining and measuring "care time." Time-use surveys based on diary methods were designed to capture "activities." Yet, much of the time that individuals devote to the care of others does not fall neatly into a specific activity, or spills over into other activities such as domestic work. The responsibilities of supervising or assisting dependents often limit the ways that caregivers can choose to allocate their time. In "Activity, proximity, or responsibility? Measuring parental childcare time," Michelle Budig and Nancy Folbre explore this issue through a critical analysis of research on historical trends in parental time with children in the United States. In "Making the invisible visible: The life and time(s) of informal caregivers," Michael Bittman, Janet Fast, Kimberly Fisher, and Cathy Thomson focus on efforts to measure the time that caregivers provide to the disabled or frail elderly in Australia and Canada. They compare the results of time-diaries with the more personal and informal accounts caregivers provide in a focus group setting. The insights gained show how the time allocation patterns of adults who provide significant care for the disabled can yield a distinctive "signature" that can lead to more accurate assessment of the costs they incur.

   The efforts to assign a monetary value to childcare and elder care time in part three illustrate many of the methodological concerns described, but also show that time-diary data can illuminate the quantitative dimensions of the care economy. Duncan Ironmonger builds a bridge between microeconomic and macroeconomic analysis in "Bringing up Betty and Bobby: The inputs and outputs of childcare time." He shows that the childcare "industry," properly defined, absorbs more labor time than any other single industry within the market economy. In "Valuing informal elder care," Douglas A. Wolf summarizes existing research and presents results of an analysis of data from the National Long Term Care Survey in the United States. While emphasizing that this monetary value of informal elder care is very high, he argues that it may be overstated by a simplistic application of a replacement cost approach that assigns the same dollar value to every hour of family care time.

   The essays in the fourth part confront the pressures faced by women and men attempting to reconcile their work and family responsibilities. Michael Bittman, Lyn Craig, and Nancy Folbre use Australian data to explore the ways parents change their patterns of time allocation when they utilize formal or informal childcare services. So-called "high quality time" devoted to activities that promote children's development is the most resistant to change. In "Parenting and employment: What time-use surveys show" Michael Bittman investigates why more people report frequent or extreme time-pressure in an era when leisure time has, if anything, increased. The solution to this riddle can be found in increased responsibilities for combining paid work and care, which are associated with leisure-time deprivation. In "The rush hour: The quality of leisure time and gender equity," Michael Bittman and Judy Wajcman use Australian data to reveal quantitative differences that bear on the quality of leisure. Largely because of the care responsibilities described in preceding chapters, women's schedules tend to be more rushed and constrained than those of men.

The last part of the volume uses international comparisons to explore the impact of cultural norms, labor market structures, and policy regimes on the social organization of care. In "The organization of time: A tale of dual-earner families in four countries," Shelley Pacholok and Anne H. Gauthier examine a wide spectrum of policies, showing that some factors contribute to lower levels of total work (paid and unpaid) while others seem to promote greater gender equity. In "Parenthood without penalty: Time-use and public policy in Australia and Finland," Michael Bittman offers a more narrowly focused consideration of similar issues. Both analyses reveal the limits of private renegotiation of care responsibilities, suggesting that public policies provide more effective levers of change.

Part I
The big picture

1 A theory of the misallocation of time

Nancy Folbre

In 1965, Gary Becker published an article entitled "A Theory of the Allocation of Time" that called attention to the productivity of nonmarket work. Laying an important cornerstone of the "new home economics," Becker extended neoclassical economic theory beyond the traditional realm of consumer choice. He also reinforced its most reassuring claim: Individuals pursuing their own self-interest by maximizing their utility make choices that are efficient not only for them, but also for society as a whole. Related contributions by Jacob Mincer (1962) and Reuben Gronau (1973, 1977, 1980) clarify the implications for gender roles: Women choose to specialize in nonmarket production within the home because this represents their best option. Efforts to restrict or modify such choices would likely impose efficiency losses on society as a whole.

This confidence in individual choice finds empirical expression in human capital models that explain wages as the outcome of individual decisions to invest in education and experience. Application to the sexual wage differential is straightforward. Women choose to specialize in nonmarket production because they have a comparative advantage in breastfeeding and infant care. As a result, they accumulate fewer market-specific skills and earn lower wages than men. While this causality is questioned by those who argue that labor market discrimination also plays a role, the underlying theory of time allocation excites little disagreement among economists.[1] New sources of high-quality data on time-use in Canada, Australia, Europe, and the United States remain underutilized by economists, who seldom integrate time-use into models of household decision making (Apps 2002). Many sociologists studying time-use discount Becker's arguments without directly confronting them.

In this essay, I argue that Becker's theory of time allocation and female specialization in nonmarket family work overstates the role of individual decisions and exaggerates the efficiency of social outcomes. Distributional conflict influences decisions made by families and also shapes the social institutions that govern the allocation of time. Time allocation does not conform to the idealized processes of competitive markets because it involves important coordination problems that cannot be solved entirely by the independent decisions of individuals. Time devoted to the care of children and other dependent family members has effects that reach beyond the household. Individuals often face strategic dilemmas in which the difficulties of establishing and enforcing agreements make it unlikely they will get what they want. The social institutions that evolve to help solve these coordination problems are shaped by collective action, and often prove resistant to change even when they lead to inefficient outcomes.

The first section of this chapter reviews the strengths and weaknesses of the neoclassical theory of time allocation, emphasizing the need for situating its insights within a more interdisciplinary approach. The second section focuses on reasons why decentralized individual choices may not lead to efficient outcomes. Time devoted to the production and maintenance of human capabilities creates positive externalities or spillover benefits. Unrestricted competition can increase the opportunity cost of time devoted to family care by contributing to "arms race" and free rider problems. The third section describes some of the social institutions that have emerged as ways of addressing these coordination problems. Cultural norms and legal rules often restrict the length of the work day; discriminatory rules against female participation in wage employment as well as public supports for childrearing have served to limit competitive pressures on the allocation of time to dependents.

That such rules have had some positive effects does not suggest that they have been either efficient or fair. Indeed, a number of explicit and implicit restrictions on maternal employment have historically contributed to the subordination of women. New efforts are underway in many countries to develop more equitable and efficient ways of coordinating paid work and family responsibilities. These efforts have much to gain from an economic analysis of factors that can contribute to the misallocation of time.

The neoclassical theory of time allocation

The strength of the neoclassical approach to human behavior lies in its elegant formulation of the logic of individual choice. In order to explore this logic, most practitioners set aside questions concerning the origins of individual preferences, the initial distribution of assets, and institutional rules. This makes it possible to focus on responses to changes in prices and incomes. It also makes it difficult to question whether a voluntary exchange is "fair" or "unfair." No voluntary exchange takes place unless both parties expect to benefit from it. Hence, voluntary exchanges should lead to a situation in which no person can be made better off without making another worse off (or, in technical terms, Pareto optimality).

Limitations of scope

Some critics reject this emphasis on rational choice out of hand; others, like myself, believe that it offers important insights.[2] The notion that individuals consider the economic consequences of their actions is endorsed by many diverse schools of social thought, and the allocation of time clearly has economic consequences. Indeed, it is difficult to explain the relationship between the historical transition from family-based to wage-based employment and fertility decline without resorting to reasoning similar to that which Becker outlines.

To illustrate the more specific mechanics of his approach, consider an individual who has a choice between specializing in producing goods and services for their own consumption (whether on a family farm or in the home) or working for a wage. The wage is determined by the forces of supply and demand in the labor market, and remains the same no matter how many hours of work are supplied to the market. However, the marginal product of labor devoted to nonmarket work is likely to decline after a certain point, simply because of diminishing returns to labor given a fixed supply of capital and other inputs.

The Rational Economic Man of neoclassical economic theory faces the situation described in Figure 1.1. If we ignore all constraints outside the graph itself, we can predict that he will allocate time to nonmarket work until the value of his product per hour equals the wage. At that point, he is better off reallocating his time to wage employment.[3] Any other choice would entail receiving less income or product for the same amount of work.

It follows that if men face a higher market wage than women, as illustrated in Figure 1.2, they allocate more time to wage employment, and if their marginal product in nonmarket production is lower than that of women, they will specialize even further. In terms of the possibilities pictured on the graph, men's decisions are efficient. Whether they are efficient (or fair) from a larger point of view depends largely on the factors determining the shapes and the shifts of these curves. What if, for instance, men earn higher wages because of discrimination against women, or are less competent in nonmarket production because they are never instructed in what are considered "feminine" skills? An answer to the larger efficiency question requires exploration of counterfactual possibilities that are not in the picture.

By focusing attention on the optimal choice for an individual, given relative prices and payoffs, the neoclassical approach carves out a small piece of a larger

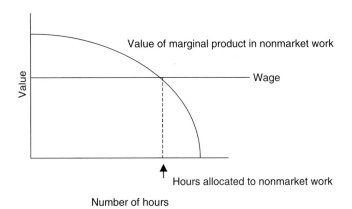

Figure 1.1 The allocation of time between nonmarket work and wage employment: simplest case.

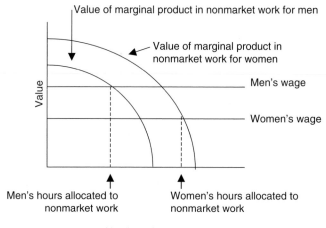

Figure 1.2 Allocation of time with gender differences in productivity and wages.

picture. It tells us something important about what is happening on a microeconomic level. For instance, we can infer that if someone chooses to do nonmarket work at home they must value that work more than the next best alternative use of their time. What we cannot infer – without buying into some very restrictive assumptions – is *why* they value it.

Most neoclassical economists not only take what people want as a given, but argue that preferences do not systematically vary, either across populations or over time (Becker and Stigler 1971). Preferences are, after all, largely unobservable, and it is easy to construct post hoc explanations based on wishful thinking. Gary Becker calls attention to preference formation within families, offering a cogent explanation of why parents might want to inculcate love and altruism in their children (Becker 1996). Yet, he never explores the related question of why societies might want to inculcate solidarity and altruism in their citizens.

Nor is there much interest in which preferences might be considered "good" and which "bad." Indeed, economists consider a type of preference that many people would consider repugnant – perfect selfishness – not only natural, but also desirable in all market transactions. On the other hand, altruism is considered natural and appropriate to family transactions, without much consideration of just how altruistic individuals in the family *should* be.

Prediction problems

Conceding the limited scope of the neoclassical approach reduces but does not eliminate its uncomfortable features. By his own account, Becker (1965) hoped to establish a framework for empirical research. Yet remarkably few studies actually set out to test hypotheses regarding time allocation generated by the neoclassical utility maximization framework.[4] Scholars have articulated a long list of misgivings, many of which relate to the difficulty of making clear predictions that can be empirically tested.

One misgiving first concerns the nature of preferences for household and family work. In nonmarket activities, it seems particularly obvious that individuals derive benefits from the activities themselves as well as from their outputs. A mother may enjoy the process of playing with her child while she provides necessary care for it. The personal pleasure she enjoys will lead her to allocate more time to this activity than she otherwise would. Her preferences are not directly observable. Therefore, it is impossible to determine to what extent her time allocation is shaped by technology (the value of the service she is providing) and to what extent it is shaped by her preferences (the direct utility derived from the activity itself) (Pollak and Wachter 1975; Pollak 1999).[5]

A second problem with empirical predictions concerns the aggregation of individual preferences. Traditional neoclassical theory focuses on individual decision making, but many individuals live in families where decisions to allocate time are shaped by their concern for the welfare of other family members (altruism) as well as strategic expectations of punishment or reward (bargaining). Becker minimizes this problem by treating the family as if it were a single unit, and much of the economic literature on household decision making follows suit.[6] But a substantial body of theoretical and empirical research suggests that individual bargaining power affects family decisions (Folbre 1986; Lundberg and Pollak 1996). Patterns of control over individual income lead to differences in the allocation of consumption; it seems likely that they also affect the allocation of time (Apps and Rees 1997; Apps 2002).

Finally, as many critics of human capital models have pointed out, it is difficult to distinguish cause and effect in family time allocation. Do women tend to devote more time to housework and childcare than men do because their wages are lower, or are their wages lower because they devote more time to housework and childcare? The interpretation can run either way (Hersch and Stratton 1997). Even controlling for hours of market work, it may be that the types of responsibilities that women shoulder within the home reduce the energy and attention that they devote to paid work (Becker 1991). Offered higher wages, however, women might happily unload some of their traditional responsibilities.

More interdisciplinary efforts to explore testable hypotheses could yield valuable insights. Economists are usually skeptical of survey results, but some acknowledge the value of measuring subjective satisfaction (Juster *et al.* 1981; MacDonald and Douthitt 1992). Psychologists offer useful tools for measuring the psychic benefits of different activities, using randomly programmed beepers on experimental subjects instructed to immediately write down their activities and describe their mood (Larson and Richards 1994).

Aggregation problems might be sidestepped by focusing on single-member households (Pollak 1999). Sociologists emphasize that cultural norms or the related process of "doing gender" affect time allocation (Brines 1994; Bittman and Pixley 1997; Bittman *et al.* 2003). Economists could explore this possibility by examining differences in the elasticity of male and female responses to changes in relative prices. Bargaining effects could be untangled by analysis of the relationship between control over nonlabor income and time allocation. The emerging field of experimental economics could also shed light on the factors influencing time allocation decisions.

Valuation problems

Neoclassical economic theory offers some tools for assigning a monetary value to nonmarket work. Not surprisingly, however, a theoretical approach that describes human interactions in terms of voluntary market exchange runs into some conceptual problems outside a market environment. In a perfectly competitive market, the intersection of supply and demand generates an equilibrium price. Outside of a market, no equilibrium price is evident. Efforts to solve this problem and arrive at reasonable estimates of the value of time are often hindered by lack of clarity and consistency in the application of principles such as the labor/leisure trade-off and the substitutability of home- and market-produced goods.

The neoclassical theory of labor supply treats labor and leisure as opposites. Labor is defined as an activity aimed only to generate income, while leisure is defined as an activity engaged in for its sake. In time-use surveys, this distinction is reflected in the so-called "third-person criterion" explicitly articulated by Margaret Reid (1934). Work is defined as an activity that you would be willing to pay someone else to do for you, or, more generally, for which market substitutes are available. That is, cooking a meal is defined as work, because you could hire someone to do this for you, whereas going skiing or watching television are defined as leisure, because you could not hire someone to do this for you.

Several rather time-consuming activities, such as sleep and study, do not seem to fit into either category. Sometimes the distinction seems based more on technological opportunities than actual preferences. Many of us, for instance, would happily pay someone else to study for us if only we could. A bigger problem is that some activities, like childcare, are leisure up to a point, and then become work. That parents are often willing to buy substitutes for their care does not imply that they do not derive intrinsic satisfaction from much of the care they provide. In sum, the third-person criterion offers only a crude approximation of the underlying principle, because it is based on a hypothetical – whether a substitute could be purchased. More relevant to the theory is whether a person would actually choose to purchase a substitute at a particular point in time, which is not directly observable.

Also significant is the evidence that people derive considerable direct satisfaction or "process benefits" from paid employment. Surveys show that most people, on average, enjoy their jobs even if they look forward to the end of the day of Friday (Juster and Dow 1985). In other words, the difficulty of distinguishing between preferences and technology, pointed out above, applies to time allocation in the labor market as well as the home. People may put in extra hours on the job because they enjoy them, not necessarily because they want the extra income. In practice, however, we always consider their extra hours as "work" valued at the market wage.

If all that matters is the satisfaction or utility of the worker, and the disutility of wage employment is simply assumed, why distinguish between nonmarket work and leisure at all? Presumably, individuals would not engage in unpaid work unless they received nonpecuniary satisfaction from it, much like the satisfaction they derive from leisure. Either both activities should be valued the same (at the opportunity cost, often assumed to be the market wage) for a measure of social welfare, and neither should be valued as part of economic output, since both are supplied at no cost other than foregone earnings. Yet if we adopt this reasoning, we arrive at the odd conclusion that an economy in which people spend eight hours a day performing nonmarket work but enjoy no leisure is no better off than an economy in which those same people engage only in leisure, and not at all in nonmarket work. Similarly, an economy in which human activities are motivated by altruism would, by definition, involve less work than an economy in which people cared only about earning money, even if the actual amount of time devoted to productive activities were exactly the same.

What is missing from a valuation based only on the utility of the worker is the consideration of the utility of the consumer. Work can be defined not as activity that necessarily causes a disutility to the worker, but as an activity that provides utility to others, as indicated by the willingness of consumers to buy substitutes for it (a criterion similar to the "third-person criterion"). Altruism complicates the picture here as well: many intrinsically motivated care activities provide unplanned or unexpected benefits for dependents who benefit even if they are incapable of purchasing a market substitute. From this point of view, the appropriate method of valuation is replacement cost (what it would cost the beneficiary to purchase a substitute or replacement) rather than opportunity cost (what the provider could have earned in his or her best alternative activity).

Complete reliance on replacement cost assumes perfect substitutability. This assumption is plausible up to a point. You can wash your own clothes or hire someone to wash them for you. But not all nonmarket activities are as simple as washing clothes. Many involve services that are personal and emotional in character, such as caring for loved ones. Children, the sick, and the infirm elderly are particularly important recipients of care services. Yet many care services are also lavished on fellow adults, often combined with particular physical activities that are better documented in time-use studies than emotional interactions.

Caring is often culturally linked to cooking someone their favorite meal, or bringing them a cup of coffee (Devault and Stimpson 1994). We often perform such activities for expressive rather than purely instrumental purposes. On the other hand, some emotional work takes place even in the absence of what we think of as physical production – taking family members out to dinner is not necessarily pure leisure. Sometimes we set ourselves the task of trying to listen to and engage with other people even when we are not in the mood for it ourselves.

The quality of care services often depends upon the development and maintenance of long-term relationships.[7] Friends offer forms of support and affection that no paid substitute can provide. Parents who purchase large quantities of childcare continue to devote large amounts of time to activities with children (Bittman *et al.*, Chapter 7, this volume). The value added of this emotional labor is difficult to measure. Yet, it is far more consequential for human development and well-being than time devoted to more mundane physical activities such as doing laundry and cleaning house.

In a world of perfect substitutability and consumer sovereignty, the worker's opportunity cost could be interpreted as one bound of the value of nonmarket work and the consumer's replacement cost another bound. But this interpretation does not hold if the value of the purchased substitute (e.g. foster care for an infant) is significantly below the actual value of the nonmarket service (e.g. parental care) measured either in terms of the child's preferences or objective measures of its well-being. Nor does it hold if a care recipient would actually prefer to purchase a substitute for the care that is offered, but is unable to do so for reasons of limited capability. An adult who values a purchased meal over a home-cooked one can simply go out and buy it. A child who would prefer the attentions of a loving foster mother over those of an abusive parent, however, cannot act on this preference.

Altruism, externalities, and coordination problems

The claim that individuals do not always allocate time efficiently does not imply that they systematically misallocate their time. But this latter possibility appears more likely if acknowledgment of the problems outlined above is combined with serious consideration of the combined impact of altruism and coordination problems on forms of time allocation that have positive externalities or spillover effects for the production of human and social capital.

Positive externalities or spillover effects

The concept of altruism can be defined in a number of ways, but economists usually apply it to instances in which someone derives satisfaction from another's well-being.[8] For instance, we usually assume that parents are happier, all else equal, when their children are happier. If you love your wife, you want to please her, etc. From this point of view, "virtue hath its own reward." Individuals may sacrifice some income or leisure for themselves, but are fully compensated by the good feelings they enjoy.

From a subjective point of view, it matters little whether persons are altruistic or not, because they are simply revealing their own preferences. Indeed, one could say (and economists often do) that altruists are simply expressing a different kind of selfishness. But altruistic preferences often lead to unexpected costs or unanticipated benefits (Simon 1992). And while many altruists make decisions, recipients of altruistic transfers often have little choice. They receive a gift whether they ask for it or not. The gift has consequences beyond the good feelings of the gift giver. In some cases, the consequences may be negative (the gift could be inappropriate or harmful). But in many cases, especially where transfers to dependents such as children, the sick, or the disabled are concerned, we expect the consequences to be positive.

One reason these consequences have something in common with externalities is that they create spillovers. For instance, Person A loves Person B, who is seriously disabled. Person A is altruistic and decides to provide Person B with constant attention and care, purely for the pleasure derived from acting on an altruistic preference. Person B benefits. So too do other friends of Person B and the taxpayers who do not need to pay for the institutional care that would otherwise be necessary.

A second example: A father happens to enjoy spending time with his kids, and decides to reduce his career aspirations and spend more time in housework and childcare. As a result, both children and the mother benefit. Neighbors benefit too, because another parent is available to help out others engaging in the same activity (Coleman 1988). Similar spillover effects can occur in the absence of altruism. Suppose that parents like to engage in thoughtful intellectual discussion around the dinner table. As a result, their children develop better verbal skills, and become more productive workers and citizens. All these happy outcomes are generated by what we think of as nice or "socially desirable" preferences, not by a set of rational decisions based on calculations of the value added (England and Folbre 2000).

The concept of externality also seems relevant because the benefits of altruism are often diffuse, with big multiplier effects. The home is a primary site for the production of both human and social capital. Parental education has a significant effect on child outcomes (Leibowitz 1974, 1975, 1977). Children are not the only ones who benefit from the improvement of their own capabilities. Fellow workers, citizens, and future spouses also gain (Folbre 1994a,b; England and Folbre 1999). Both kin work and time devoted to the development of social networks and trusting relationships outside the family increase economic efficiency (Putnam 1995; World Bank 1997).

Neoclassical economists often argue that rational individuals should be able to negotiate an efficient contract that takes the effects of externalities into account (Coase 1960). However, this argument holds only if all the relevant parties can negotiate, which is obviously not the case where young children and other dependents are concerned. The argument also depends on the assumption that property rights can be established for all the relevant resources. Most modern societies, however, reject the concept of property rights over other people. A mother who devotes much of her time and energy to raising a son without any assistance from anyone else, including his father, may hope that her love will be returned, but she knows it will be unlikely that she will ever be literally repaid. She does not enjoy any property rights over his future wealth or earnings (Burggraf 1993, 1997; Wax 1999).

Whatever we decide to call them, the positive spillovers of altruistic forms of time allocation probably increase the social value of some uses of time more than

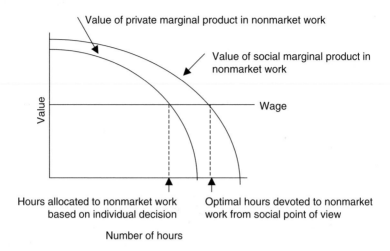

Figure 1.3 Misallocation of time when social returns are greater than private returns.

others. If the social benefits of time devoted to the care of family and community members exceed the private benefits, then individuals making decisions to allocate time between wage work and care work on the basis of the private benefits will over-allocate time to wage employment (see Figure 1.3). The result is a social misallocation of time.

The graph is simplistic, because positive spillovers probably characterize paid employment as well as nonmarket production. For example, people who prefer to take jobs in daycare or nursing even though they are relatively underpaid create positive benefits for society as a whole (England *et al.* 2002). Consider the following counterfactual: How much more would employers need to pay these workers (and how much more would consumers of these services be charged) if the quantity and quality of their labor supply were not increased by altruistic motivation? Even within the family, there can be positive spillovers to paid employment of mothers, when this increases self-respect and provides healthy role models for children (a common rationale for imposing work requirements on welfare recipients).

However, it seems likely that the spillovers created by the altruistic care of dependents and the development of children's capabilities in the family are proportionately greater than those derived from market-based activities. Therefore, it is important to consider the factors that may affect the opportunity cost of such forms of time allocation.

Rat race effects

The classic illustration of circumstances in which decentralized individual decisions can leave all individuals worse off is the Prisoner's Dilemma. If Prisoner A could be assured that Prisoner B will not confess his best strategy is also not to confess. But because A fears that B will confess, he confesses as well (and vice versa). This is the worst outcome for both A and B (although good for the police). They are forced to make a decision in a strategic situation in which the actions of others will influence their own payoffs. The game might just as easily be termed the Free Man's Dilemma, because it describes circumstances in which two actors, unable to make a binding agreement, face uncertainty about the results of their own decisions (Folbre 2001).

This strategic complexity conforms more closely to the everyday world than the neoclassical theory of time allocation, in which individuals do not have to guess what other people will do, but simply take relative prices as given. In Figure 1.1 discussed above, for instance, individual decisions about how many hours to work do not affect wages in the labor market or the marginal product of labor outside the market. In the real world, however, the consequences of time allocation may depend on the structure of payoffs to other workers. Employers may interpret willingness to work long hours as a signal of work effort or commitment (Landers *et al.* 1996). The result can be a race in which the rat that works the longest hours wins, even though the amount of cheese offered as a reward remains unchanged. A "winner take all" tournament leads to a "squirrel-cage" work regime (Schor 1991; Frank and Cook 1995).

For a more specific illustration using a payoff matrix, consider two individuals, Robin and Terry, with identical preferences (see Figure 1.4). Each would prefer to say "no" to overtime in a well-paying job and receive individual payoffs of 5 each. But if one says "no" and the other says "yes" the naysayer will be demoted to a less well-paid job, receiving a payoff of 2, while the other will remain in the well-paid job, but be forced to work over-time, for a payoff of 3.

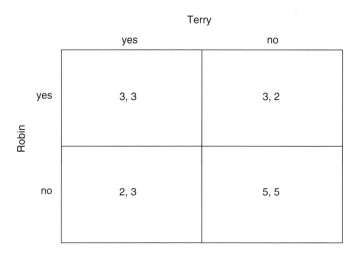

Figure 1.4 Commitments to work "overtime" (payoff to Robin, payoff to Terry).

If Robin and Terry could make a binding agreement with each other and all potential competitors not to work overtime, they could both attain their favored jobs, enjoying a payoff of 5 each for a total of 10. In the absence of such an agreement, they compete with one another by promising to work overtime, settling for a payoff of 3 each or a total of 6.

This model has obvious applications to professional jobs where the length of the working day is seldom fixed. For instance, in prestigious law firms, individuals without job security (i.e. lawyers who are not yet partners in the firm) are not free to choose their hours worked. If they choose to work less than the expected number, which is close to a biological maximum, they will be fired (Williams 2000). Such forms of competition obviously disadvantage those workers who must find time not merely to meet their own basic subsistence needs, but also to care for other people. Do their higher wages fully compensate for their lack of care time? Not unless time and money are perfect substitutes.

Do their extra work hours increase total output? If they come at the expense of leisure time, the answer is probably yes. But if their extra hours come at the expense of time that would otherwise have been devoted to family activities that benefit their children and society as a whole, the answer is probably no.

Children as luxury goods

The rat race outcome depends on a relative shortage of cheese, which is to say a relative abundance of rats. The basic point can be generalized beyond a game-theoretic framework to a competitive labor market with an infinite supply of labor, the world envisioned by many nineteenth-century political economists and often applied to developing countries.

Thomas Robert Malthus argued that if the wage ever exceeded the subsistence level (or if public assistance interfered with the market) workers would marry earlier, conceive more children, increase the supply of labor in the long run, and push wages back to subsistence level. Assume that all workers must sell the services of human capital (or, in Marxian parlance, labor power) by the hour.

In long-run competitive equilibrium, the price of a unit of labor should be exactly equal to its subsistence or maintenance cost and profits should equal zero. Wages should equal subsistence in terms of time as well as money. If we define leisure as a form of surplus, above and beyond the activities needed to actually generate a productive flow of services from human capital in the market, we must conclude that leisure will be driven to zero. Similarly, all nonmarket work that does not offer a rate of return equal to or higher than the wage, such as that involving the unreciprocated care of other people, will be driven to zero. If workers have no fall back at all beyond the sale of labor time to a perfectly competitive market, it is conceivable that the production of children would become an unaffordable luxury.

Gary Becker rightly points out that natural selection should reward altruism within the family (1991). But economic competition among humans is measured in terms of money, unlike competition among species whose success is measured in reproductive fitness. Economic competition can penalize kin-based altruism precisely because such altruism generates externalities not captured by the market. In a capitalist system, unlike a feudal or slave society, employers have no property rights over the next generation of workers. As a result, we would expect them to be reluctant to subsidize time devoted to their care.

The price of love

What if labor is not infinitely abundant, and the demand for it exceeds the supply? In this case, we would expect wage workers to be able to claim not only higher wages but also greater flexibility of choice regarding the length of the paid working day. In general, highly educated workers who are in short supply are in a better position to avoid the competitive pressures described above. In the United States, for instance, women in high-paying occupations generally have greater access to paid and unpaid family leave than do women in other occupations (Gornick and Meyers 2003: 118). But, increases in the bargaining power of workers do not necessarily increase time available for family work. Male dominated trade unions, for instance, tend to bargain for more vacation time rather than the shorter paid workweek that many women would prefer.

Furthermore, increases in wages also lead to increases in the opportunity cost of time devoted to family members. Suppose that individuals are somewhat altruistic, as Becker hypothesizes with respect to family life. This implies constant calculation of the tradeoffs between their own happiness and that of others.[9] Just as a consumer has a set of preferences that determines how she or he will respond to changes in the price of an apple or an orange, a family member will have a set of preferences that determine how she or he will respond to changes in the price of devoting time to the care of another person.

As the opportunity cost of altruistic activities goes up, the relative gain from these activities diminishes, and we would expect their supply to diminish as well. To be more specific, suppose that a father derives pleasure from the well-being and happiness of his infant, but also from the amount of money that he can earn in wage employment. As his wage goes up, the cost of paternal time also increases. All else equal, this should lead to a reduction in the amount of time he allocates to infant care. This is especially true if it is difficult for him to measure the exact value of his time to the infant. As Al and Tipper Gore put it, "at any given moment when a decision between work and family must be made, the workplace has a much stronger ability to quantify and express the immediate cost of neglecting work" (2002: 205).

Should economists worry about this? Not on the father's behalf, since no matter what he decides, he is presumably maximizing his own utility. Should they worry about the infant's welfare? Not if money and time are perfect substitutes, because the increase in paternal income should lead to a compensating increase in money spent on the infant – used, for instance, to purchase someone else's time, or allow another family member, such as the mother, to provide care. But what if neither money and time nor paternal and maternal time are perfect substitutes?

Becker avoids these questions by defining "child quality" as expenditures per child, ignoring possible lack of substitutability with time. In his world, parents respond to the increased opportunity cost of their time by reducing fertility, never by reducing their children's welfare (or opting out of parenting responsibilities altogether, as do many unmarried and divorced fathers). Even if increases in opportunity cost threaten to reduce parental time with children, Becker argues that the demand for child quality goes up with income, a factor that should countervail increases in its price. The actual effects of increases in the opportunity cost of time on altruistic commitments can only be determined by empirical research.

We should worry about the possible under-allocation of parental time to children not only because children have little power to act on their own preferences but also because their choices are constrained by public policies such as paid work requirements for receipt of public assistance (Folbre 2003). Children are not the only ones potentially affected by decreases in the supply of unpaid care time. Some adults are unable to buy the care they need. And, most adults find it necessary to pay a higher price for forms of care that were once taken for granted.

The social regulation of time

Although individuals make many decisions regarding the allocation of their time, many social institutions influence the options available to them. These social institutions evolved for a reason: to help solve the coordination problems described in this chapter. Collectively enforced limits on the working day can be found in most economies. The limits are accomplished by a social norm, such as "no work on the Sabbath" or by an explicit law limiting the length of the workweek or requiring extra or overtime pay. Nor are governments the only regulators of time; most private firms set explicit requirements for participation in employment that restrict individual flexibility.

Social institutions governing time-use are not necessarily efficient or fair. Their evolution is influenced by many forms of collective aggrandizement. The historical record reveals a distinct pattern of restrictions on women's choices in order to ensure a generous and inexpensive supply of domestic labor (Folbre 1994). The founding fathers of neoclassical economics were eloquent advocates of such restrictions. Alfred Marshall argued that women should not be admitted to graduate study at Cambridge University because this might tempt them to neglect their family duties. Stanley Jevons favored a law prohibiting the mothers of children younger than three from wage employment (Folbre and Hartmann 1988). One might conclude that such policies were aimed to solve the "externality" problems described above at women's expense.

In the twentieth century, women's individual freedom and their collective power increased along with their participation in wage employment. In much of Europe, the United States, and Australia, women's right to vote played an important part in the evolution of the welfare state. Many public policies, such as provision of public education and subsidized childcare can be interpreted as efforts to socialize the costs of caring for dependents. Yet many other public policies, especially high rates of marginal taxation on second earners, continue to reduce married women's participation in paid employment in ways that increase the supply of unpaid caring labor in the home (Apps 2002).

Work–family policies designed to reduce the private costs of devoting time to family responsibilities are a focal point of many political campaigns, as are efforts to reduce the length of the paid workweek and minimize the penalties for engaging in part-time work. Such policies can have the effect of reinforcing the traditional gender division of labor, but they can also be designed to encourage greater male participation in family work (Gornick and Meyers 2003).

Neither individual choice nor social regulation guarantee efficient time allocation. But efforts to design institutional rules that provide both individual flexibility and social coordination can benefit from the economic reasoning outlined above. Bargaining within the family over the distribution of care responsibilities can help explain bargaining within the larger polity over policies that affect the relative supply of market and nonmarket labor. And empirical studies of family time that look beyond the effects of individual choices can help explain why caregivers, in particular, often feel unfairly constrained.

Acknowledgments

This paper grew directly out of discussions with Michael Bittman, who also suggested the title. I would like to acknowledge the support of the Visiting Fellows Program of Australian National University, and the MacArthur Research Network on the Family and the Economy. I also benefited from general discussions of these issues with members of the National Academy of Science Panel on the Valuation of Non-market Work. None of the above bear any responsibility for any errors (or opinions) here.

Notes

1 For a broad review of early debates, see England and Farkas (1986). For a clear statement of the argument that discrimination against women in the market "crowds" them into overspecialization in household production, see Apps (1982). For an historical analysis of changes in women's labor force participation based on a neoclassical framework, see Goldin (1990).
2 For a more detailed exposition of these points see chapters 1–3 of Folbre (1994).
3 The total length of the working day would be determined by the marginal utility of income/product compared to the marginal utility of leisure.
4 Kooreman and Kapteyn (1987) also emphasize this point. For an example of a recent application of neoclassical theory to nonmarket time allocation see Hamermesh (2002).
5 Note, however, that the same objection applies to time allocation in market work, once it is conceded that most paid work also yields utility or "process benefits." See later discussion.

6 For an excellent critical review, see Apps (2002).
7 For more discussion of this issue see England and Folbre (1999) and Folbre and Nelson (2001).
8 For a review of this literature, as well as presentation of alternative approaches, see Andreoni (1990) and Margolis (1982). Both scholars point out that altruism may involve a preference for personally providing assistance, rather than simply improving the welfare of another. This distinction is interesting and important but does not have direct implications for the argument developed here.
9 The assumptions of traditional neoclassical theory make it difficult to see how individuals measure the well-being of others in comparison to their own (Folbre and Goodin, forthcoming).

References

Andreoni, J. (1990) "Impure Altruism and Donations to Public Goods. A Theory of Warm Glow Giving," *The Economic Journal*, 100(401): 464–77.

Apps, P. (1982) "Institutional Inequality and Tax Incidence," *Journal of Public Economics*, 18: 217–42.

—— (2002) "Gender, Time Use, and Models of the Household," manuscript, Faculty of Law, University of Sydney, Sydney, Australia.

—— and Rees, R. (1997) "Collective Labor Supply and Household Production," *Journal of Political Economy*, 105: 178–90.

Becker, G. and Stigler, G. (1971) "De Gustibus non Est Disputandum," *American Economic Review*, 67: 76–90.

Becker, G. S. (1965) "A Theory of the Allocation of Time," *The Economic Journal*, 75: 493–517.

—— (1991) *A Treatise on the Family*, Cambridge: Harvard University Press.

—— (1996) *Accounting for Tastes*, Cambridge: Harvard University Press.

Bittman, M. and Pixley, J. (1997) *The Double Life of the Family. Myth, Hope, and Experience*, Sydney: Allen and Unwin.

——, England, P., Sayer, L., Folbre, N., and Matheson, G. (2003) "When Does Gender Trump Money? Bargaining and Time in Household Work," *American Journal of Sociology*, 109: 1.

Brines, J. (1994) "Economic Dependency, Gender, and the Division of Labor at Home," *American Journal of Sociology*, 100: 652–88.

Burggraf, S. (1993) "How Should the Cost of Child Rearing be Distributed? *Challenge*, 37: 48–55.

—— (1997) *The Feminine Economy and Economic Man*, New York: Addison-Wesley.

Coase, R. (1960) "The Problem of Social Cost," *Journal of Law and Economics*, 3: 1–45.

Coleman, J. (1988) "Social Capital in the Creation of Human Capital," *American Journal of Sociology*, 94 (Supplement), S95–120.

Devault, M. J. and Stimpson, C. R. (1994) *Feeding the Family: The Social Organization of Caring as Gendered Work*, Chicago: University of Chicago Press.

England, P. and Farkas, G. (1986) *Households, Employment, and Gender. A Social, Economic, and Demographic View*, New York: Aldine Publishers.

—— and Folbre, N. (1999) "Who Should Pay for the Kids?" *Annals of the American Academy of Political and Social Science*, 561: 39–51.

—— and —— (2000) "Reconceptualizing Human Capital" in Werner Raub and Jeroen Weesie (eds), *The Management of Durable Relations*, Amsterdam: Thela Thesis Publishers.

——, Budig, M. and Folbre, N. (2002) "The Public Benefits and Private Costs of Caring Labor" (with Paula England and Michelle Budig), *Social Problems*, 49: 455–73.

Folbre, N. (1986) "Hearts and Spades: Paradigms of Household Economics," *World Development*, 14: 245–55.

—— (1994a) *Who Pays for the Kids? Gender and the Structures of Constraint*, New York: Routledge.

—— (1994b) "Children as Public Goods," *American Economic Review*, 84: 86–90.

—— (2001) *The Invisible Heart: Economics and Family Values*, New York: The New Press.

—— (2003) "Disincentives to Care: A Critique of U.S. Family Policy," manuscript, Department of Economics, University of Massachusetts.

—— and R. Goodin (2004) "Revealing Altruism," *Review of Social Economy* (Forthcoming).

—— and Hartmann, H. (1988) "The Rhetoric of Self Interest: Selfishness, Altruism, and Gender in Economic Theory," in Arjo Klamer, Donald McCloskey, and Robert Solow (eds), *The Consequences of Economic Rhetoric*, Cambridge: Cambridge University Press, pp. 184–200.

—— and Nelson, J. (2001) "For Love or Money—Or Both?" *The Journal of Economic Perspectives*, 14: 123–40.

Frank, R. and Cook, P. J. (1995) *The Winner-Take-All Society*, New York: Free Press.

Goldin, C. (1990) *Understanding the Gender Gap. An Economic History of American Women*, New York: Oxford University Press.

Gore, A. and Tupper Gose (2002) *Joined at the Heart: The Transformation of the American Family*, New York: Henry Holt and Company.

Gornick, J. C. and Meyers, M. K. (2003) *Families That Work. Policies for Reconciling Parenthood and Employment*, New York: Russell Sage.

Gronau, R. (1973) "The Intrafamily Allocation of Time: The Value of the Housewives' Time," *American Economic Review*, 68: 634–51.

—— (1977) "Leisure, Home Production, and Work—The Theory of the Allocation of Time Revisited," *The Journal of Political Economy*, 85: 1099–124.

—— (1980) "Home Production—A Forgotten Industry," *Review of Economics and Statistics*, 62: 408–16.

Hamermesh, D. S. (2002) "Timing, Togetherness and Time Windfalls," *Journal of Population Economics*, 15: 601–23.

Hersch, J. and Stratton, L. (1997) "Housework, Fixed Effects, and Wages of Married Workers," *Journal of Human Resources*, 32: 285–307.

Juster, F. T. and Dow, G. K. (1985) "Goods, Time, and Well-Being: The Joint Dependence Problem," in F. T. Juster and Frank P. Stafford (eds), *Time, Goods, and Well-Being*, Survey Research Center, Institute for Social Research, University of Michigan.

—— and Courant, P. N. and Dow, G. K. (1981) "A Theoretical Framework for the Measurement of Well-Being," *The Review of Income and Wealth*, 27: 1–31.

Kooreman, P. and Kapteyn, A. (1987) "A Disaggregated Analysis of the Allocation of Time Within the Household," *Journal of Political Economy*, 95(2): 223–49.

Landers, R., Taylor, L., and Rebitzer, J. (1996) "Rat Race Redux: Adverse Selection in the Determination of Work Hours in Law Firms," *American Economic Review*, 86: 329–48.

Larson, R. and Richards, M. H. (1994) *Divergent Realities. The Emotional Lives of Mothers, Fathers, and Adolescents*, New York: Basic Books.

Leibowitz, A. (1974) "Home Investments in Children," *Journal of Political Economy*, 82: S111–31.

—— (1975) "Education and the Allocation of Women's Time," in F. T. Juster (ed.), *Education, Income, and Human Behavior*, New York: McGraw-Hill.

Leibowitz, A. (1977) "Parental Inputs and Children's Achievements," *Journal of Human Resources*, 12: 242–50.

Lundberg, S. and Pollak, R. A. (1996) "Bargaining and Distribution in Marriage," *Journal of Economic Perspectives*, 10: 139–58.

MacDonald, M. and Douthitt, R. A. (1992) "Consumption Theories and Consumers' Assessments of Subjective Well-Being," *The Journal of Consumer Affairs*, 26: 243–61.

Margolis, H. (1982) *Selfishness, Altruism, and Rationality. A Theory of Social Choice*, New York: Cambridge University Press.

Mincer, J. (1962) "The Labor Force Participation of Married Women," in H. G. Lewis (ed.), *Aspects of Labor Economics*, Princeton, NJ: Princeton University Press.

Pollak, R. (1999) "Allocating Time," Draft, Department of Economics, Washington University, St Louis, MO.

Pollak, R. A. and Wachter, M. L. (1979) "The Relevance of the Household Production Function and its Implications for the Allocation of Time," *Journal of Political Economy*, 83: 255–77.

Putnam, R. (1995) "Bowling Alone: America's Declining Social Capital," *Journal of Democracy*, 6: 65–78.

Reid, M. (1934) *The Economics of Household Production*, New York: John Riley.

Schor, J. (1991) *The Overworked American*, New York: Basic Books.

Simon, H. A. (1992) "Altruism and Economics," *Eastern Economic Journal*, 18: 73–83.

Wax, A. (1999) "Is There a Caring Crisis?" *Yale Journal of Regulation*, 16: 327–58.

Williams, J. (2000) *Unbending Gender: Why Family and Work Conflict and What to Do About It*, New York: Oxford University Press.

World Bank (1997) *Expanding the Measure of Wealth. Indicators of Environmentally Sustainable Development*, Washington, DC: The World Bank.

2 Family time and public policy in the United States

Timothy M. Smeeding and Joseph T. Marchand

The analysis of family time-use data and its implications for social policy is a relatively underdeveloped area in the United States.[1] Researchers have only recently come to realize the contribution that nationally representative surveys of time-use could make to important policy debates.[2] Caregiving, volunteer time-use, inputs into human capital formation, time-use by children and adolescents, and more generally the division of work and leisure time within and across households have become topics of controversy in all major industrial countries. The value of time spent in various activities is the last major under-explored resource in the field of household survey research in many nations, especially in the United States.

Macroeconomists have long expressed an interest in measuring the value of nonmarket as well as market production (Kendrick 1970; Eisner 1989; Goldschmidt-Clermont 1993). While these activities remain outside the official system of national accounts, statistical agencies are moving toward "satellite" accounts that include imputations or estimates of their value (Statistics Canada 1995; Australian Bureau of Statistics 2000; Holloway *et al.* 2002). This process is complicated by the difficulty of assigning a market value to nonmarket time.

The economic theory of household production stresses the importance of time as an input into the production of goods that increase well-being as well as a direct source of well-being (Becker 1965). But nonmarket inputs are more difficult to measure than those purchased in the market. Difficult conceptual problems arise as a result of joint production (when nonmarket work produces outputs *and* satisfaction simultaneously) (Pollak and Wachter 1975; Pollak 1991; Gronau 1997). Much depends on assumptions made concerning which activities represent work, and which leisure, and whether a particular use of time is valued by its replacement cost (the price of purchasing a substitute) or its opportunity cost (potential earnings in another activity). All methods of valuation require accurate data regarding time allocation.

In this essay, we provide a broad overview of the literature describing patterns and determinants of time devoted to family and community in the United States, with particular attention to implications for public policy. We focus on studies derived from household surveys and time diaries designed to answer basic questions about time allocation (e.g. Juster and Stafford 1985; Robinson and Godbey 1997) rather than the "experience sampling method" designed to assess psychological well-being (Larson 1989). We cover five major topics: adult time devoted to the care of children and other dependents, the impact of time-use on children's human capital, patterns of time devoted to volunteer work, economic assessments of inequality and poverty, and intra-household inequalities. Age and gender differences in time-use cut through all these topics, and many conceptual overlaps are evident. In the conclusion, we urge greater attention to the issue of who counts what type of time, for what purpose and in what context, and emphasize the need for improved survey design.

Care of children and other dependents

Large amounts of family care are provided to children, the very aged, and the sick or disabled of every age group. Caregiving has many dimensions of quality, quantity, and satisfaction. Some caregiving is intrinsically rewarding (e.g. playing ball with an 8-year-old); some is stressful (e.g. the burden of caring for a demented loved one twenty-four hours a day). Despite these similarities, most studies tend to focus on one demographic group of care recipients. The paths of researchers studying childcare and those studying care for the elderly or disabled seldom intersect.

Time devoted to children

Caregiving for younger healthy children is an important part of every parent's commitment to their children. The topic of trends in overall time spent by parents with children appears to be a straightforward research question but has in fact proven to be difficult to pin down (Budig and Folbre, Chapter 3, this volume). If time spent with children is a normal consumption good, individuals should demand more of it as incomes rise (even if work time interferes with parental time). Some evidence suggests that husbands and wives in two-parent families in the United States are spending *more* time in activities with their children today than twenty years ago (Bryant and Zick 1996; Bianchi 2000). Gauthier *et al.* find a similar trend in four additional countries (2003).

Declines in family size have played a role, reducing overall demands on parental time. But mothers have also reduced the time they devote to both housework and to leisure. The "time crunch" that many families experience seems to reflect efforts to devote quality time to children despite increased participation in paid employment (Schor 1991; Goodin *et al.* 2002). Women spend more time with children than do men, but the trends in these measures suggest that coresident parents, at least, are not reducing the time in activities with their own children. Less is known about trends in "secondary time" with children (participating with children in simultaneous activities such as cooking or watching television) or about time when a parent is "on call" or available.

Furthermore, time devoted to subgroups of children, such as those under the age of three, has not been closely tracked.

Differences in the time burden on single- versus two-parent families also deserve closer attention. According to studies based on the 1987–88 National Survey of Families and Households (NSFH), single mothers have less leisure and sleep time and higher levels of stress than do married mothers (Folk 1995). Time-diaries from the mid-1980s indicate that single mothers spent about three hours a week less than married mothers in activities with children, and did not make up the time that children would otherwise have spent with fathers (Robinson and Godbey 1997: 106). Other estimates suggest that children in fatherless households receive about six hours less of parental care per week (Nock and Kingston 1988).

Low earnings and lack of assistance with transportation and other fixed time demands contribute to the constraints that single mothers face (Solberg and Wong 1992; Folk 1995). Issues of child support in terms of money have dominated the policy agenda in the United States for over twenty years. Yet little is known about the way that enforcement of financial responsibilities affects the amount of time that fathers spend with children (Mincy 2002).

The economic costs of caregiving are reflected in low money income (lower future pension entitlements, less pay from work, slower advancement at market work, higher poverty rates) and greater stress. The opportunity costs of time, as well as the cost of other nonmarket goods, seem to be rising (Costa and Kahn 2003). Women provide a disproportionate share of unpaid parental care time, a factor that increases gender inequality. Mothers pay a high price for their commitments to meet family needs (Folbre 1994). Especially large earning penalties are imposed on women who take time out of paid employment to care for children (Shelton 1992; Waldfogel 1997; Budig and England 2001). In addition to lower market income and increased risk of poverty in the event of nonmarriage or divorce, mothers enjoy less leisure time than fathers. Hirsch and Stratton (1997) estimate that the birth of a child adds about five hours of nonmarket work per week for women, but only 0.5 hours for men. The tradeoff between rewards for market work and caregiving appears to be steep.

The United States is the only major rich nation that fails to provide paid parental leave from work. Subsidies for childcare are also far less generous and universal than in most European countries. Societies with pension provisions for homemakers, effective child support enforcement and family leave policies provide better protections for those who specialize in nonmarket work (Shaver and Bradshaw 1995; Jacobs and Gornick 2002). Greater public support for childrearing could reduce the burdens on parents (England and Folbre 2002). A rich literature describes these policy issues in more detail (Gianarelli and Barsimantov 2000; Adams 2001; Jacobs and Gornick 2002; Joesch and Spiess 2002). Public policies have a discernible impact on parental time allocation and more detailed studies of this impact remain a high priority (Pacholok and Gauthier, Chapter 10, this volume; Bittman, Chapter 11, this volume).

Caring for the elderly, ill, and disabled

In a comprehensive study of unpaid caregiving for ill and disabled household members of all ages, 16 percent of all adults and more than 20 percent of women aged 35–64 reported providing care at least once during 1987–88 (Marks 1996). About 40 percent of these caregivers were provided coresidential care; about 60 percent were provided care away from their own home. A full third of disabled or ill care recipients were under age 65. Both the care and the financial assistance provided to coresident frail elders by other household members help lower poverty rates for this population (Rendall and Bahchieva 1997).

Using the 1991 Commonwealth/ICF Survey of those aged 55 and over, Doty (1995) found that 26 percent of those aged 65 and over are involved in caregiving for another person, with 7 percent of all elders providing at least twenty hours of care to another person not living with them. Hunt *et al.* (1997) cite similar findings from the 1997 National Caregiver Survey sponsored by the American Association for Retired Persons. This estimate roughly doubles the fraction of elders who reported receiving regular care on the 1989 National Long Term Care Survey (NLTCS).

Given the large gerontological and disability literature devoted to these issues, it is surprising to find so little in the time-use literature on this topic. As far as we can tell, there are few recent national studies of the intensity of caregiving for the entire population (but see Doty 1995). A recent paper based on the Asset and Health Dynamics of the Oldest Old (AHEAD) survey and covering the 70+ population only begins to tackle the question (Wolf *et al.* 1997). Others have studied how many individuals need long-term care (Stone and Kemper 1990) and the substitution of formal for informal care (Soldo *et al.* 1989). Interest also focuses on the decision of who provides care (e.g. which sibling), the decision of whether any care is provided (e.g. in cases of divorced parents), and the decision of which younger adult provides care within intergenerational households (Pezzin and Schone 1997, 1999; Wolf *et al.* 1997). The amount of care provided in quantitative terms is less well studied and most studies of the quality of that care in terms of respondent burdens are limited to small samples.

Within the literature on caregiving by and for the elderly there is considerable controversy over the definition of "caregiving." For instance, Stone (1991) found that between 2 and 23 percent of the caregivers of the frail elderly were also working in the paid labor market, depending on the definition of caregiving used. Marks (1996), using the 1987 NSFH, found that roughly 12 percent of the elderly provide care to other frail elderly, compared to 26 percent found in the 1991 Commonwealth/ICF Survey. Doty (1995) reported that fewer than 5 percent of primary caregivers of the ADL-impaired elderly have children under age 18, calling into doubt the hypothesis of the "sandwich generation" of women simultaneously caring for their children and their parents. McLanahan and Munson (1990) have noted that childcare has a much larger effect on paid hours worked of middle-aged women than elder care.

While these findings raise the possibility that the burden of elder care is overestimated, the most recent major study of US time-diary data does not even mention the topic (Robinson and Godbey 1997). As with childcare, time spent on behalf of or simply being available or "on call" for the aged and disabled may be as relevant as time actually devoted to activities with them (see Wolf, Chapter 6, this volume; Bittman *et al.*, Chapter 4, this volume). Given the pressures expected in a rapidly aging society where individuals who are 85 and older (about half of whom need assistance) are the fastest growing group in America, time devoted to elder care requires more explicit attention.

We recently attempted to investigate the economic burden of disabled children among a population of low-income women in California (Lukemeyer *et al.* 1998, 2000). While we did not directly assess time inputs into caregiving, we did assess monetary expenses for disabled children and the effect of childhood disability on parental market work. We found that low-income families with severely disabled children spent about 10 percent of their incomes on this disability. These families were more likely to suffer economic hardships (e.g. lack of food, unpaid rent), and were less likely to perform market work than mothers in similar economic circumstances but without disabled children. We found no other recent studies that attempted to measure the economic burden of disabled children in the United States.

The time dimensions of caregiving for severely disabled elders, adults, and children are poorly documented. Equally unclear are the time costs of performing various basic activities by or on behalf of the disabled themselves (Bittman *et al.*, Chapter 4, this volume). Common sense indicates that disability should create extra time costs for achieving basic activities of daily living, but the magnitude of these costs remains unknown. In an era when public policy increasingly stresses the importance of market work for the disabled, via the Americans with Disabilities Act and related policy measures, we know precious little about the time costs of disability to the disabled themselves or to their caregivers (Burkhauser 1997; Yelin 1997).

It has recently been suggested that the childless elderly should pay higher taxes to compensate for the higher costs they will place on society compared to those whose children willingly provide these services at a zero tax price (Wolf 1997). But before we can fully understand these trade-offs we need to better understand the time dimensions of caregiving: its definition, incidence, prevalence, and burden. The effects of parental time allocation on the well-being and development of children deserve special attention.

Time-use and children's human capital

Research on investments of time in human capital in the United States has mainly focused on the costs of education, including foregone earnings (Jorgenson and Fraumeni 1991). In other nations, more attention has been devoted to parental time (Klevmarken and Stafford 1996; Ironmonger, Chapter 5, this volume). Raising children is a far more time-intensive activity than investment in equipment or machinery. Tax laws offer greater subsidies for investments in physical capital than for investments in human capital. Still, high monetary returns to enhanced skills have increased the demand for education and training. The proportion of youths aged 18–22 attending school has risen from 50.1 to 65.5 percent from 1984 to 1994 alone in Organization for Economic Cooperation and Development (OECD) nations and is probably rising still in most countries (Blanchflower and Freeman 1996).[3]

The payoffs to human capital formation for both children and adults go far beyond additional future earnings (Wolfe and Zuvekas 1997; England and Folbre 2000; Meyers *et al.* 2002). They include many other benefits such as greater capabilities for physical functioning (e.g. improved health) and for cognitive functioning (e.g. increased efficiency in household production). These benefits provide returns which largely accrue to individuals and their families and which can be roughly quantified. They also produce external spillovers or benefits for all citizens in the form of greater civic engagement and future tax payments (Dee 2003; Milligan *et al.* 2003). By some estimates, additional years of schooling produce total private returns twice as high as the returns from increased earnings alone (Haveman and Wolfe 1984; Wolfe and Zuvekas 1997). The social benefits add to these private returns. Interest in family time allocation to children overlaps with issues of caregiving and maternal employment relevant to public policy concerns (Presser 1989; England and Folbre 2002).

Time and early child development

Parental time devoted to children lays the foundation for future acquisition of formal human capital. Analysis of the Child Development Supplement of the Panel Study of Income Dynamics offers some important insights (Hofferth and Sandberg 2001; Sandberg and Hofferth 2001). Different levels of completed schooling by children, test scores, and other child outcomes that will eventually produce higher child earnings are one measure of the value of parental investments in young children. Less easily measured, but perhaps equally important, are improvements in noncognitive capabilities that benefit others (England and Folbre 2000). For instance, increased self-regulation among youth can reduce crime and lead to greater social responsibility (Chase-Lansdale *et al.* 1995).

Increased ability to provide high quality care for family members and friends also represents an individual and social benefit. These aspects of human capital development are particularly important in early childhood. Developmental psychologists emphasize the importance of both parents and preschools in developing caregiving capabilities in children (Klebanov *et al.* 1994; Chase-Lansdale *et al.* 1995; Brooks-Gunn *et al.* 2002). The impact of fathers' time allocation on children's capabilities is significant and merits further study (Duncan *et al.* 1996; Yeung *et al.* 2000; Mincy 2002).

While the great bulk of early childhood investment is time provided by parents, we know little about which types of parental activities promote desirable outcomes. Some evidence suggests that reading aloud to children pays large dividends in terms of children's future school performance (Duncan and Brooks-Gunn 1997). A recent thorough survey of the literature suggests that formal early childhood education varies greatly across family types (Meyers *et al.* 2002). Quality of care influences early child and school readiness, but little is known about the way that disparities in care type (informal, formal, family, others) translate into disparities in quality outcomes (Karoly *et al.* 1998). More information concerning differences in time inputs between rich and poor families could help explain the impact of economic circumstances on children's development (Smith *et al.* 1997; Morris *et al.* 2003).

Time investments in and by older children: mentoring and homework

The time-use of adolescents, particularly during nonschool hours, remains something of a mystery (Carnegie Corporation 1992; Harding 1997; Aizer 2002). Considerable evidence shows that children from single-parent families tend to do less well than children from other types of families (McLanahan and Sandefur 1994). This differential may reflect differences in overall parental time inputs. Recent studies (especially Aizer 2002) suggest that children with adult supervision (parent or other adult) are less likely to use harmful substances such as alcohol or drugs, injure someone, or commit petty crimes. It appears that these problems are more likely to arise in dual-earner and single-parent families than in two-parent families with a full-time homemaker. Problems are likely to become particularly acute when adolescents have emotional contact with only one parent.

A growing body of research indicates that adolescent problem behaviors (teen pregnancy, crime, drug use, failure at school) can be reduced by investing time in adolescent human capital building activities. Several small group studies show the effort of mentoring programs on both the prevention of bad adolescent behaviors and the promotion of good behaviors such as college attendance (Johnston 1996). But issues of selection into after-school programs, uneven quality of programs, and low participation rates are problematic (Granger and Gianinno 2003). More research on this topic is sorely needed. The impact of time that individuals invest in themselves through activities such as homework also merits closer study (Leone and Richards 1989).

Maternal employment

The most important policy issue related to parental time-use concerns the impact of maternal employment on young children, a highly contentious issue in the United States (England *et al.* 1994). Much has been written on the effects of welfare reform and the subsequent large increases in paid work time by former TANF (Temporary Assistance to Needy Families) recipients. While policy changes appear to have stabilized and even increased family incomes (especially after taking account of the Earned Income Tax Credit), far less is known about the effects on adult time investments in children, child time-use, and educational outcomes. The effects of welfare reform on child achievement are difficult to ascertain (e.g. see Morris *et al.* 2003 and compare to Chase-Lansdale *et al.* 2003). Maternal employment has not been shown to have a negative effect on academic achievement or child development among pre-teens. However, there is some contention about its effects on adolescent children (Duncan *et al.* 2001; Chase-Lansdale *et al.* 2003; Morris *et al.* 2003).

The literature recently surveyed by Meyers *et al.* (2002) suggests that differences in the quality and quantity of formal care may create serious developmental disadvantages for low-income children who come from less stable homes and face multiple changes in care arrangements as they age. The effects of out-of-home care on infant well-being and child development are highly relevant. A series of studies recently publicized in major newspapers paint a complex picture of outcomes that demand further study (Lewin 2001, 2002; Brooks-Gunn *et al.* 2002; Waldfogel 2002). While full-time employment by both parents during infancy *may* have negative effects on early childhood development, these findings must be put into the context of overall parental time spent with children, quality of care provided, other family and home inputs, and a large array of intervening and confounding variables. These studies suggest that more generous allowances for family leave, better quality childcare for infants, and more flexible working arrangements can offset many potential problems (Duncan and Magnuson 2003).

Volunteer time

At least one widely publicized study of time-use tells Americans that we have more free time than we once did (Robinson and Godbey 1997). But most of this increase in free time comes after retirement from market work. Discretionary time has increased among the elderly from 1880 to 1995, and is forecast to continue (Fogel 1997a,b). OECD data indicates declining labor force participation rates from 1975 to 1995 among older men, particularly those aged 55–64, in almost every nation (OECD 1996). The question of what these retirees do with their time in general, and the extent to which it is devoted to socially useful volunteer activities, is therefore of considerable interest. Of course, elder volunteerism is only one part of the larger question of contributions to building the resources of trust and reciprocity often labeled "social capital."

Robert Putnam's work on social capital (1996) has fostered interest in the extent to which adults engage in activities which build community and neighborhood ties. Recently, Sampson *et al.* (1997) have suggested that "socially cohesive activities" which they term "collective efficacy" can make an important difference in the level of criminal activity in central city neighborhoods. Additional information on time and effort spent in building community ties by all age groups would greatly help clarify many of these debates.

Among adults, Putnam (1996) and others seem to have identified some decline in overall civic activity in America. Freidman (1996) cites Gallup poll studies that show a decline in the incidence of volunteer activity among all adults from 54 to 48 percent from 1983 to 1993. Former President Clinton seized the issue, called a national town meeting, and assigned Colin Powell to reverse the tide. But since then the issue has disappeared from the headlines. What do we know about patterns of volunteering by age?

Voluntary time-use at older ages

Elders seem to have increased capacity to engage in volunteer activities (Bass 1995). Recent studies have cited both the potential and the incidence of such activities (Commonwealth Fund 1993). While those over age 55 providing care outnumber those providing volunteer services by 2 to 1, volunteer work is still an important elder activity (Coleman 1995). This volunteerism takes many forms, not all of which might be considered "charitable giving" (Commonwealth Fund 1993). So far, the research on time-use and volunteering has failed to distinguish between true aid for the disadvantaged (e.g. mentoring troubled youth, working in a soup kitchen), and time spent in more consumption-oriented activities (e.g. serving on the board of the local senior center, or arranging senior citizens bus trips to Atlantic City).

Moreover, a recent paper by Gauthier and Smeeding (2003) suggests that when market work ends, older adults tend to disperse their time among many different areas, with no particular increase in either home production time or volunteer time. A number of programs and policies (e.g. Senior Corps, Foster Grandparents), while small, show great potential to increase altruistic volunteer work among the aged (Peterson and Wendt 1995; Freidman 1996). So far, this potential remains largely unrealized. Questions regarding the determinants of volunteer time (such as differences between those with and without children) remain largely unanswered (Wilson and Musick 1997).

Volunteering and youth

Only in recent years have we come to realize the positive effects of increased volunteer and community work on teens (Allen *et al.* 1994, 1997). This literature mainly emphasizes the positive effects of community-based volunteer efforts on youth themselves (e.g. reduced pregnancy and school dropout rates). Child development researchers have found positive effects of increased community activities among adolescents (Allen *et al.* 1997). Encouragement of teen participation in volunteer work has gone beyond the bounds of demonstration projects such as the Term Outreach Program cited by Allen *et al.* (1994) to become a requirement for graduation in some cities such as Salt Lake City, Utah. National data on the extent of this activity and its effects on those assisted is lacking. However, new evidence suggests that elementary and secondary schooling can help produce the sort of "civic engagement" that improves citizenship (Dee 2003).

Our knowledge of the extent and nature of unpaid volunteer work, community involvement, and their determinants among various age groups is very thin, despite a "national campaign" to increase volunteerism and an increasingly heated debate about the value and determinants of community-level social capital. Periodic collection of detailed data on the nature, extent, and determinants of time devoted to volunteer work and its value to others and to communities is clearly needed.

Economic measurement and time-use

Conventional measures of the money value of output and its distribution are misleading because they ignore the value of nonmarket production. The assumption that only goods and services with an explicit price tag on them affect economic welfare can be termed "money illusion."

This illusion can distort measurement of aggregate output and related economic indicators such as productivity, technological change, and consumer price indices. It can also distort measures of the distribution of real economic well-being across households (Michael 1996). The impact of time-use on income distribution and international comparisons of well-being and its distribution among affluent countries requires far more attention than it has yet received (O'Connor *et al.* 1997).

Macroeconomic measurement

Macroeconomists have a special interest in measurement of the growth of total economic output and related issues of technological change and increased productivity. The movement of economic activity from the home to the market, exemplified by the increase in married women's labor force participation rates in the twentieth century, means that measures of output based on market output alone are misleading (Goldschmidt-Clermont 1993; Harvey and Mukhapadhyay 1996). Much of the gain in family income in the United States in the 1980s and 1990s resulted from increased market hours worked rather than from increased wages due to higher productivity (Levy 1987, 1996).[4] By most measures, the wages of men have declined while increases in hours worked by wives and other workers have kept family income constant.

Research on implicit price-time trade-offs and time spent searching for "best values" are central to accurate measurement of consumer prices (Boskin 1995). If individuals enjoy lower prices only because they spend a longer time shopping, are they really better off? Concerns about the accuracy of national income accounts have prompted many national statistical agencies to begin collecting time-use data as a way of providing "satellite" accounts of the value of nonmarket production (e.g. Statistics Canada 1995). While such aggregate measures of total economic output are useful, the value of unpaid work has important social and political ramifications as well. Because housework, caregiving, and related activities provide benefits to families and to society, it is important to go beyond the conventional macroeconomic perspective and examine the allocation of time across the economic and social spectrum (Goodin *et al.* 2002; Hamermesh 2003; Jacobs and Gerson 2003).

Microeconomic perspectives

"Money illusion" may make some families (such as those with two employed adults) appear better off than families with lower money incomes and only one employed adult, because of failure to account for the value of the nonmarket work that nonemployed adults do in the home. Money illusion may also over-state the economic well-being of low-income single mothers who work for pay compared to those who devote more hours to childcare and housework. Increased labor force participation of women is associated with significant declines in time devoted to household tasks (Juster and Stafford 1991).

Many recent studies of widening income inequality suggest that a prime rea-son for upward money income mobility among households is increased labor force participation by married women, particularly those with children (Karoly and Burtless 1995; Gottschalk and Smeeding 1997; Juhn and Murphy 1997). Downward mobility, on the other hand, is associated both with nonmarital childrearing and divorce (Duncan *et al.* 1994). Differences in female labor force participation and the incidence of single-parent households have significant effects on the level and distribution of money income.

Rough estimates compiled by Gottschalk and Mayer (1995) indicate that fam-ily income in the United States, adjusted for the value of home production, is more equally distributed than conventionally measured income, although trends in both measures of inequality over time are similar. Similar results have been reported for Norway (Aslaksen and Koren 1996). Using a measure of potential market earning capacity of adults, O'Connor *et al.* (1997) found that inequality within each nation narrowed, as did inequalities across countries, although rank ordering of countries by inequality did not change. Additional research on these issues should be a high priority.

Employment is associated with specific costs for childcare, transportation, and clothing, which vary widely by income level and type of worker.[5] A National Academy of Sciences report by Citro and Michael (1995) recommends that some of these costs be deducted from family income in determining poverty status. While this approach offers advantages over conventional measures, it is impor-tant to note that it fails to take account of lost home production (such as cook-ing and cleaning services), differences in the quality of home-produced versus market-purchased services, or lost hours of leisure (Firestone and Shelton 1988). Ethnographic research among recipients and former recipients of public assistance shows that wide differences in market income between families in which a mother works for pay and other families are associated with much smaller differences in consumption levels (Edin and Lein 1997). Some scholars make a strong case for taking account of differences in time available for household production and leisure when calculating poverty rates (Douthitt 1994; Vickery 1997).

Hours worked controversy

Americans spend more time working for pay, on average, than the citizens of other affluent countries. When GDP or "total income" is presented on a "per hour employed" basis, Americans are no richer than Germans, Swedes, or French citizens (Osberg 2002a,b). Yet lack of adequate data has made it difficult to precisely determine trends in time devoted to paid employment. In 1991, Juliet Schor's book *The Overworked American* became a best seller that attracted significant media attention. Its claim that Americans were working more and longer hours for pay was met by a strong critical reaction from time-use scholars, and continues to attract controversy (Juster and Stafford 1992; Robinson and Godbey 1997). Much depends on how time devoted to paid work is defined, but time-use surveys show declining hours of market work for men from 1965 to 1985, while labor force surveys over the 1970–93 period show little change in hours worked but high variance across groups.[6] Furthermore, high variance in hours worked over a specific time period (such as a month or a year) is typical for workers who are self-employed, working on temporary contracts, or outside prime employment age (Bluestone and Rose 1997).[7]

Differences based on age, gender, and family composition are significant. Market work has declined among individuals under age 24 as a result of increased schooling, and among those over age 55 as a result of increased early retirement. Women, overall, have increased their hours of market work. The rise of dual-earner households has increased working hours within an important subset of the larger population (Jacobs and Gerson 1998, 2001, 2003). Many affluent households have at least one member devoting forty-nine or more hours a week to market work. Particularly, dual-earner households with young children are likely to experience time stress (Bittman, Chapter 8, this volume; Jacobs and Gornick 2002). It seems likely that the distribution of work time is becoming more unequal, with some households working many more hours than they would prefer, while others experience unemployment or involuntary part-time employment.

Efforts to pull apart the relative significance of these factors are hampered by the low quality of time-use data available in the United States. While most of the interest in working hours focuses on the late 1990s, the best data available was collected in the 1980s by Robinson and Godbey (1997). Furthermore, their 1985 data are based on a 51 percent response rate to a mail-back survey (1997: 72). One might expect nonrespondents to be more likely to work long hours in employment, but the issue of selective nonresponse is not directly addressed by Robinson and Godbey (1997), Robinson and Bostrom (1994), or Juster and Stafford (1991, 1992). The new American Time Use Survey (ATUS), which will collect information on both time-use and labor force participation, may shed light on this issue in the future (see later discussion).

Intra-household allocation of time

The literature on bargaining in the household and time allocation dates back to research on divorce and the allocation of time to market and nonmarket work (Manser and Brown 1980; McElroy and Horney 1981). Rather than treating households as unitary decision making units, this approach emphasizes individual preferences and bargaining within households based on market income and on power relationships. Non-cooperative bargaining models provide theory and evidence that resources are not simply pooled but are bargained for (Schultz 1990; Lundberg and Pollak 1993, 1994, 1996).

This literature has evolved rapidly toward consideration of such issues as the intrafamily distribution of income (Jenkins and O'Leary 1995; Sutherland 1996), time-use within marriage (Lundberg and Pollak 1996; Bittman *et al.* 2003), the allocation of resources for caregiving and living arrangements (Pezzin and Schone 1997, 1999), the allocation of expenditures and lack of monetary resource pooling (Lundberg *et al.* 1997), and the effects of domestic violence on bargaining and household time-use (Lundberg and Pollak 1997). These models could be extended to include decisions on childbearing and childrearing, geographic location, and other household behaviors which have significant time-use allocation implications.

Some public policy decisions can have obvious household time allocation effects. For instance, Michael (1996) suggests that child support decisions should involve both time (e.g. hours requirements of support by absent parents) and money (normal child support) requirements. And the 1997 US new welfare reform legislation removes some of the bargaining power of low-income women who would otherwise seek divorce as an alternative to a bad marriage and household violence (Lundberg and Pollak 1997; Raphael and Tolman 1997). In each of these instances the allocation of time resources within the household to market versus nonmarket work plays an important role. With better information on time-use for all adults, researchers could develop a better picture of the impact of public policies regarding taxation, family leave, and income transfers (Waldfogel 1997) and the way that individuals value time spent in caring (Folbre 1995, 2001).

Conclusion

The moral of this story is that there is a burgeoning demand by social policy analysts for time-use data. This demand far exceeds the basic needs of macro-economists for estimating aggregate values of nonmarket production. In closing we would like to comment on the prospects for meeting this demand. The US Bureau of Labor Statistics has recently inaugurated the ATUS, with the first wave collected in January 2003 and data to be available in 2004. The ATUS will be included as part of the annual Current Population Survey (CPS), which also collects data on hours of employment, income, and household characteristics. It represents a significant step forward in the analysis of US time-use, and will likely prove valuable for the construction of satellite national income accounts.

However, the ATUS is unlikely to meet the needs of social policy researchers. Because it will collect data on only one individual within each of the sampled households, it will offer only limited insights into the intrafamily distribution of time. Longitudinal data following time-use patterns for the same individuals and households over time would be more useful (Fenstermaker 1996). From an economic perspective, time-use data is of most value when it can be combined with data that also indicates prices for other inputs into household production, such as wages and purchased inputs. Ideally, detailed information on assets and consumption (such as that collected in the Consumer Expenditure Survey) would be included. From a human capital perspective, data on child and adult well-being within surveyed households would be desirable.

We believe that the ATUS could and should be supplemented by other time-use diary collection efforts. Addition of a micro-family time oriented segment to an existing household panel survey, such as the Panel Survey of Income Dynamics (PSID), National Longitudinal Survey of Youth (NLSY), or Survey of Income and Program Participation (SIPP), would yield valuable data. While repeated observations of time-use for the same persons need not be annual, they should be periodic and with special emphasis on significant life events. Specific supplements could investigate particular topics, such as volunteer use of time, or caregiving activities, in greater depth. Another possibility would be addition of a supplement to the regular Consumer Expenditure Survey. This would permit better measurement of the substitutability between time and money, and related issues crucial to measuring prices of goods, services, productivity, and family economic well-being more generally.

Diverse groups of researchers – government, policy analysts, and academics – should be involved in the design of such supplementary surveys, with the resulting questionnaire evaluated by each group before data collection proceeds. This model, followed by the Health and Retirement Study (HRS), and the AHEAD survey sponsored by the National Institutes of Health (NIH), produced a lean "user driven" survey vehicle which contains the maximum amount of valuable information and a minimal amount of waste. It also produced a ready audience of researchers who are eager to make good use of their survey design investment.

Public agencies seeking academic support for data collection activities are well advised to seek and make use of academic and other data user inputs before fielding surveys. A ready armada of survey users who feel they have a vested interest in the data collected by public agencies and its research use are an effective method for building support for the national data infrastructure which is now so heavily under-funded.

One specific vehicle for funding more collection of time-use data might be a National Science Foundation (NSF) funded competition for one or more supplemental modules on time-use to be added to an existing household panel survey (such as the PSID or NLSY) with the competition sponsoring both module planning and implementation of the survey. One criterion for ranking applications for this supplement should be a multi-disciplinary team approach to data collection and initial analysis. The module could be general or more specifically focused on topics such as human capital building, monitoring, volunteerism, or caregiving.

Five years ago, the lack of an ongoing commitment to collecting household based time-use data in the United States was an embarrassment. The new ATUS data is only a partial response to this shortcoming, and in time it will only add to the demand for micro-level studies of time-use. As demonstrated by other chapters in this volume, there is much to be learned by social science researchers and policy analysts from analysis of time-diary data.

Acknowledgments

The authors would like to thank Nancy Folbre, the members of the MacArthur Network on the Family and the Economy, and Robert Michael for their support, reactions, and input into this chapter. We would also like to thank Matt Lyon, Katherin Ross, Kati Foley, and Ann Wicks for their assistance with an earlier draft prepared for a Bureau of Labor Statistics Conference in 1997. In so doing, the authors accept full responsibility for all errors of commission and omission.

Notes

1 While many writers using time-use data address the policy implications of their specific topical interest, our literature search has uncovered only one article specifically addressing the more general issue of time and social policy making (Michael 1996).
2 After a spate of US surveys in the 1960s and 1970s, only one major survey was fielded in the 1980s and one in 1995, before two important new surveys in the late 1990s: the Panel Study of Income Dynamics Child Development Supplement (1997) and the Maryland Family Time Use Survey (1989). The US Bureau of Labor Statistics has begun an annual ATUS as an ongoing supplement to the CPS in 2003. Other nations, especially Australia and Canada, do a much better job at fielding regular, comparable time-use surveys as the papers by Bittman *et al.* (Chapter 4, this volume) and Pacholok and Gauthier (Chapter 10, this volume) attest.
3 Interestingly, the United States has experienced an increase from 62 to 65 percent of 18-year olds in school between 1984 and 1994, among the smallest increase of all OECD nations (Blanchflower and Freeman 1996: 118, table 4.6).
4 Uchitelle (1997) came to the same conclusion for 1995–96 changes in family income.
5 Short *et al.* (1996) report that work-related expenses including transportation averaged about $2,058 per year for those incurring such expenses in 1987 dollars. Childcare costs averaged $3,263 in these 1987 dollars, bringing the total to $5,321. These adjustments can raise poverty rates by 1.5–2.5 percentage points.
6 Robinson and Godbey (1997) do not include time on the job for phone calls or lunch hours in their definition of paid work. Inclusion of work-related travel may differ across surveys. While the CPS has improved methods of data collection on hours worked (as indicated by a declining respondent "spike" at forty hours), significant differences in household- and labor force-based survey methodologies remain problematic. Compare, for instance, Rones *et al.* (1997) to Robinson and Bostrom (1994).
7 A separate but related controversy concerns the issue of overtime and shift work. During an economic boom, the marginal cost to employers of overtime may be less than the cost of new employees, thus increasing overtime hours in some industries. Higher wage workers may decrease evening and night work in response to higher pay and/or rising real incomes from partners' work (Hamermesh 1996).

References

Adams, G. (2001) "Child Care Funding: How Much is Needed and is There Enough?" Paper presented at Brookings Institution Forum, Washington, DC, June 13.

Aizer, A. (2002) "Home Alone: Supervision after School and Child Behavior," Department of Economics Working Paper No. 807. Los Angeles: University of California.

Allen, J. P., Kuperminic, G. P., Philliber, S., and Herre, K. (1994) "Programmatic Prevention of Adolescent Problem Behaviors: The Role of Autonomy, Relatedness, and Volunteer Service in the Teen Outreach Program," *American Journal of Community Psychology*, 22(5): 617–38.

Allen, J. P., Philliber, S., Herrling, S., and Kuperminc, G. P. (1997) "Preventing Teen Pregnancy and Academic Failure: Experimental Evaluation of a Developmentally Based Approach," *Child Development*, 64(4): 729–42.

Aslaksen, I. and Koren, C. (1996) "Unpaid Household Work and the Distribution of Extended Income: The Norwegian Experience," *Feminist Economics*, 2(3): 65–80.

Australian Bureau of Statistics (ABS) (2000) *Unpaid Work and the Australian Economy, 1997*, Canberra: Australian Bureau of Statistics.

Bass, S. A. (ed.) (1995) *Older and Active: How Americans over 55 are Contributing to Society*, New Haven, CT: Yale University Press.

Becker, G. (1965) "A Theory of the Allocation of Time," *Economic Journal*, 75: 483–517.

—— (1981) *A Treatise on the Family*, Cambridge, MA: Harvard University Press.

Bianchi, S. (2000) "Maternal Employment and Time with Children: Dramatic Change or Surprising Continuity?," *Demography*, 37: 401–14.

Bittman, M., England, P., Folbre, N., Matheson, G., and Sayer, L. (2003) "When Does Gender Trump Money? Bargaining and Time in Household Work," *American Journal of Sociology*, (July): 109:1.

Blanchflower, D. G. and Freeman, R. B. (1996) "Growing into Work: Youth and the Labour Market over the 1980s and 1990s," in *The OECD Employment Outlook*, Paris: Organization for Economic Cooperation and Development.

Bluestone, B. and Rose, S. (1997) "Overworked and Underemployed: Unraveling an Economic Enigma," *The American Prospect*, 31: 58–69.

Boskin, M. (1995) "Toward a More Accurate Measure of the Cost of Living," report to Senate Finance Committee from the Advisory Commission to Study the CPI, September 15, 1995.

Brooks-Gunn, J., Han, W., and Waldfogel, J. (2002) "Maternal Employment and Child Cognitive Outcomes in the First Three Years of Life: The NICHD Study of Early Child Care," *Child Development*, 73(4): 1052–72.

Bryant, W. K. and Zick, C. (1996) "Are We Investing Less in the Next Generation? Historical Trends in Time Spent Caring for Children," *Journal of Family and Economic Issues*, 17(Winter): 365–91.

Budig, M. and England, P. (2001) "The Wage Penalty for Motherhood," *American Sociological Review*, 66: 204–25.

Burkhauser, R. V. (1997) "Post-ADA: Are People with Disabilities Expected to Work?," *The Annals*, 549: 71–83.

Carnegie Corporation (1992) *A Matter of Time: Risk and Opportunity in the Nonschool Hours*, New York: Carnegie Corporation.

Chase-Lansdale, P. L., Wakschlag, L. S., and Brooks-Gunn, J. (1995) "A Psychological Perspective on the Development of Caring in Children and Youth: The Role of the Family," *Journal of Adolescence*, 18: 515–56.

——, Moffitt, R. A., Lohman, B. J., Cherlin, A. J., Levine Coley, R., Pittman, L. D., Roff, J., and Votruba-Drzal, E. (2003) "Mothers' Transitions from Welfare to Work and the Well-Being of Preschoolers and Adolescents," *Science*, 299: 1548–52.

Citro, C. and Michael, R. (1995) *Measuring Poverty: A New Approach*, Washington, DC: National Academy of Sciences Press.

Coleman, K. A. (1995) "The Value of Productive Activities of Older Americans," in S. A. Bass (ed.), *Older and Active: How Americans Over 55 are Contributing to Society*, New Haven, CT: Yale University Press.

Commonwealth Fund (1993) *The Untapped Resource: The Final Report of the Americans Over 55 at Work Program*, New York, NY: The Commonwealth Fund, November.

Costa, D. L. and Kahn, M. E. (2003) "The Rising Price of Nonmarket Goods," unpublished manuscript, Massachusetts Institute of Technology.

Dee, T. S. (2003) "Are There Civic Returns to Education?," unpublished manuscript, Swarthmore College.

Doty, P. (1995) "Older Caregivers and the Future of Informal Caregiving," in S. A. Bass (ed.), *Older and Active: How Americans Over 55 are Contributing to Society*, New Haven, CT: Yale University Press.

Douthitt, R. (1994) "Time to Do the Chores? Factoring Home-Production Needs into Measures of Poverty," Discussion Paper no. 1030-94. Institute for Research on Poverty. Madison, WI: University of Wisconsin-Madison, March.

Duncan, G. J. and Brooks-Gunn, J. (1997) *The Consequences of Growing Up Poor*, New York: Russell Sage Foundation.

—— and Magnuson, K. A. (2003) "Promoting the Healthy Development of Young Children," in I. Sawhill (ed.), *One Percent for the Kids: New Policies, Brighter Futures for America's Children*, Washington, DC: Brookings Institution Press, pp. 16–39.

——, Smeeding, T. M., and Rodgers, W. (1994) "Whither the Middle Class?" in D. B. Papadimitriou and E. Wolff (eds), *Poverty and Prosperity in the U.S.A. in the Late Twentieth Century*, New York: Macmillan.

——, Dunifon, R., and Knutson, D. (1996) "Vim Will Win: Long Run Effects of Motivation and Other 'Non-Cognitive' Traits on Success," IPR working papers 96-23, Institute for Policy Research at Northwestern University.

——, Dunifon, R. E., Ward Doran, M. B., and Yeung, W. J. (2001) "How Different are Welfare and Working Families? And Do These Differences Matter for Children's Achievement?" in G. J. Duncan and P. L. Chase-Lansdale (eds), *For Better and For Worse: Welfare Reform and the Well-Being of Children and Families*, New York: Russell Sage Foundation.

Edin, K. and Lein, L. (1997) *Making Ends Meet: How Single Mothers Survive Welfare and Low-Wage Work*, New York: Russell Sage Foundation.

Eisner, R. (1989) *The Total Incomes System of Accounts*, Chicago, IL: The University of Chicago Press.

England, P. and Folbre, N. (2000) "Reconceptualizing Human Capital," in W. Raub and J. Weesie (eds), *The Management of Durable Relations*, Amsterdam: Thela Thesis Publishers, pp. 126–8.

—— and —— (2002) "Reforming the Social Family Contract," in Lindsay Chase-Lansdale and Greg Duncan (eds), *For Better or Worse: Welfare Reform and the Well-Being of Children and Families*, New York: Russell Sage Foundation.

——, Herbert, M. S., Stanek Kilbourne, B., Reid, L. L., and McCreary Megdal, L. (1994) "The Gendered Valuation of Occupations and Skills: Earnings in 1980 Census Occupations," *Social Forces*, 73(1): 65–100.

Fenstermaker, S. (1996) "The Dynamics of Time Use: Context and Meaning," *Journal of Family and Economic Issues*, 17: 231–43.

Firestone, J. and Shelton, B. (1988) "An Estimation of the Effects of Women's Work on Available Leisure Time," *Journal of Family Issues*, 9: 478–95.

Fogel, R. W. (1997a) *The Fourth Great Awakening: The Political Realignment of the 1990s and the Future of Egalitarianism*, Chicago, IL: The University of Chicago Press.

—— (1997b) "Using Secular Trends to Forecast the Scope of the Retirement and Health Problems in 2040 And Beyond," prepared for the Economics of Aging International Health and Retirement Surveys Conference, Oudesijds Voorburgwal, Amsterdam, August.

Folbre, N. (1994). *Who Pays for the Kids? Gender and the Structures of Constraint*, New York: Routledge.

—— (1995) "'Holding Hands at Midnight': The Paradox of Caring Labor," *Feminist Economics*, 1(1): 73–92.

—— (2001) *The Invisible Heart: Economics and Family Values*, New York: The New Press.

Folk, K. F. (1995) "Single Mothers in Various Living Arrangements: Differences in Economic and Time Resources," Working Paper No. 1075-95. Institute for Research on Poverty. Madison, WI: University of Wisconsin-Madison.

Freidman, M. (1996) "The Aging Opportunity: America's Elderly as a Civic Resource," *American Prospect*, 29: 38–43.

Gauthier, A. H. and Smeeding, T. M. (2003) "Historical Trends in the Pattern of Time Use of Older Adults," unpublished manuscript, Center for Policy Research, Syracuse University, Syracuse, NY.

——, ——, and Furstenberg, F. F. Jr (2003) "Do We Invest Less Time in Children? Trends in Parental Time in Selected Industrialized Countries Since the 1970s," unpublished manuscript, Center for Policy Research, Syracuse University, Syracuse, NY.

Giannarelli, L. and Barsimantov, J. (2000) "Child Care Expenses of America's Families," Occasional Paper No. 40. Washington, DC: The Urban Institute.

Goldschmidt-Clermont, L. (1993) "Monetary Valuation of Nonmarket Productive Time: Methodological Considerations," *Review of Income and Wealth*, 39: 419–33.

Goodin, R. E., Rice, J. M., Bittman, M., and Saunders, P. (2002) "The Time-Pressure Illusion: Discretionary Time Versus Free Time," SPRC Discussion Paper No. 115. Social Policy Research Center. Sydney, Australia: University of New South Wales.

Gottschalk, P. and Mayer, S. (1995) "Changes in Home Production and Trends in Economic Inequality," unpublished manuscript, Boston College.

—— and Smeeding, T. M. (1997) "Cross-National Comparisons of Earnings and Income Inequality," *Journal of Economic Literature*, XXXV (June): 633–86.

Granger, R. C. and Gianinno, L. (2003) "Our Evolving Program," William T. Grant Foundation Annual Report, New York, pp. 11–19.

Gronau, R. (1997) "The Theory of Home Production: The Past Ten Years," *Journal of Labor Economics*, 15(2): 197–205.

Hamermesh, D. S. (1996) "The Timing of Work Time over Time," NBER Working Paper No. 5855. Cambridge, MA: National Bureau of Economic Research.

—— (2003) "Routine," NBER Working Paper No. 9440. Cambridge, MA: National Bureau of Economic Research, January.

Harding, D. J. (1997) "Measuring Children's Time Use: A Review of Methodologies and Findings," Working Paper No. 97-1. Bendheim-Thoman Center for Research on Child Wellbeing. Princeton, NJ: Princeton University.

Harvey, A. S. and Mukhapadhyay, A. K. (1996) "The Role of Time Use Studies in Measuring Household Outputs," paper prepared for the Conference of the International Association for Research on Income and Wealth, Lillehammer, Norway.

Haveman, R. and Wolfe, B. (1984) "Schooling and Economic Well-Being: The Role of Nonmarket Effects," *Journal of Human Resources*, 19: 378–407.

Hirsch, J. and Stratton, L. (1997) "Housework, Fixed Effects, and Wages of Married Workers," *Journal of Human Resources*, 32: 285–306.

Hofferth, S. and Sandberg, J. (2001) "How American Children Spend Their Time," *Journal of Marriage and the Family*, 63: 295–308.

Holloway, S., Short, S., and Tamplin, S. (2002) "Household Satellite Account (Experimental) Methodology," London: National Statistics.

Hunt, G., Howe, D., and Takeuchi, J. (1997) "National Caregiver Survey – New Profile," paper presented to the Gerontology Society of America, Cincinnati, Ohio, November.

Jacobs, J. A. and Gerson, K. (1998) "Who are the Overworked Americans?," *Review of Social Economy*, 56: 442–59.

—— and —— (2001) "Overworked Individuals or Overworked Families? Explaining Trends in Work, Leisure and Family Time," *Work and Occupations*, 28: 40–63.

—— and —— (2003) "The Overworked American or the Growth of Leisure?," in J. A. Jacobs and K. Gerson (eds), *The Time Divide: Work, Family and Social Policy in the 21st Century*, Cambridge, MA: Harvard University Press.

—— and Gornick, J. C. (2002) "Hours of Paid Work in Dual-Earner Couples: The U.S. in Cross-National Perspectives," *Sociological Focus*, 35(2): 169–87.

Jenkins, S. and O'Leary, N. (1995) "Modeling Domestic Work Time," *Journal of Population Economics*, 8: 265–79.

Joesch, J. M. and Spiess, C. K. (2002) "European Mothers' Time Spent Looking after Children: Differences and Similarities Across 9 Countries," EPAG working paper no. 31.

Johnston, A. (1996) "Pre-College Programs for At-Risk Youth: Recent Findings and Issues," paper presented to the Association for Public Policy Analysis and Management Annual Research Conferences, Pittsburgh, Pennsylvania, October.

Jorgenson, D. W. and Fraumeni, B. M. (1991) "Investment in Education and U.S. Economic Growth," Discussion Paper No. 1573. Harvard Institute of Economic Research. Cambridge: Harvard University, October.

Juhn, C. and Murphy, K. (1997) "Wage Inequality and Family Labor Supply," *Journal of Labor Economics*, 15: 72–97.

Juster, F. T. and Stafford, F. P. (eds) (1985) *Time Goods and Well-Being*. Ann Arbor, MI: Survey Research Center, Institute for Social Research, University of Michigan.

—— (1991) "The Allocation of Time: Empirical Findings, Behavioral Models and the Problems of Measurement," *Journal of Economic Literature*, 24: 471–523.

—— (1992) "Changes Over The Decades in Time Spent at Work and Leisure: An Assessment of Conflicting Evidence," paper presented at the International Association for Research in Income and Wealth 22nd General Conference. Flims, Switzerland.

Karoly, L. A. and Burtless, G. (1995) "Demographic Change, Rising Earnings Inequality and the Distribution of Personal Well-Being, 1959–1989," *Demography*, 32(3): 379–405.

——, Greenwood, P. W., Everingham, S. S., Hoube, J., Kilburn, M. R., Rydell, C. P., Sanders, M., and Chiesa, J. (1998) *Investing in Our Children: What We Know and Don't Know About the Costs and Benefits of Early Childhood Interventions*, Washington, DC: RAND Corporation.

Kendrick, J. W. (1970) "The Historical Development of National-Income Accounts," *History of Political Economy* II (Fall): 284–315.

Klebanov, P. K., Brooks-Gunn, J., and Duncan, G. J. (1994) "Does Neighborhood and Family Poverty Affect Mothers' Parenting, Mental Health, and Social Support?," *Journal of Marriage and the Family*, 56: 441–5.

Klevmarken, N. A. and Stafford, F. P. (1996) "Measuring Investment in Young Children with Time Diaries," paper presented at the Conference in Honor of Tom Juster, Ann Arbor, MI, December.

Larson, R. (1989) "Beeping Children and Adolescents: A Method for Studying Time Use and Daily Experience," *Journal of Youth and Adolescence*, 18: 511–30.

Leone, C. M. and Richards, M. H. (1989) "Classwork and Homework in Early Adolescence: The Ecology Of Achievement," *Journal of Youth and Adolescence*, 18: 531–48.

Levy, F. (1987) *Dollars and Dreams*, New York: Russell Sage Foundation.

—— (1996) "Where Did All the Money Go? A Laymen's Guide to Recent Trends in U.S. Living Standards," MIT/IPC working paper no. 96-008. MIT Industrial Performance Center, July.

Lewin, T. (2001) "Study Says Little Has Changed in Views on Working Mothers," *New York Times*, September 10.

—— (2002) "A Child Study is a Peek. It's Not the Whole Picture," *New York Times*, July 21.

Lukemeyer, A., Meyers, M. K., and Smeeding, T. M. (1998) "The Cost of Caring: Childhood Disability and Poor Families," *Social Service Review*, 72(2)(June): 209–33.

—— (2000) "Expensive children in poor families: Out-of-pocket expenditures for the care of disabled and chronically ill children in welfare families," *Journal of Marriage and the Family*, 2(62)(May): 399–415.

Lundberg, S. and Pollak, R. A. (1993) "Separate Spheres Bargaining and the Marriage Market," *Journal of Political Economy*, 101(6): 988–1010.

—— and —— (1994) "Noncooperative Bargaining Models of Marriage," *American Economic Review*, 84(2): 132–7.

—— and —— (1996) "Bargaining and Distribution in Marriage," *Journal of Economic Perspectives*, 10(4): 139–58.

—— and —— (1997) "An Intergenerational Model of Domestic Violence," unpublished paper, University of Washington.

——, Pollak, R. A., and Wales, T. J. (1997) "Do Husbands and Wives Pool Their Resources? Evidence From the U.K. Child Benefit," *Journal of Human Resources*, (November): 403–80.

McElroy, M. and Horney, M. J. (1981) "Nash-Bargained Household Decisions: Toward a Generalization of the Theory of Demand," *International Economic Review*, 22(2): 333–49.

McLanahan, S. and Munson, R. (1990) "Caring for the Elderly: Prevalence and Consequences," NSFH working paper no. 18. Madison, WI: University of Wisconsin.

—— and Sandefur, G. (1994) *Growing Up With a Single Parent Family*, Cambridge, MA: Harvard University Press.

Manser, M. and Brown, M. (1980) "Marriage and Household Decision-Making: A Bargaining Analysis," *International Economic Review*, 21(1): 31–44.

Marks, N. F. (1996) "Caregiving Across The Lifespan: National Prevalence and Predictors," *Family Relations*, 45: 27–36.

Meyers, M., Rosenbaum, D., Ruhm, C., and Waldfogel, J. (2002) "Inequality in Early Childhood Education and Care: What Do We Know?," unpublished manuscript, New York: Russell Sage Foundation.

Michael, R. (1996) "Money Illusion: The Importance of Household Time Use in Social Policy Making," *Journal of Family and Economic Issues*, 17: 245–60.

Milligan, K., Moretti, E., and Oreopoulos, P. (2003) "Does Education Improve Citizenship? Evidence from the U.S. and the U.K.," NBER working paper no. 9584. Cambridge, MA: National Bureau of Economic Research, March.

Mincy, R. B. (2002) "Who Should Marry Whom? Multiple Partner Fertility Among New Parents," Fragile Families Working Paper 2002–03-FF, February.

Morris, P., Duncan, G. J., and Clark-Kaufmann, E. (2003) "Child Well-Being in a Year of Welfare Reform: The Sensitivity of Transitions in Development to Policy Change," unpublished manuscript, New York: Manpower Demonstration Research Corporation, April.

Nock, S. and Kingston, P. (1988) "Time With Children: The Impact of Couples' Work-Time Commitments," *Social Forces*, 67: 59–85.

O'Connor, I., Saunders, P., and Smeeding, T. M. (1997) "The Distribution of Welfare: Inequality, Earnings Capacity, and Household Production in a Comparative Perspective," in S. Jenkins, A. Kapteyn, and B. Van Praag (eds), *The Distribution of Household Welfare and Household Production*, Cambridge, UK: Cambridge University Press.

OECD (1996) *Employment Outlook*, Paris: Organization for Economic Cooperation and Development.

Osberg, Lars (2002a) "Time, Money, and Inequality in International Perspective," Luxembourg Working Paper no. 334. Syracuse, New York: Center for Policy Research.

—— (2002b) "How Much Does Work Matter for Inequality? Time, Money, and Inequality in International Perspective," Luxembourg Working Paper no. 326. Syracuse, New York: Center for Policy Research.

Peterson, D. A. and Wendt, P. F. (1995) "Training and Education of Older Americans as Workers and Volunteers," in S. A. Bass (ed.), *Older and Active: How Americans Over 55 are Contributing to Society*, New Haven, CT: Yale University Press.

Pezzin, L. E. and Schone, B. (1997) "The Allocation of Resources in Intergenerational Households: Adult Children and their Elderly Parents," *The American Economic Review*, 87(2): 460–4.

—— and —— (1999) "Parental Marital Disruption and Intergenerational Transfers: An Analysis of Lone Elderly Parents and their Children," *Demography*, 36(3).

Pollak, R. A. (1991) "Welfare Comparisons and Situation Comparisons," *Journal of Econometrics*, 50: 31–48.

—— and Wachter, M. (1975) "The Relevance of the Household Production Function and its Implications for the Allocation of Time," *Journal of Political Economy*, 83(2): 255–77.

Presser, H. (1989) "Can We Make Time for Children? The Economy, Work Schedules, and Child Care," *Demography*, 26: 523–43.

Putnam, R. (1996) "The Strange Disappearance of Civic America," *The American Prospect*, 7(24) December: 34–48.

Raphael, J. and Tolman, R. M. (1997) *Trapped by Poverty/Trapped by Abuse: New Evidence Documenting the Relationship Between Domestic Violence and Welfare*, report from the Project for Research on Welfare, Work, and Domestic Violence. Taylor Institute and the University of Michigan Research Development Center on Poverty, Risk and Mental Health, April.

Rendall, M. S. and Bahchieva, R. A. (1997) "An Old-Age Security Motive for Fertility in Developed Countries? The Large Contribution of Coresident Family to the Poverty Alleviation of Unmarried and Disabled Elderly in the United States," Population and Development Working Paper, 1997 Series. Ithaca, NY: Cornell University, June.

Robinson, J. P. and Bostrom, A. (1994) "The Overestimated Workweek? What Time Diary Measures Suggest," *Monthly Labor Review* (August): 11–23.

—— and Godbey, G. (1997) *Time for Life: The Surprising Ways Americans Use Their Time*. University Park, PA: The Pennsylvania State University Press.

Rones, P. L., Ilg., R. E., and Gardner, J. M. (1997) "Trends in Hours of Work Since the Mid-1970s," *Monthly Labor Review* (April): 3–14.

Sampson, R., Raudenbusch, W., and Earls, F. (1997) "Neighborhoods and Violent Crime: A Multilevel Study of Collective Efficiency," *Science* (August): 2–8.

Sandberg, J. F., and Hofferth, S. L. (2001) "Changes in Children's Time with Parents: United States, 1981–1997," *Demography*, 38: 423–36.

Schor, J. B. (1991) *The Overworked American: The Unexpected Decline of Leisure*, New York: Basic Books.

Schultz, T. P. (1990) "Testing the Neoclassical Model of Family Labor Supply and Fertility," *Journal of Human Resources*, 25(4): 599–634.

Shaver, S. and Bradshaw, J. (1995) "The Recognition of Wifely Labor by the Welfare State," *Social Policy and Administration*, 29(1): 10–25.

Shelton, B. (1992) *Women, Men, and Time: Gender Differences in Paid Work, Housework, and Leisure*, New York: Greenwood Press.

Short, K., Shea, M., and Eller, T. J. (1996) "Work Related Expenditures in a New Measure of Poverty," Poverty Measurement Working Paper. Mimeo, Washington, DC: US Census Bureau.

Smith, J. R., Brooks-Gunn, J., and Klebanov, P. K. (1997) "The Consequences of Growing Up Poor," in G. J. Duncan and J. Brooks-Gunn (eds), *The Consequences of Growing Up Poor*, New York: Russell Sage Foundation.

Solberg, E. and Wong, D. (1992) "Family Time Use: Leisure, Home Production, Market Work, and Work Related Travel," *Journal of Human Resources*, 27: 485–510.

Soldo, B. J., Agree, E. M., and Wolf, D. A. (1989) "The Balance Between Formal and Informal Care," in M. G. Ory and K. Bond (eds), *Aging and Health Care: Social and Policy Perspectives*, London: Routledge.

Statistics Canada (1995) *Households' Unpaid Work: Measurement and Valuation*, Studies in National Accounting, ISSN 1192–0106. Ottawa: Statistics Canada.

Stone, R. (1991) "Defining Family Caregivers of the Elderly: Implications for Research and Public Policy," *Gerontologist*, 31: 724–5.

—— and Kemper, P. (1990) "Spouses and Children of Disabled Elders: How Large a Constituency for Long-Term Care Reform?," *Milbank Memorial Fund Quarterly*, 76: 485-505.

Sutherland, H. (1996) "Households, Individuals and the Re-Distribution of Income," Microsimulation Unit Discussion Paper MU9601, Department of Applied Economics, Cambridge.

Uchitelle, L. (1997) "More Work, Less Play Make Jack Look Better Off," *New York Times*, October 5.

Vickery, C. (1997) "The Time Poor: A New Look at Poverty," *Journal of Human Resources*, 12(1): 27–48.

Waldfogel, J. (1997) "The Effect of Children on Women's Wages," *American Sociological Review*, 62(2): 209–17.

—— (2002) "Child Care, Women's Employment, and Child Outcomes," *Journal of Population Economics*, 15: 527–48.

Wilson, J. and Musick, M. (1997) "Who Cares? Toward an Integrated Theory of Volunteer Work," *American Sociological Review*, 62: 694–713.

Wolf, D. A. (1997) "Efficiency in the Allocation and Targeting of Community-Based Long-Term Care Resources," unpublished paper, Center for Policy Research, Syracuse University, June.

——, Freeman, V., and Soldo, B. J. (1997) "The Division of Family Labor: Care for Elderly Parents," *The Journals of Gerontology: Series B: Psychological and Social Sciences*, 52B: 102–9.

Wolfe, B. and Zuvekas, S. (1997) "Nonmarket Outcomes of Schooling," *International Journal of Educational Research*, 27(6): 491–502.

Yelin, E. H. (1997) "The Employment of People with and Without Disabilities in an Age of Insecurity," *Annals of the Association of American Political and Social Science*, 549(1): 117–28.

Yeung, J., Duncan, G., and Hill, M. (2000) "Putting Fathers Back into the Picture: Parental Activities and Children's Adult Outcomes," *Marriage and Family Review*, 29(2/3): 97–113.

Part II

Using the yardstick of time to capture care

3 Activity, proximity, or responsibility?

Measuring parental childcare time

Michelle J. Budig and Nancy Folbre

"Study Sees No Change in Mothering Time" and "Kids Seeing More of Mom and Dad." Newspaper headlines trumpet the claim that parents in the United States spend as much – or more – time with their children than they did twenty or thirty years ago.[1] Widespread concern about the effects of mothers' increased labor force participation creates an eager audience for research on trends in parental time with children. Analysis of time-use surveys provides a scientific way of addressing these concerns.

Yet, the empirical analysis of parental time devoted to the care of children remains a relatively new field. Most surveys of time-use were not designed with the specific characteristics of care work in mind. US researchers have been forced to rely on a patchwork of small surveys that make it difficult to go beyond a superficial level of analysis. The new annual American Time Use Survey (ATUS) launched by the US Bureau of Labor Statistics (BLS) in 2003 represents a significant step forward in data availability, but makes it all the more important to directly confront a basic conceptual problem: how should parental care time be defined?

Does "maternal time with children" include only the time a mother spends engaging in activities with her child or does it also include time when she is available in the same room, or even "on call" elsewhere in the home while the child is sleeping? The qualitative dimensions of time-use pose additional conceptual problems. Most existing surveys fail to capture important dimensions of timing and intensity, including overlaps among those providing and those receiving care. A mother and a father may both report an hour of care activity, but it is often difficult to ascertain if this care is provided simultaneously or at separate times. Likewise, it is often difficult to determine whether one, two, or more children are being cared for at the same time. Simply dividing total care time by number of children gives misleading results.

Time-use diaries capturing childcare time in the United States often rely on imprecise measures, and many are based on unrepresentative samples. Three surveys (those conducted by Thomas Juster and others at the University of Michigan, by John Robinson and Suzanne Bianchi at the University of Maryland, and by the Children's Development Supplement of the Panel Study of Income Dynamics) are sufficiently consistent and representative to allow comparisons of national trends over time. However, small sample sizes make it difficult to ascertain potentially important differences in trends among subgroups of the population, such as unmarried parents and those with children under the age of three.

Our criticisms do not invalidate the important findings reported by Bryant and Zick (1996a), Bianchi (2000), Sandberg and Hofferth (2001), or Sayer *et al.* (2002). These researchers mobilize considerable evidence to support their claim that mothers resist reductions in time devoted to activities with children as they increase hours of paid employment. Other national and international studies corroborate the finding that maternal employment has much smaller effects on time-use than might be expected (Hill and Stafford 1985; Gershuny 2000). The rise in maternal employment in the United States has not significantly reduced maternal time in care activities, and seems to be associated with small increases in married fathers' time in such activities. These trends however, do not imply that maternal care time has remained unchanged or that all families have successfully adjusted to increases in hours of maternal employment. In this chapter, we point to the need for more precise definition and measurement of parental childcare time.

Studies of parental time allocation in the United States

As early as the 1920s, researchers asked homemakers to fill out a time-diary recording their daily activities against the clock (Vanek 1974). Yet the time devoted to nonmarket work has received surprisingly little systematic attention, considering its implications for both family well-being and economic growth.

Time-use diaries

Time-diaries ask individuals to record the activities they engage in over a given period of time, either through recall or by responding to a beeper programmed to give random cues. Individuals typically report their own activities, which are then coded by others into distinct categories in order to facilitate empirical tabulation. These time-diaries represent the preferred methodology for examining time-use. They yield responses that are more reliable than answers to stylized questions such as "How much time did you spend providing childcare last week?" Such questions require recall over a longer period and tempt respondents to report what they think interviewers would like to hear rather than what actually occurred, leading to "social desirability" bias. For instance, most parents recognize that it is socially desirable to read aloud to their children. Asked a stylized question about how much time they spend in this activity, their answers are almost twice as high as estimates derived from time-diaries (Hofferth 1999).

But while time-diaries represent a distinct improvement over stylized questions, they may also be susceptible to misreporting. Cultural norms as well as social expectations affect the ways people perceive their own activities. Because childcare is often considered a greater responsibility for mothers than for fathers, women may be more likely than men to report engagement in a care activity (Press and Townsley 1998). Similarly, growing social concern about the amount of time that mothers spend with their children may lead mothers to reclassify their own use of time, perceiving care activities as more salient and therefore reporting them in more detail.

Time-use surveys generally call attention to *activities* such as sleep, personal care, leisure, and work. Both survey design and the categorization of activities reflect the influence of studies conducted in the 1960s by Alexander Szalai and others (1972). The focus on time-use *activities*, rather than on constraints or responsibilities has important implications for measuring childcare. A parent may rush home to be there when a child returns from school, but not necessarily engage in an activity with the child once he or she arrives. Furthermore, individuals often engage in more than one activity at once. One of these activities usually takes precedence, and is construed as the "primary" activity. Some surveys probe "secondary" activities by asking questions such as "were you doing anything else at the same time?" Questions regarding the presence of other individuals or the location of the activity may also be asked, allowing for measures of "contact" time. Surveys differ considerably in their attention to these issues, contributing to problems of comparability.

An additional complication is that activities conducted on behalf of children, rather than directly with children, are not typically considered care. Time picking up a child's toys, for instance, is generally counted as housework. Preparation of a child's meal is counted as part of meal preparation. Transporting children to activities, or making phone calls to arrange a child's health care or music lessons are sometimes explicitly coded as childcare, and sometimes not.[2] The distinction between time spent in activities with children and time spent in activities on behalf of children has significant quantitative implications. One analysis of the Multinational Time Use Survey finds that the presence of a child under the age of 5 is associated with an additional 62 minutes per day of unpaid work including, but not limited to, childcare itself (Gershuny 2000: 149).[3]

An overview of time-use surveys of childcare in the United States

At least twenty studies of maternal time-use in the United States have been conducted over the past twenty-five years.[4] Many of these categorize childcare in different ways. About one-third of the studies rely on generic categories such as "childcare," "baby care" or "amusing/playing with children."[5] Relatively few studies explicitly state that they include activities such as feeding, bathing, diapering, and dressing children, though it seems likely that they do. What difference do definitions make? Limited comparability across surveys makes it difficult to answer this question.[6] Variation is notable even among studies using the same data set. Analysis of University of Michigan time-use data for 1975 yields conflicting estimates: 51 minutes of childcare per day for all women (Coverman and Sheley 1986: 416) and 42 minutes per day by Hill (1985: 149) for all married women, which would likely be lower if unmarried women were included. Juster (1985: 191) also analyzes the 1975 Michigan data with a view to measuring women's childcare time, but restricts his attention to what he terms "investment," defined as time spent helping children make or do things, teaching them new skills, and providing for their health care. He considers only half the time spent caring for, reading to, talking for, or playing with and being the chauffeur of one's children as investment rather than consumption (Juster 1985: 186).

Survey design also limits comparability. Most surveys ask parents how much time they spend in activities with children. The recent Child Development Supplement of the Panel Study of Income Dynamics (PSID-CD) asks individual children how much time they spend in activities with parents (caregivers report time-use for infants) (Hofferth 2001; Hofferth and Sandberg 2001; Sandberg and Hofferth 2001). Parent-focused surveys cannot reveal the total amount of time that individual children enjoy, unless they specify the name and number of children being cared for. Child-focused surveys cannot reveal the total amount of time parents spend in childcare unless all children in families (and stepfamilies) are surveyed.

One consistent pattern emerges: parents devote relatively little time, on average, to activities with children. According to studies explicitly examining primary activities, such as Bryant and Zick (1996a), Robinson and Godbey (1997: 105), and Bianchi (2000: 405), mothers devote less than two hours a day, and fathers less than an hour a day in every time period covered. This is notably less than the total amount of time devoted to other nonmarket activities such as "core" housework (not including shopping), which Robinson and Godbey estimate at almost four hours a day for women in 1965, and more than two and a half hours in 1985.

Parental time declines dramatically with the age of the child. Virtually all children over the age of 6 attend school and those over the age of 12 are able to take care of themselves for significant periods. Duncan Ironmonger's analysis (Chapter 5, this volume) of Australian data suggest that children under the age of two spend about twice as much time in activities with parents as those between two and four, who in turn spend about two and a half times more than children between 5 and 9. Time devoted to secondary childcare activities shows a similar though less steep decline as children mature.

Evidence suggests that the amount of time that women devote to housework has declined since 1965 (Robinson and Godbey 1997: 105). Time devoted to children has clearly been more resistant to change. Actually documenting historical trends, however, is difficult. In one of the first efforts to show that parental time might actually be increasing, Bryant and Zick (1996a) rely on US Department of Agriculture surveys from the late 1920s and early 1930s that asked married women about time devoted to family care. They compare these with data from the National Time-Use in Economic and Social Accounts sample collected at the University of Michigan for 1975 and 1981 (Juster and Stafford 1985; Juster et al. 1988). This comparison hinges on the assumption that USDA survey category "care of family members" is comparable to detailed categories for childcare available in the later surveys. This seems problematic since Bryant and Zick cannot account for the presence of grandparents (who could be consumers or providers of family care).

Using these "spliced" data, they report that mean minutes per day that married women devoted to family care increased from 80 minutes in 1924–31 to 81 minutes in 1975 and 89 minutes in 1981. The definitions they rely on for the two later years are consistent, and thus represent a valuable finding. However, a difference of 8 minutes a day is a small one, and its statistical significance is not reported.[7] Interestingly, Bryant and Zick's analysis shows that employed mothers spent less than half as much time as nonemployed mothers with their children in both 1975 and 1981 (1996a: table 6). Furthermore, their estimates show that employed mothers of children under the age of 1 spent less time with children in 1981 than in 1975 (1996a: 382).

Maternal time devoted to primary activities with children seems resistant, but not immune to decline (Hill and Stafford 1985; Gershuny 2000). Using the same 1981 University of Michigan sample that Bryant and Zick analyze, Nock and Kingston (1988) show that employed married mothers spend less time overall with their children, but that most of the reduction comes in activities "that involve children only peripherally, not in directly child-oriented activities" (1988: 59). Similar results are reported in the analysis of Australian data (Bittman *et al.*, Chapter 7, this volume).

A number of studies suggest that mothers' hours of work have no significant effects on fathers' hours of childcare time (Nock and Kingston 1988; Bryant and Zick 1996a; Pleck 1997). Furthermore, most noncustodial parents (primarily fathers) have relatively little contact with their children (Furstenberg *et al.* 1983; McLanahan and Sandefur 1994; Nord and Zill 1996). Therefore, one would expect the combined effect of greater maternal employment and increased single-parenthood to lower overall parental time in activities with children. A focus on married couple, two-parent households deflects attention from this probable trend.

The effects of parental employment seem to vary considerably across households, reflecting differences in temporal flexibility. Nock and Kingston (1988) emphasize that the effects of maternal employment are influenced by work schedules. Harriet Presser (1994) shows that many married parents accommodate childcare needs by engaging in split-shift employment strategies. Professional couples may actually be more constrained in this respect than working-class families, because their career tracks make it difficult to substitute night- or swing-shift work for regular hours. Single parents have far less flexibility in scheduling childcare than two parents, but often participate in a low-wage employment market that requires nontraditional hours of work.

New and improved studies of parental time

Partly in response to limitations described above, new efforts have recently sought improved benchmarks for meaningful analysis of trends in parental time allocation. Suzanne Bianchi and John Robinson conducted a survey in 1998–99 designed for comparability with Robinson's earlier survey of 1965 (Bianchi 2000). The 1997 PSID-CD collected data on children's activities that have been extensively analyzed and compared to the 1981 University of Michigan study (Hofferth and Sandberg 2001; Sandberg and Hofferth 2001). Studies based on these three data sets show that maternal employment has surprisingly small effects and that parental time devoted to activities with children has not declined significantly over time. However, their findings should be interpreted with caution.

In her presidential address to the Population Association of America, published in *Demography*, Suzanne Bianchi (2000) warns against a tendency to exaggerate the potentially negative effects of increased maternal employment. Seconding Nock and Kingston's emphasis on the distinction between activity time and more peripheral activities, she also presents results showing that mothers devoted an average of 103 minutes to childcare as a primary activity in 1998 compared to 90 minutes per day in 1965, a statistically significant increase. When secondary time was included the change was even more dramatic, to 168 minutes per day from 132 minutes per day. However, time spent with children in any activity remained relatively constant, between 318 and 330 minutes per day (2000: 405). Clearly, much depends on how childcare is defined.

Bianchi's results are based on interviews with 1,151 individuals (including 79 single mothers and 358 married mothers) and a relatively low response rate (56 percent). A surprisingly large proportion of respondents (34 percent of single mothers and 28 percent of married mothers) report no activities with children on the diary day.[8] The results are not perfectly consistent with those reported by Robinson and Godbey (1997: 105) for the 1965–85 period, which show a decrease from 9.9 hours per week or 85 minutes per day for women who were parents in 1965 to 8.9 hours per week or 76 minutes per day in 1985. Nor is it clear why the more recent studies omit reporting the results for 1975 and 1985, which Robinson and Godbey treated as comparable with the 1965 survey. Trend continuity over four points in time would be more persuasive than merely between the two end-points.

Setting this issue aside, these results are based on households with children under age 18, and do not break out trends for children under the age of 6, probably due to small sample size. Bianchi reports that married fathers increased their activity time with children over the period, but her data do not allow her to examine trends for unmarried or noncoresident fathers. Sayer *et al.* (2002) use multivariate analysis of the same data set to examine trends controlling for a number of factors. The results suggest that increases in the average amounts of time that both mothers and fathers devote to care of their children have more than compensated for compositional changes such as the increase in single parenthood and maternal employment. However, the large percentage of mothers and fathers who report no childcare activity at all on the diary day also suggests an increase in the overall inequality of childcare time that could make average trends somewhat misleading.

The recent PSID-CD offers an additional opportunity to systematically examine differences across households. The PSID is a longitudinal survey of a representative sample of US men, women, and children, and the families in which they live. In 1997, information was collected on one or two randomly selected 0- to 12-year children of PSID respondents, both from the primary care-giver and from the children themselves. About 3,563 children were included. Econometric analysis of this data shows that the impact of maternal employment on maternal time with children is small. Time in which mothers are available declines more than time in which they are engaged in activities with children (Hofferth 2001; Hofferth and Sandberg 2001). However, it is important to remember that employment is, to some extent, endogenous. Many mothers are able to choose their hours of employment in order to preserve "quality time" with children; the effect of employment would likely differ if it were imposed from without (e.g. in the form of a work requirement).[9]

Analysis of the PSID-CD also supports previous findings that children's time with parents tends to be lower in single parent than two-parent families. That is, mothers raising children on their own are unable to fully compensate for the reduction in paternal time. Furthermore, the negative effect of maternal employ-ment is greater in single-parent households. In families in which women are household heads, children of employed mothers receive five hours per week less of engaged time than children of mothers who stay home (Hofferth 2001; Sandberg and Hofferth 2001).

The PSID-CD covers only one year. In order to analyze change over time, Sandberg and Hofferth (2001) compare their results with the University of Michigan survey of 1981. They make the questionable assumption that the time parents spent in activities with children in the 1981 can be compared with time par-ents spend either in activities or are "available" to children in the 1997 survey. Since the earlier study omitted children under the age of 3, they restrict their 1997 sam-ple accordingly. While this limitation is clearly acknowledged in the text of the article, both the title and headings for tables and figures omit this detail, which may explain why it is often lost in citation.[10] The age composition is relevant since children under the age of 3 require more care. Furthermore, an increase in age at marriage along with postponed childbearing over the period could contribute to a decline in the average age of children between the ages of 3 and 12, which would bias measures of parental time upward. Such limitations point to the need for care-ful reassessment of conceptual issues as well as additional empirical research.

Defining care time

The advantages of focusing on individual activities are obvious. Activities are simpler to categorize and calibrate than are more subjective indicators such as purposes or goals. Yet the focus on activities inherited from Alexander Szalai also creates problems that are particularly relevant to the analysis of work that involves care for others. Care often takes the form of joint production or "multi-tasking" that is difficult to capture, and it also entails diffuse responsibilities such as "on call" time (see Bittman *et al.*, Chapter 4; Wolf, Chapter 6, this volume). The appropriate choice of emphasis on primary activities, secondary activities, or responsibilities that cannot be reduced to explicit activities depends on the researcher's larger goal.

Primary activities

Primary activities are likely to have direct implications for child outcomes such as emotional well-being and cognitive attainment. Feeding and dressing a child is often an opportunity for emotional bonding as well as physical contact. Time spent reading aloud to children has positive implications for later school performance (Ortiz 1986). The time that children spend watching television is widely believed to have negative effects (though much depends on what kinds of programs children watch).

But not all primary activities or forms of what Hofferth and Sandberg (2001) call "engaged" time are equal, and researchers might do better to focus on those activities that are explicitly "developmental" such as reading aloud or playing with a child (Bittman *et al.*, Chapter 7, this volume). Different activities imply different levels of personal engagement. Time spent chauffeuring children to activities comprises a surprisingly large component of parental time. Results from the PSID-CD show that in 1997 children under the age of 3 in the United States spent about as much time with their mother on a weekday in transportation as they did in personal care (Fuligni and Brooks-Gunn 2003). Most were probably riding in a car on their way to childcare, shopping, or errands. Should this time be considered "available" or "engaged," "developmental" or "low intensity"? The answer to this question is not obvious.

Secondary activities

The specific nature of care responsibilities also invites reconsideration of the conventional distinction between primary and secondary activities. Most respondents seem to prioritize activities in terms of the level of energy or attention they require (Bittman 1999). Cooking or doing laundry may be considered more primary than overseeing a child, even if supervisory responsibility is the primary determinant of time allocation. Over the last thirty years, changes in the technology of housework have reduced the physical effort required, possibly making it more likely that mothers will list childcare as a primary activity (Gershuny 2000: 200).

Since both primary and secondary activities are defined using similar activity codes, we would expect ratios of primary and secondary time to be similar across surveys. Yet, these ratios vary considerably. Time-diaries administered in Australia in 1992 report three hours of secondary childcare for every one hour of primary childcare activity (Australian Bureau of Statistics 1994). US surveys tend to report a much lower ratio, less than one hour of secondary for every two hours of primary childcare time (Zick and Bryant 1996: 277; Robinson and Godbey 1997: 106). Studies that examine both primary and secondary time in the United States reveal significant differences in their relative importance. Robinson and

Godbey report that adding secondary activities increases the total amount of time devoted to childcare by 50 percent, indicating that it represents about a third of the total (1997: 107). Similarly, in their analysis of the 11-State Survey of two-parent, two-child families, Keith Bryant and Kathleen Zick find that secondary childcare time accounts for about 44 percent of primary childcare time (1996a,b). However, in her analysis of 1998 data that is otherwise treated as comparable to the data analyzed by Robinson and Godbey, Suzanne Bianchi (2000: 405) reports that secondary time amounts to about 65 percent of primary care time. These differences in secondary/primary time ratios probably reflect differences in explicit definitions of care or wording of survey questions.

The ways in which respondents prioritize their activities introduce considerable potential for subjective variation. Variability across countries in definitions of secondary activities prompted the Eurostat Task Force on Time Use to exclude measures of secondary time-use from satellite income accounts (Stinson 1999: 19). As Michael Bittman puts it, official statistical offices are "haunted by the idea that the amount of secondaries recorded has more to do with how much effort a respondent is willing to commit to completing the time-diary than the real number of simultaneous activities."[11] In recent cognitive pre-testing for the ATUS, the BLS found that participants "strongly suggested that the concept of secondary childcare is not intuitively meaningful, because most parents would consider those activities, 'just part of being a parent'" (Schwartz 2002: 35). On the other hand, reliance on primary activities alone almost certainly understates the amount of time parents devote to childcare (Ironmonger, Chapter 5, this volume).

Responsibility time

Childcare is not just a set of activities. It is also a state of mind. Children are generally aware of their parents' presence and availability, as well as their hours of shared activities. Parents' concerns about their children's needs for monitoring and supervision often constrain their activities (Leslie *et al.* 1991; Walzer 1996). These constraints are particularly relevant to estimates of total inputs of parental time, an important component of the cost of children. Parental "on call" responsibilities are normally excluded from measures of both primary and secondary time, suggesting the need for a separate category of "responsibility" time.[12]

The 1997 Australian Time Use Survey goes further than any US survey by specifying a category called "Minding Children," defined as "caring for children without the active involvement shown in the codes above. Includes monitoring children playing outside or sleeping, preserving a safe environment, being an adult presence for children to turn to in need, supervising games or swimming activities including swimming lessons. Passive childcare" (ABS 1997: 37). This category probably explains why estimates of secondary relative to primary time are so high in Australia.

Parental awareness of supervisory responsibilities could help explain why their answers to stylized questions such as "How much time did you spend providing care for your children last week?" typically yield much larger estimates than time-diaries (Juster 1999: 17). While stylized estimates may be biased upward by social desirability pressures, time-diary estimates may be biased downward by their emphasis on explicit activities, which have less overall impact on parental time than the indirect pressures imposed by responsibility for young children.

For instance, time that children spend sleeping never registers as an activity, but it may prevent parents from accepting paid employment that requires night-time hours or travel away from home. Activity-based measures may capture the number of hours a parent spends reading aloud, but they do not capture parental ability to stay home from work if a child is sick, or show up at a soccer game or school play that a child considers important. Detailed studies of low-income families suggest that maternal monitoring and supervision may be particularly relevant to the well-being of young adolescents (Gennetian *et al.* 2002). Parents may try to compensate for loss of temporal flexibility by adding hours of direct activity time that can be more conveniently scheduled.

Mothers are more likely than fathers to experience the indirect pressure of responsibility for children. Concepts of leisure itself are shaped by gender roles (Deem 1996; Henderson 1996). Analysis of Australian time-use data shows that mothers are more likely than fathers to engage in leisure activities while children are present (Bittman and Wajcman, Chapter 9, this volume). Analysis of Canadian data shows that mothers, unlike fathers, tend to report that they are looking after their children for a longer time than the conventional measures of social contact suggest (Frederick 1994).

Some time-use surveys go beyond activity-based measures, asking, for instance, "who else was present?" Childcare is occasionally defined as "contact time," encompassing all activities in which a child is present, such as time spent eating meals together, even in a restaurant (Almeida and McDonald 2000; Hallberg and Klevmarken 2000). The PSID-CD asks not only "Who was doing the activity with child" but also "Who (else) was there but not directly involved in the activity?"[13] Hofferth and Sandberg (2001) describe this as "accessible" time, as distinct from "engaged" time. Likewise, the surveys administered by Robinson and Bianchi ask "While you were (REPEAT ACTIVITY), who was with you?"

But even such direct questions leave considerable room for interpretation. They call attention to who else was in the same room, or in visual contact. Children who are napping in another room or playing in the backyard are unlikely to be listed. The PSID-CD stipulates that the "who else was there" question should not be answered if the child was sleeping or engaged in personal care. Yet, parents can be charged with child abandonment or neglect if they leave a sleeping child under the age of 8 alone in a house for a lengthy period of time.[14] If they cannot be "on call" they typically ask a family member, friend, or babysitter to take their place.

Researchers should devote more attention to development of new instruments for measuring care time. The US BLS plans carefully scripted supplementary questions on childcare responsibilities (see later discussion). Another way to address measurement problems would be to calibrate quantitative surveys by conducting intensive qualitative observation of a small subset of surveyed families.

Timing, sequencing, and overlaps

Qualitative surveys could also shed light on issues such as timing, sequencing, and overlaps. From a parental point of view, time devoted to playing with children or reading to them may be more enjoyable than time in routine activities such as feeding or changing diapers. Fathers are more likely than mothers to specialize in "fun" activities (Pleck 1997). Periods of time in which childcare is combined with another activity may be highly productive but particularly stressful and tiring (Floro 1995; Floro and Miles 2001). Mothers are more likely than fathers to experience high intensity overlaps (caring for many children at one time) as well as constant interruptions to leisure time (Bittman and Wajcman, Chapter 9, this volume). Another overlap issue concerns the presence of two parents at the same time, which offer children more adult attention as well as the opportunity to learn from parental interaction. Similarly, siblings often spend time together with one or both parents.

Unless time-use data is collected for all members of a household (as in Australia), rather than from one individual within each household (as in the United States) it is difficult to ascertain overlaps among adults.[15] But the "who else was there?" question on the PSID-CD shows that fathers are much more likely to provide care in conjunction with mothers than on their own. For instance, the time that fathers in married-couple families spend in activities with 6-year-old children with a mother present is more than twice what they spend on their own. Mothers, on the other hand, spend almost twice as much time alone in activities with children as they do with a father present. This asymmetrical overlap has important implications for analysis of differences in mothers' and fathers' time inputs.

A related issue concerns the ways in which time-use is averaged across children, which raises questions concerning economies of scale, or the increased efficiency of caring for more than one child at a time. Triple the number of children in a household and the amount of time devoted to childcare activities does not triple. Three children are far cheaper than two, in terms of per capita expenditures of parental time. The average number of children per family has declined over the course of the twentieth century, despite a temporary bulge caused by the baby boom of the 1950s. As a result, the average amount of childcare time divided by the number of children would have increased even if the average amount of time devoted to childcare overall had declined, because of a loss of economies of scale.

But parental time does not always benefit one child rather than another; it may benefit all children at once.[16] The average amount of childcare time divided by the number of children may be substantially less than the average amount of parental time each child enjoys (in the company of other children). Consider a family in 1952 with three children, one a newborn, another 3 years old and the eldest 6 years old. The parents might have spent 24 hours a week in primary childcare activities, for an average of 8 hours per week per child. On the other hand, a family in 1992 with only two children might have spent only slightly less time, say 20 hours a week in primary childcare, for an average of 10 hours per child. We might look at the averages and celebrate the fact that the later-born children enjoyed more time per capita.

But, is parental time necessarily "diluted"? Even developmentally rich activities such as reading aloud or giving instruction can benefit more than one child at a time. Take the example given previously to the opposite extreme: if all three children were always together with at least one parent in the earlier family, they each received 24 hours of care per week; likewise, if two children were always together with at least one parent in the later family, they each received only 20 hours of care per week. By this measure of total hours of parental care from children's point of view, children in the later year were receiving fewer hours of care time.

Neither way of calculating care time per child is entirely satisfactory. But the example shows that it can be misleading to divide the number of hours of parental care by the number of children, as do Bryant and Zick (1996a: 373, 386). There is no a priori reason to believe that every hour that parents devote to two children at once is only the equivalent of a half-hour for each.[17] Ideally, time-use surveys would look at levels of parental attention and engagement children enjoy both from the parents' point of view (what they provide both individually and together) and from the children's point of view (what they receive and whether another sibling is there when they receive it).

The American national time-use survey

In 2003, the BLS launched the first annual nationally representative time-use survey, with significant implications for future research on time devoted to the care of children and other family members. Respondents will be drawn from the monthly samples used for the Current Population Survey, which are nationally representative of American households. Annually, the ATUS will target 34,000 individuals aged 16 and above living in separate households; a 70 percent response rate is expected for a total of 24,000 respondents per year. Sample size and design should enable future analyses of single versus married parents and comparisons across racial/ethnic groups. The sample will be stratified by family size (number of children in the family), education level of respondent, sex, age, employment status, family type (marital status), location, and race/ethnicity. Each respondent is randomly assigned one day during the survey week and is surveyed the day after this day, creating a one-day recall time-diary.

The ATUS measures both active childcare and passive childcare. After extensive field testing of various measures, the BLS decided to measure passive childcare in the following way: after the respondent completes the 24-hour time-diary activity report, the interviewer asks if, at any time during those activities, a child was "in your care." If respondents are unclear about what "in your care" means, the interviewer provides this definition: "By 'in your care' I mean that you were generally aware of what your child was doing, and you were near enough that you could provide immediate assistance, if necessary" (Schwartz 2002). Children are not considered in a parent's care if asleep during the evening or night (daytime naps are counted). Children are also not considered in the care of the parent if the parent is asleep (such as a parent napping with a child during the day). Moreover, activities done on the behalf of the child, but not directly "on" the child – such as making phone calls to arrange a child's health care appointments or preparing a meal for a child – are not counted as active child-care, nor as passive childcare if the child is not in the company of the parent (such as telephone calls made from the parent's workplace).

Other activities excluded from childcare measures are travel related to child-care, eating with children, and other administrative/organizational activities done for children if the child is not also in the parent's physical location. While the inclusion of the passive time parents spend with children on the ATUS is an excellent step, the exclusion of time parents spend in activities on the behalf of (but not directly "on") their children will make it difficult for researchers to calculate the full-time costs of parental commitments.

Conclusion

As opportunities for collection of time-use data grow, researchers should grapple more directly with the problems of definition and measurement raised above. More consistency in survey instruments and sample design could improve comparability of family time estimates across different groups and over time. Qualitative studies could add valuable insights. Clearly, the direct activities parents engage in with children consume far less time than the responsibility for overseeing them. Many parents work nonstandard hours and split shifts in order to make sure that one parent is at home during the night, and one during the day – even if spending part of that time sleeping (Presser 1994). The specific activities that parents engage in with their children may be particularly relevant for understanding developmental outcomes (Datcher-Loury 1988). But the time that parents are available to monitor or supervise probably also affects children's welfare. Moreover, these broader care responsibilities provide a better picture of parental contributions to the production of the next generation of workers and citizens.

Broad generalizations regarding trends in maternal care activities may con-ceal variability among families. Even the best studies available in the United States are based on highly aggregated data. Yet we know that parental activi-ties, as well as responsibilities, are particularly demanding for children under the age of 3. Differences in family structure and income also have important ramifications. Women in high-income two-earner families enjoy more discre-tion over their hours and timing of paid employment than low-income single mothers. Therefore, they are probably better able to defend "quality" time with their children. As Bianchi (2000) notes, the increased income inequality of the 1980s and 1990s may have led to increased inequality in time devoted to children.

In general, studies that examine the quality of parental time seem less optimistic than those which focus on quantity. For instance, interviews with children of working parents show that they are much less concerned about the hours their parents work than how tired and stressed out they are when they come home (Galinsky 2000). Even parents who maintain a relatively high average activity time with children may lack access to paid or unpaid family leave to deal with unexpected problems such as illness. Low-income families are particularly likely to lack such flexibility (Heymann 2000; Chin and Newman 2002).

Interest in hours of parental time engaged in activities with children should not distract from other issues, including the role that grandparents and siblings play in providing care. Studies of childcare utilization show that many low-income mothers who work for pay are able to take advantage of free care provided by kin, friends, or neighbors. Those lacking such informal assistance pay an average of over 20 percent of their income for childcare (Giannarelli and Barsimantov 2000).

In the past, concerns about the effects of maternal labor force participation on children have been overstated. Recent research on time-use helps allay these concerns. Even if based on imperfect measures and small samples, the finding that maternal time devoted to activities with children has been relatively stable over time is an important one. However, it is also important to qualify this generalization and to urge more detailed attention to the indirect demands of paid employment and the impact of single-parenthood. Future research should focus more carefully on time devoted to children under the age of 3, mothers affected by paid employment requirements, and overlaps among both caregivers and care recipients.

Acknowledgments

We gratefully acknowledge the comments and criticisms of Michael Bittman, Paula England, Naomi Gerstel, Sandra Hoffreth, Natasha Sarkisian, and Liana Sayer and the financial support of the MacArthur Research Network on the Family and the Economy. An earlier version of this chapter was presented at the International Association for Time Use Research Annual Conference, Lisbon, Portugal, October 2002.

Notes

1 See Jacqueline L. Salmon, "Study Sees No Change in Mothering Time" (*Washington Post*, March 26, 2000) reporting on the research of Suzanne Bianchi and Jacqueline L. Salmon, "Kids Seeing More of Mom and Dad," (*Washington Post*, May 9, 2001), reporting on the work on John Sandberg and Sandra Hofferth.

2 Of US studies, the Robinson/Bianchi data include these activities as childcare, but the Child Development Supplement of the Panel Study of Income Dynamics (PSID-CD) does not.

3 Unfortunately, Gershuny's presentation makes it impossible to disaggregate the two components.

4 We reviewed all studies of maternal childcare time based on time diaries we could find published in books or scholarly journals, as well as one unpublished study: Robinson (1977), Berk and Berk (1979), Coverman (1983), Hill (1985), Juster (1985), Coverman and Sheley (1986), Nock and Kingston (1988), Douthitt *et al.* (1990), Hiatt and Godwin (1990), Sanik (1990), Shelton (1990), Bryant and Zick (1996a,b), Zick and Bryant (1996), Robinson and Godbey (1997), Almeida and McDonald (2000), Bianchi (2000), Hofferth (2001), Sandberg and Hofferth (2001), Sayer *et al.* (2002).

5 The majority of studies (seventeen) call attention to specific activities such as reading to, talking with, and/or instructing and teaching children (Robinson 1977; Berk and Berk 1979; Fuligni and Brooks-Gunn 2003; Hill 1985; Hill and Stafford 1985; Juster 1985; Coverman and Sheley 1986; Nock and Kingston 1988; Douthitt *et al.* 1990; Hilton 1990; Sanik 1990; Shelton 1990; Bryant and Zick 1996a,b; Zick and Bryant 1996; Robinson and Godbey 1997; Bianchi 2000). Fifteen studies explicitly code time spent on child health care and time spent chauffeuring children as childcare.

6 Many studies rely partly on convenience samples (Douthitt *et al.* 1990; Sanik 1990, Bryant and Zick 1996a). Some samples are limited to married couples only (Sanik 1990, Bryant and Zick 1996a), whites (Bryant and Zick 1996a), urban dwellers (Juster 1985; Coverman and Sheley 1986), residents of a small number of states (Douthitt *et al.* 1990; Sanik 1990; Bryant and Zick 1996a;), first-time parents (Sanik 1990), or graduates of elite eastern colleges (Bryant and Zick 1996a).

7 While the authors engage in considerable statistical analysis, they do not report either the significance of the difference in the means or the standard deviation of the estimates of time use.

8 Based on table 1, Sayer *et al.* (2002).

9 Furthermore, the size of estimated coefficents is likely to be affected by the specification of the model. Hofferth (2001) measures employment both as a set of dummy variables and through the number of hours employed. She includes a set of employment dummies indicating dual earner, female-only earner, and no earners (with male-only earner as the omitted category) in the same model with number of mothers' and fathers' work hours and the number of fathers' work hours (as well as dummies capturing the relative size of mothers' and fathers' contribution to family income). This confuses interpretation of the effects of employment. Hofferth states that "maternal employment does not reduce the time children are engaged with employed mothers, after adjusting for other factors" (p. 21, manuscript version) where one of those "other factors" is the number of hours of mother's employment. This result is hardly surprising.

10 Bianchi (2000), referring to the Sandberg/Hofferth results on p. 411, incorrectly describes them as pertaining to all children under 13.

11 Michael Bittman, personal communication.

12 Blanke (1994) refers to the need for a concept of "tertiary" time, but this implies more of a quantitative ranking (primary–secondary–tertiary) than a qualitative difference.

13 See www.isr.umich.edu/src/child-development/home.html, for more details regarding the PSID-CD.

14 Exact definitions of child neglect vary across states within the United States. The National Child Care Information Center reports explicit rules for several communities that stipulate that children 10 years and under should be under direct supervision at all times.

15 For more discussion of this issue see Winkler (2002).

16 In more technical terms, parental time may be nonexcludable in consumption and represent a household public good.

17 Hofferth and Sandberg cite Bryant and Zick (1996a) to the effect that "studies have found that the time parents spend with any given child declines as the number of children in the family increases" (2001: 425). What they are referring to, however, is

not a finding, but an assumption. Bianchi (2000: 404) and Sayer *et al.* (2002: 10) also uncritically accept this definition of per capita time.

References

Almeida, D. M. and McDonald, D. A. (2000) "The Time Americans Spend Working for Pay, Caring for Families, and Contributing to Communities," Paper prepared for the Conference on Work, Family, and Democracy, Racine.

Australian Bureau of Statistics (ABS) (1994) "How Australians Use Their Time," Cat. No. 4153.0, Canberra: ABS.

—— (1997) Time Use Survey, Australia, Users' Guide.

Berk, R. A. and Berk, S. F. (1979) *Labor and Leisure at Home: Content and Organization of the Household Day*, Beverley Hills: Sage Publications.

Bianchi, S. (2000) "Maternal Employment and Time with Children: Dramatic Change or Surprising Continuity?," *Demography*, 37: 401–14.

Bittman, M. (1999) "An International Perspective to Collecting Time Use Data," Paper presented at the Committee on National Statistics Workshop on Measurement of and Research on Time Use, Washington, DC.

Blanke, K. (1994) "Time Use Data and the (In)Visibility of Child Care – Methodological Aspects," Paper presented at the International Sociological Association, Statisches Bundestaat, D-65189 Wiesbaden.

Bryant, W. K. and Zick, C. D. (1996a) "Are We Investing Less in the Next Generation? Historical Trends in Time Spent Caring for Children," *Journal of Family and Economic Issues*, 17: 385–92.

—— and —— (1996b) "An Examination of Parent–Child Shared Time," *Journal of Marriage and the Family*, 58: 227–37.

Chin, M. M. and Newman, K. S. (2002) "High Stakes: Time Poverty, Testing and the Children of the Working Poor," Working Paper, Foundation for Child Development. New York.

Coverman, S. (1983) "Gender, Domestic Labor Time, and Wage Inequality," *American Sociological Review*, 48: 623–37.

—— and Sheley, J. F. (1986) "Change in Men's Housework and Child-Care Time, 1965–1975," *Journal of Marriage and the Family*, 48: 413–22.

Datcher-Loury, L. (1988) "Effects of Mother's Home Time on Children's Schooling," *Review of Economics and Statistics*, 70: 367–73.

Deem, R. (1996) "'No Time for a Rest?' An Explanation of Women's Work, Engendered Leisure and Holidays," *Time and Society*, 5(5): 5–25.

Douthitt, R. A., Zick, C. D., and McCullough, J. (1990) "The Role of Economic and Demographic Factors in Explaining Time-Use of Single and Married Mothers," *Lifestyles: Family and Economic Issues*, 11: 23–51.

Floro, M. (1995) "Women's Well-Being, Poverty, and Work Intensity," *Feminist Economics*, 1: 1–25.

—— and Miles, M. (2001) "Time Use and Overlapping Activities. Evidence from Australia," Social Policy Research Centre Working Paper, Sydney, Australia.

Frederick, Judith (1994) "Measuring Child Care and Sleep. Some Results from the 1992 Canadian General Social Survey," unpublished manuscript, Statistics Canada.

Fuligni, A. S. and Brooks-Gunn, J. (2003) "Measuring Mother and Father Shared Caregiving: An Analysis Using the Panel Study of Income Dynamics – Child

Development Supplement," in R. Day and M. Lamb (eds), *Conceptualizing and Measuring Paternal Involvement*, Mahwah, NJ: Erlbaum.

Furstenberg F. C., Jr. Nord, W., Peterson, J. L., and Zill, N. (1983) "The Life Course of Children of Divorce: Marital Disruption and Parental Conflict," *American Sociological Review*, 48: 656–68.

Galinsky, E. (2000) *Ask The Children*, New York: Quill.

Gennetian, L. A., Duncan, G. J., Knox, V. W., Vargas, W. G., Clark-Kauffman, E., and London, A. S. (2002) "How Welfare and Work Policies for Parents Affect Adolescents: A Synthesis of Research," New York: Manpower Demonstration Research Corporation.

Gershuny, J. (2000) *Changing Times: Work and Leisure in Postindustrial Society*, New York: Oxford.

Giannarelli, L. and Barsimantov, J. (2000) "Child Care Expenses of America's Families," Occasional Paper Number 40. Washington, DC: Urban Institute.

Hallberg, D. and Klevmarken, A. (2000) *Time for Children? A Study of Parents' Time Allocation*, Department of Economics, Uppsala University, Sweden.

Henderson, K. A. (1996) "One Size Doesn't Fit All: The Meanings of Women's Leisure," *Journal of Leisure Research*, 28: 139–54.

Heymann, J. (2000) *The Widening Gap*, New York: Basic Books.

Hiatt, A. R. and Godwin, D. D. (1990) "Use of Time and Preferences for Time Allocation Among Urban, Employed, Married Women," *Lifestyles: Family and Economic Issues*, 11: 161–81.

Hill, C. R. and Stafford, F. P. (1985) "Parental Care of Children: Time Diary Estimates of Quantity, Predictability and Variety," in F. T. Juster and F. P. Stafford (eds), *Time, Goods, and Well-Being*, Ann Arbor: Institute for Social Research, University of Michigan, pp. 415–37.

Hill, M. S. (1985) "Patterns of Time Use," in F. T. Juster and F. P. Stafford (eds), *Time, Goods, and Well-Being*, Ann Arbor: Institute for Social Research, University of Michigan, pp. 133–76.

Hilton, J. M. (1990) "Differences in Allocation of Family Time Spent on Household Tasks Among Single-Parent, One-Earner, and Two-Earner Families," *Lifestyles: Family and Economic Issues*, 11: 283–98.

Hofferth, S. (1999) "Family Reading to Young Children: Social Desirability and Cultural Biases in Reporting," Paper presented at Workshop on Measurement of and Research on Time Use, Committee on National Statistics, National Research Council, Washington, DC.

—— (2001) "Women's Employment and Care of Children in the United States," in T. Van der Lippe and L. Van Dijk (eds), *Women's Employment in a Comparative Perspective*, New York: Aldine de Gruyter, pp. 151–74.

—— and Sandberg, J. (2001) "How American Children Spend Their Time," *Journal of Marriage and the Family*, 63: 295–308.

Juster, F. T. (1985) "Investments of Time by Men and Women," in F. T. Juster and F. P. Stafford (eds), *Time, Goods, and Well-Being*, Ann Arbor: Institute for Social Research, University of Michigan, pp. 177–204.

—— (1999, May) "Time Use Data: Analytic Framework, Descriptive Findings, and Measurement Issues," Paper presented at the National Research Council, Committee on National Statistics, Workshop on Measurement of Time Use, Washington, DC.

—— and Stafford, F. P. (eds) (1985) *Time, Goods, and Well-Being*, Ann Arbor: Institute for Social Research, University of Michigan.

Juster, F. T., Hill, M. S., Stafford, F. P., and Parsons, J. E. (1988) *Time Use Longitudinal Panel Study, 1975–1981*, (2nd ICPSR edition) Ann Arbor: University of Michigan, Inter-University Consortium for Political and Social Research.

Leslie, L. A., Anderson, E. A., and Branson, M. P. (1991) "Responsibility for Children, the Role of Gender and Employment," *Journal of Family Issues*, 12(2): 197–210.

McLanahan, S. and Sandefur, G. (1994) *Growing Up with a Single Parent: What Hurts, What Helps?*, Cambridge: Harvard University Press.

Nock, S. and Kingston, P. (1988) "Time with Children: The Impact of Couples' Work Time Commitments," *Social Forces*, 67: 59–85.

Nord, C. W. and Zill, N. (1996) *Non-Custodial Parents' Participation in Their Children's Lives: Evidence from the Survey of Income and Program Participation, Volume II*, Washington, DC: Office of Assistant Secretary for Planning and Evaluation, US Department of Health and Human Services.

Ortiz, V. (1986) "Reading Activities and Reading Proficiency among Hispanic, Black, and White Students," *American Journal of Education*, 95: 58–76.

Pleck, J. H. (1997) "Paternal Involvement: Levels, Sources, and Consequences," in Michael E. Lamb (ed.), *The Role of Father in Child Development*, 3rd edn, New York: John Wiley, pp. 66–103.

Press, J. E. and Townsley, E. (1998) "Wives' and Husbands' Housework Reporting: Gender, Class, and Social Desirability," *Gender and Society*, 12: 188–219.

Presser, H. B. (1994) "Employment Schedules among Dual-Earner Spouses and the Division of Labor by Gender," *American Sociological Review*, 59: 348–69.

Robinson, J. (1977) *How Americans Use Time: A Social-Psychological Analysis of Everyday Behavior*, New York: Praeger.

—— and Godbey, G. (1997) *Time for Life: The Surprising Ways Americans Use Their Time*, University Park: Pennsylvania State University.

Sandberg, J. F. and Hofferth, S. L. (2001) "Changes in Children's Time with Parents: United States, 1981–1997", *Demography*, 38: 423–36.

Sanik, M. M. (1990) "Parents' Time Use: A 1967–1986 Comparison," *Lifestyles: Family and Economic Issues*, 11: 299–316.

Sayer, L. C., Bianchi, S. M., and Robinson J. P. (2002) "Are Parents Investing Less in Children? Trends in Mothers' and Fathers' Time with Children," manuscript, January 2002, revised version of a paper presented at the American Sociological Association Annual Meeting, August 2000.

Schwartz, Lisa K. (2002) "The American Time Use Survey: Cognitive Pretesting," *Monthly Labor Review*, February: 34–44.

Shelton, B. A. (1990) "The Distribution of Household Tasks. Does Wife's Employment Status Make a Difference?," *Journal of Family Issues*, 11(2): 115–35.

Stinson, L. (1999) "Measuring How People Spend Their Time: A Time-Use Survey Design," *Monthly Labor Review*, August: 12–19.

Szalai, A. et al. (eds) (1972) *The Use of Time: Daily Activities of Urban and Suburban Population in Twelve Countries*, The Hague: Mouton.

Vanek, J. (1974) "Time Spent in Housework," *Scientific American*, 231(5): 116–20.

Walzer, S. (1996) "Thinking about the Baby: Gender and Divisions of Infant Care," *Social Problems*, 43: 219–34.

Winkler, A. E. (2002) "Measuring Time Use in Households with more than one Person," *Monthly Labor Review* (February): 45–52.

Zick, C. D. and Bryant, W. K. (1996) "A New Look at Parents' Time Spent in Child Care: Primary and Secondary Time Use," *Social Science Research*, 25: 1–21.

4 Making the invisible visible

The life and time(s) of informal caregivers

Michael Bittman, Janet E. Fast, Kimberly Fisher, and Cathy Thomson

Care for people with a disability or the frail elderly can be provided either formally (through organized services and special residential facilities) or informally by relatives, friends, or others within the home. Interest in the situation of informal caregivers arises from two sources – theoretical issues and practical policy concerns.[1] In the theoretical realm, the development of feminist analyses of social policy led to the "discovery" of the informal care routinely supplied by women in families (Land 1978; Ungerson and Kember 1997). This coincided with a change in policy direction, away from institutional care toward "care in the community."

Since the late 1970s, governments have become increasingly aware of the value of informal caring. As populations have aged and the costs of social support systems for the oldest members of society have increased, national policies across Organization for Economic Cooperation and Development (OECD) countries increased the proportion of care provided by informal (and therefore less expensive) caregivers in the home (Hennessy 1995; Jacobzone 1999; Jenson and Jacobzone 2000; Neysmith 2000).[2] The public discussion of informal care has simultaneously emphasized its social and financial benefits and revealed anxiety about the hidden demands placed on women caregivers (Brody 1981; Finch and Groves 1983).

Time-diaries offer a potentially unique opportunity to capture the daily labor process of caring and to study how caregiving affects day-to-day activities. Fleming and Spellerberg (1999) note that time-use methodologies are valuable aids in studying the lives of caregivers "as they record caring or voluntary work in the context of the other activities of people's lives" (Fleming and Spellerberg 1999: 29).[3] However, studying caregiving using time-diaries is susceptible to many of the problems raised by Budig and Folbre (Chapter 3, this volume) regarding childcare – diaries are designed to capture activities, not responsibilities or constraints. Furthermore, as Wolf's chapter in this volume points out, coresident caregivers often engage in forms of joint production and simultaneous activity that make it difficult to measure their contribution. Provision of assistance across households is often more visible than within households.

In this chapter, we address these problems by comparing patterns of time-use across households with coresiding caregivers, noncoresiding caregivers, and no caregivers. Our analyses of Canadian and Australian data show that time-diary data can provide important insights into the life and time(s) of informal caregivers. We begin with a review of the social and political changes that lie behind the emergence of intense interest in caregiving.

Nonmarket provision of care

Informal care has been described as the submerged portion of the "iceberg of welfare." There is little documentation of its dimensions, but available evidence suggests that across the OECD countries a large proportion of caring services are provided informally by family and friends (Jenson and Jacobzone 2000). Informal caregivers are estimated to provide care for about 75 percent of elderly persons in Australia, who need assistance with the activities of daily living. Despite the fact that Australia has a comparatively young age structure, the proportion of informal caregiving is similar to that in other OECD countries (Bittman and Thomson 2000; Jenson and Jacobzone 2000: 12). The reason that informal care has remained largely unnoticed is because it is unpaid and, therefore, does not register in conventional accounting for welfare expenditure.

Although unpaid activities leave no cash trail, they do leave a trace in terms of the expenditure of time. Smeeding and Marchand (Chapter 2, this volume) note that time-use may be as important as income, consumption, and wealth data for informing public policy. Household time represents "the ultimate resource" (Fleming and Spellerberg 1999: 5). Douglas Wolf (Chapter 6, this volume) emphasizes that methods that assign an hourly wage rate to family time devoted to informal care may lead to overstatement of the costs of purchasing market substitutes. Nonetheless, the value of the time family members provide is staggeringly large. The Australian Institute of Health and Welfare estimates that the total value (of a rather artificially limited range) of caring activities is greater than the total value of government expenditure on welfare services (2001: 42).[4] In other words, the informal or household sector of the economy is probably the most important supplier of long-term care in Australia's welfare system. Similarly, in the United Kingdom "the input from all six million informal carers in 1986 was estimated as equivalent to five times the total expenditure on long-term care by central and local government and charities combined" (Hennessy 1997: 27). Arno *et al.* conclude that:

> The economic value of informal caregiving in 1997 dwarfs national spending for formal home health care (US$32 billion) and nursing home care (US$83). At the midrange estimate of US$196 billion annually, the economic value of informal caregiving is equivalent to 18 percent of the total national health care spending.
>
> (1999: 185)

Fast *et al.* (2000) estimate that it would have taken the equivalent of 276,509 full-time employees, at a cost of C$4.9–6.4 billion, to replace the informal care provided to seniors by Canadians in 1996.

Policy shifts in the OECD countries

Policy makers in the OECD countries have placed increasing priority on developing policies to address the long-term care needs of frail elderly people (Hennessy 1995). Hennessy notes that "the demand for long-term care is growing, and it will continue to do so for least another 50 years" due to political as well as demographic forces. He adds that "by 2020 over 50 percent of the *electorate* of the current European Union will be aged 50 or more." He argues that policy-makers should learn to treat long-term care as part of the "normal risk of living and growing old" and "create a balanced delivery system that is capable of responding to individual need" (1997: 36).

In particular, the balance should tilt more towards supporting people in their own homes or in carefully designed group housing in local communities. Currently, public expenditure on long-term care is, in most countries, heavily focused on institutional forms of care. Home-based care often requires housing adaptations and rent allowances, but is generally preferred by elderly people (Hennessy 1997: 37). However, with the exception of Italy and Japan, an increasing proportion of households across the OECD include only one adult generation, which means that fewer household members are immediately available to provide informal care (Casey and Yamada 2002). While caregivers generally prefer to avoid institutionalizing family members, the process of providing care themselves often limits their opportunities for employment, leisure pursuits, and sleep (Linsk *et al.* 1992: 9; Merrill 1997: 89–98; Jenson and Jacobzone 2000: 34).

In response to these pressures, many OECD countries have established some systems of support for caregivers, including tax breaks or direct payments (Linsk *et al.* 1992; Jenson and Jacobzone 2000). Nevertheless, these payments and supports thus far have proved more symbolic than practical, and do little to redress the economic disadvantages incurred by those who take on the caregiving role (Jenson and Jacobzone 2000: 33).

Gender dimensions

The growing public recognition of women's contributions to the care of the disabled and elderly has been advanced by feminist emphasis on the invisibility of women's unpaid work in general. Gender roles virtually dictate women's responsibility for care. Women are more likely than men to make adjustments to their paid work (like reducing their hours of work or switching to less taxing and often lower paid tasks) to provide unpaid care (Merrill 1997: 74; Jenson and Jacobzone 2000: 14). Women provide the majority of informal care, especially for their close relatives (Linsk *et al.* 1992: 8–9, 42; Merrill 1997: 4; Jenson and Jacobzone 2000; Neysmith 2000). Even when men and women share care tasks, men often leave women in charge of overall coordination (Merrill 1997: 7). Women play a greater role than men in helping with personal and daily tasks, while men (except for spouses) more often undertake occasional help, such as doing repairs, putting together items like furniture, or installing equipment in the home

(Merrill 1997: 6; Jenson and Jacobzone 2000: 14). Even paid work in elder care across OECD countries tends to be low-paid, part-time, female-dominated work that lacks career advancement opportunities (Christopherson 1997).

What nondiary sources tell us

Researchers have uncovered some information about the consequences of assuming the caring role (1) for care providers themselves, (2) for the people for whom they care, and (3) for other stakeholders, such as the employers of care providers. Caring can have an enormous impact on the daily lives of caregivers, constraining their ability to engage in other activities, including paid employment, routine domestic work, social engagements, leisure activities, and personal care (Keating *et al.* 1999).

Prior research also reveals that assuming a caring role influences the long-term future of caregivers, limiting their career development, the accumulation of pension funds for their own retirement and increasing their risk of poverty (Arber and Ginn 1997; Neysmith 2000). A significant proportion of working-age caregivers are employed. In Australia, for example, 36 percent of caregivers fall into this category (Australian Bureau of Statistics (ABS) 1998a). However, employed caregivers often find the competing demands too great and are forced to leave employment, thereby reducing their income.

Caregiving can also lead to social isolation. According to the ABS publication *A Focus on Families* (1995), for example, 17 percent of principal caregivers were unable to go out during the day unless the care recipient accompanied them or alternate caring arrangements were organized (ABS 1995). Caregivers often report high levels of stress as a result of providing help (Merrill 1997; Henwood 1998; Schofield *et al.* 1998). Many of the negative consequences of caring escalate as the time devoted to caring increases (Fine and Thomson 1995; Keating *et al.* 1999).

Despite the vast literature on informal caregiving, very little is known about the quantitative dimensions of caregiving – "its definition, incidence, prevalence and burden" – even in the data-rich OECD countries (Smeeding and Marchand, Chapter 2, this volume). Research in the United Kingdom distinguishes between the amount and the intensity of caring, between "informal helping" and "heavily involved caring" (Parker 1992; Twigg 1996; Henwood 1998). "Heavily involved" is variously defined, but may include coresident care as opposed to less intense extra-resident care (Arber and Ginn 1992). Involvement may also be defined in terms of the caregivers' levels of responsibility and whether they are the sole or main caregivers. Parker (1992) finds that helping with personal care and/or physical care may be used as a proxy measure of heavy involvement.

One US study by Moss *et al.* (1993) compares time allocation patterns of caregivers who reside with the care receiver and those who live elsewhere. Coresidential caregivers spend more than twice as much time on care tasks and about half as much time on paid work and on recreation as caregivers who live separately from the care receiver.

When a care receiver subsequently moves into a nursing home, the caregiver's care time is reduced by more than 75 percent, time they reallocate largely to recreation, family interaction, and paid work. Canadian research reveals that people informally caring for an elderly person estimate that they spend an average of 4–6 hours per week in caring activities for each senior to whom they provide assistance, though the estimated hours of care range widely (Keating *et al.* 1999).[5]

A paradoxical mismatch

The most striking finding to emerge from the study of caregiver's time-diaries is that the activities most clearly related to caring appear to consume only a small proportion of the day. This means that the time-diary information is completely at odds with self-reported estimates of the weekly hours spent in caring. Two different Australian surveys, using the same basic definition of a "caregiver", produced markedly different estimates of time devoted to unpaid care work. Estimates based on the 1997 national time-diary data indicate that primary caregivers who did not live with the care receiver devoted an average of 4.5 hours per week to care work, while coresidential primary caregivers spent over 8 hours caring per week. In contrast, respondents to the Survey of Disability, Ageing and Carers (ABS 1998a) who were caring for someone with a profound or severe handicap estimated their own care time to be much greater. Forty-four percent thought they spent 40 hours or more on care work, and another 17 percent estimated that they provided care for 20–39 hours per week. Only one-third of respondents thought they spent less than 20 hours per week on caregiving.

On the face of it, there seem to be two possible solutions to this paradox. First, self-reports may be inflated. This possibility is explored by Wolf (Chapter 6, this volume). A second possibility is that time-diaries fail to capture the real burden of caregiving and underestimate the time inputs.

As Ironmonger observes (Chapter 5, this volume), self-reported hours of childcare may reflect the constraints of supervision, needing to be "on call." As Budig and Folbre emphasize (Chapter 3, this volume), diaries are designed primarily to record activities, and being "on call" seldom shows up as an activity. An additional complication is that care activity may be embedded in and absorbed into normal domestic activity. Even the time spent in caring activities can be obscured by the ways these activities are embedded in and absorbed into normal domestic activities in diary data. In time-diaries, joint production of a meal to be consumed by both caregiver and care recipient is already assigned to a domestic activity code and does not register as a specific activity associated with caregiving.

An additional complication is that caregivers often fail to recognize much of the care work they perform as care. Some misidentification arises because they do not distinguish care from normal family responsibilities. In other cases, caregivers cope with their circumstances by denying the severity of the condition of the person for whom they care. The reclassification of caregiving activities as other kinds of activities is an integral part of the denial strategy. Denial is a frequently used, and not necessarily dysfunctional, method for dealing with the deteriorating autonomy (the onset of dementia, Alzheimer's, mobility restrictions and collapsing self-care functions) of a spouse, especially when open recognition would involve a great deal of grief and psychic pain (Andolsek *et al.* 1988; Harris Interactive 2002).

One strategy for addressing these measurement problems is to develop a more intensive and focused instrument for assessing specific activities, giving attention to qualitative as well as quantitative factors. Another strategy is to use diary data to compare the time adults spend in domestic activities in households with and without a disabled person requiring care.

Disability

Following the World Health Organization guidelines, ABS defines disability as any restriction or lack (resulting from an impairment) of ability to perform an action in the manner or within the range considered normal for a human being. A person has a disability if he/she has a limitation, restriction or impairment which has lasted, or is likely to last, for at least six months and restricts everyday activities. To qualify as a carer (caregiver) in ABS surveys, a person must provide assistance to someone with a long-term condition who cannot manage the core Activities of Daily Living (ADLs) – self-care (bathing, eating, dressing), mobility (getting in and out of bed or getting around the house), or communication (cannot understand or be understood in their native language or can communicate more easily using sign language). Estimating the marginal effect of a disabled person resembles methods used to estimate equivalent household income for families of different sizes and compositions. It also resembles the method of estimating "net replacement cost" advocated by Wolf (Chapter 6, this volume). We pursue each of these strategies here.

Caregiver focus groups

In May 2000, the organization Carers NSW in Australia recruited participants for a series of six focus groups with 21 caregivers, using their Carer Contact Database as a sampling frame. The sample included both carers of people with physical disabilities and carers of people with a mental and cognitive illness of varying levels of severity. Caregivers were asked to record their activities in a time-diary and then participate in a focus group the day after to discuss the experience. They had the opportunity to reflect on the picture that time-diaries provided.

Most focus group participants lived with the person to whom they provided care. The focus-group time-diaries differed from those distributed by the ABS in that they were divided into 30-minute intervals rather than the five-minute intervals, and in that they asked participants to record all activities which occurred during the half-hour slot (rather than only recording a main activity and up to one simultaneous activity as required by the ABS diary). One particularly revealing diary is described here. The caregiver was looking after her daughter with multiple disabilities and was supported by her husband. She began her diary at 6 a.m., when she went into her daughter's room to roll her as the daughter could not move independently. This caregiver then gave her daughter medication and assisted her daughter with eating breakfast. At 7 a.m., the caregiver fed the dog, made a cup of tea and put in a load of washing. She then packed her daughter's school bag, wrote in her communication book and made the beds. At 8.30 a.m., the caregiver suctioned her daughter and then gave her medication. At 9 a.m., she fed her daughter and changed her diaper. The husband then accompanied their daughter to school.

The caregiver's next task was to hang the washing out and put in another load of wash. At 10 a.m., the caregiver got dressed, answered the phone, and put the second load of washing out. At 11 a.m., she put in another load of washing and went shopping with her granddaughter. When she returned home, she prepared her daughter's eight small meal portions. At 1 p.m., she sterilized the tracheotomy equipment, washed the morning dishes, answered the phone and made a cup of tea. At 2 p.m., she made and ate lunch, then read stories with her granddaughter for half an hour. At 3 p.m., her daughter came home from school, and the caregiver talked and played with her. Next she washed her daughter's feeding equipment and drank the cup of tea made at 1 p.m. Then the caregiver suctioned her daughter again, prepared the family dinner, ate, and washed the dishes. At 7 p.m., the caregiver changed her daughter's diaper and helped her exercise. After concluding the exercises, she suctioned her daughter's tracheotomy tube again and gave her medication. The caregiver put her daughter to bed at 10 p.m. At 12 midnight, she got up and went to her daughter's bedroom to roll her daughter and to suction her tracheotomy tube. At 3 a.m., the caregiver got out of bed to roll her daughter again. At 5 a.m., this caregiver woke, did some knitting, watched TV, and then made milk and meals for her daughter. At 6 a.m., the caregiver fed her daughter, then changed her daughter's diaper, and put in another load of washing. Thus, another day began.

In the example given here, the caregiver spent approximately 8 hours providing direct assistance to the child or maintaining the special equipment required; if some proportion of joint production (of laundry, clean crockery, etc.) was on behalf of the care recipient the direct time spent in caregiving was still higher. Furthermore, it became evident in the focus groups that many caregivers, including this caregiver, were on-call 24 hours per day. This aspect of caring was not adequately captured in the time-diaries because time-diaries are instruments for recording activities. Being on-call is a state of readiness, like that of a fire-fighter in a station, a potential to perform an activity when needed, rather than an activity itself.

In addition, diaries did not readily reveal the severe restrictions on caregivers' ability to go out to and enjoy leisure activities, such as eating dinner in restaurants or going to the movies. Joint production is also evident in the example given. Washing for the care recipient is usually combined with washing for the family, even in cases where incontinence or some other medical requirement greatly increased the labor involved. Similarly, shopping, cleaning, and cooking tend to be coded as domestic work rather than as care. Caregivers often overlooked the number of hours they spent organizing services and appointments, as well as the associated time spent traveling to those appointments. During the focus group discussions, many participants realized for the first time that some of their domestic activities constituted part of the care they provided. Other issues raised in the discussions included the problems associated with interrupted sleep. While focus groups reveal the complexity of constraints on the activities of caregivers, they do not lend themselves to the collection of systematic data in large-scale samples. Therefore, it is important to apply these qualitative insights to the quantitative analysis of time-diaries.

Identifying the time signatures of Australian caregivers

A time signature is a distinguishing profile of time allocation. A time signature for caregivers can be constructed from analysis of how their time is distributed across the entire range of activity categories when compared with the typical time allocations of people with no caregiving responsibilities. While this is an activity-based measure and therefore does not solve the problem of measuring on-call responsibility, it does provide some insight into the effects of care responsibilities. The 1997 Australian Time Use Survey asked a battery of the standard questions used to officially identify caregivers. This sequence of questions is based on identifying those who provide assistance to persons who are unable to perform core ADLs (self-care, mobility, and communication) unassisted. Having this caregiver's flag associated with the time-diary information cleared the way for analyzing distinctive time signatures, which vary according to their residential arrangements and the age of the care recipient. The distinctive time signature of coresidential caregivers includes a substantially lower rate of participation in the labor market and in education, increased time spent in domestic work activities and, in the case of caregivers of children, the time spent in direct childcare. These patterns hold even after controlling for the effects of age and employment status (Bittman and Thomson 2000).

Perhaps the most distinctive feature of the broad time signature of the coresidential caregiver is the small, and hence apparently unremarkable, average time spent in "voluntary work and care" activities, the very category designed to capture caregiving. This group of activity classifications contains the category "support for adults," embracing physical and emotional care, and is designed to capture the assistance one adult provides for another, even if they coreside. The ABS has taken the unusual step of classifying this narrow band of caregiving activities as "voluntary work and care" even if the exchanges take place in a single residence and the parties to the exchange are spouses or parents and children. So it comes as a great surprise to find that principal caregivers of "adult in own household" spend less than 5 hours per week in voluntary work and care activities.

Somehow, the principal caregivers of "adult in another household" average over 8 hours per week in voluntary work and care activities, almost double the average hours of coresidential caregivers. It is perhaps less surprising that the coresidential caregivers of children spend less than 2 hours per week in this activity, since the bulk of their caring activities are captured in the "childcare" category. The hours devoted to voluntary work and care activities across the Australian population average out at 2.5 hours per week. Although the hours spent by principal caregivers are approximately double (coresident caregivers) or triple (caregivers of adults living in another household) the national average, on the face of it these hours seem to underestimate the caregiving burden.

All this points to the displacement of the time signature of coresidential caregivers from voluntary work and caring activities to domestic activities. The category domestic activities embraces "indoor tasks" (cooking, cleaning, and laundry) and "outdoor tasks" (lawn and pool care, household repair, and car care). Coresidential caregivers work longer hours in most of the major categories of domestic activities. Compared with the rest of the population, on average, coresidential caregivers work almost twice as long in laundry and clothes care, more than 60 percent longer in food preparation, clean-up and housework, and nearly 40 percent longer in gardening and lawn care. Compared with all other Australians those caring for children at home have even more extraordinary increases than the caregivers of adults – working double the mean population time in food preparation, clean-up, laundry, and housework, and increasing time spent in gardening and lawn care by over 60 percent.

Time signatures in Australia and Canada

To further develop the concept of caregiver time signatures, we apply similar methods to multivariate analysis of Australian and Canadian data. We compare three groups of respondents: those without any adult care responsibilities, those caring for an adult who lives apart from them, and those caring for an adult who resides with them. Three major activity categories are disaggregated into component parts. For domestic work, the subcategories include: cooking, cleaning, clothing care, home maintenance and repair, and other domestic chores. For recreation and leisure, the subcategories include: attending entertainment events, participating in active sports, other active leisure, reading and writing, and media. For social and community interaction, the subcategories include: socializing with family and friends, participating in religious activities, and participating in community organizations.

Data

We use the most recent national sample time-diary surveys conducted by Statistics Canada in 1998 and the ABS in 1997. Statistics Canada collected data over the telephone using a 24-hour yesterday-recall method, while ABS collected data for two consecutive days using leave-behind, self-completed diaries. All persons aged 15 and above in sampled households in Australia were asked to keep diaries, while the Canadian study collected a diary from one random person aged 15 or more in each household.[6]

Statistics Canada collected diaries between February 1998 and January 1999, with sampling spread over the 12 months and over all days of the week, in order to capture seasonal and daily variations in time-use patterns. The response rate was 77.6 percent yielding a sample size of 10,749. Australian data were collected at four separate periods over the calendar year (for more detailed information on the Australian survey methodology, see Note, pp. 238–9). Approximately 7,000 people in around 4,000 households completed diaries, resulting in a sample of 14,315 diary days. The response rate was 84.4 percent.

In both cases, enough information was collected about the people for whom activities were performed to allow caregivers to be identified. In the Australian survey, respondents were asked whether the person provided help with core ADLs. In the Canadian survey, personal or medical care provided to a household adult was coded as such. For other activities, respondents were asked whether they had performed that activity for someone else who lived outside the household. If the activity was performed for someone living in another household, interviewers asked the respondent for the age of the care recipient, the degree to which the care recipient could live normally without help, and the relationship between the respondent and the person to whom he or she had provided care.

Since the purpose of the analysis is to estimate the marginal effect of caregiving, it is important to control for other personal characteristics that might affect time-use. For this reason, we first provide Ordinary Least Squares (OLS) regression analysis of hours per week spent caring for adults compared to time spent in four other key broad categories of activity: paid work; domestic work; recreation and leisure; and social and community interaction.[7] In addition to type of dependent care responsibilities (coresidential or nonresidential), independent variables include many of the factors that determine how people spend their time: age; employment status; education; gender; presence and age of children in the household; marital status; income; and day of the week. These analyses, run separately for men and women, allow us to determine whether, and what type of, adult care responsibilities are related to how respondents spent the rest of their time.

The results presented in Table 4.1 demonstrate that whether a respondent provides care to a dependent adult on the diary day(s) helps to explain differences in how their time is spent. It also shows that the type of care situation (coresidential or nonresidential) matters.

Caring for an adult who lives apart is negatively associated with weekly hours of paid work in Canada. Canadian women and men caregivers spend 8.25 and 16.75 fewer hours per week, respectively, at a paid job than those without caregiving responsibilities. These coefficients probably reflect the fact that caregivers were not employed, or were employed part-time (it would be redundant to include employment status in an equation designed to explore the impact of caregiving on weekly hours of paid work). Coresidential caregivers similarly spent less time on paid work than non-caregivers, but the effect was not quite as

Table 4.1 Net effect of caregiving on weekly hours spent in selected activities

		Paid work	Domestic work	Recreation and leisure	Social/ community
Men					
Canada	Coresidential	−11.63**	0.64	−3.34	1.79
	Nonresidential	−16.74***	0.66	−7.45**	11.12***
Australia	Coresidential	−12.09***	5.20***	−5.49**	0.23
	Nonresidential	−10.68***	0.76	−3.92	4.14**
Women					
Canada	Coresidential	−4.82*	4.47**	−5.39**	−2.85
	Nonresidential	−8.25***	0.55	−6.38***	6.50***
Australia	Coresidential	−5.15**	3.80***	−4.14***	1.13
	Nonresidential	−5.34**	1.75	−3.70**	5.15***

Notes: $* P < 0.05$; $** P < 0.01$; $*** P < 0.0005$.

great as it was for those caring for someone who lived apart from them (4.8 and 3.3 hours per week for women and men, respectively). It is likely that commuting time to the care recipient's residence (which is not accounted for as care time) places constraints on the caregiver's time over and above the care time itself. The Australian figures exhibit a similar pattern, showing almost as large an impact on time spent in paid work (5 hours per week fewer for women and between 10.5 and 12 fewer for men), although coresidence increases the impact for men only.

Caring for an adult in one's own household infringes on leisure time for all caregivers, regardless of gender or nationality. However, the differential is a little smaller for Canadian coresidential caregivers than for their counterparts caring for an adult outside the household. Canadian women and men caring for an adult outside their own household enjoy 6.4 and almost 7.5 hours per week less leisure time, respectively, than noncarers. Canadian coresidential caregivers spend about 5.4 (women) and 3.3 (men) hours less on recreation than noncarers. According to Table 4.1, Australian women also spend less time on recreation and leisure if they are caring for a dependent adult (4.1 and 3.7 hours per week less for coresidential and nonresidential carers, respectively). Among Australian men, only those who are coresidential caregivers have less leisure time (5.5 hours less per week) than men without care responsibilities.

Interestingly, nonresidential caregiving is positively associated with hours per week of social and community interaction for both men and women, in both Canada and Australia. Caregivers whose care receiver lives apart from them spend between 4 and 11 hours more on social and community interaction activities than noncarers. Perhaps these patterns reflect the civic connections forged through joining self-help groups.

Nonresidential caregivers spend about the same time on domestic work as noncaregivers. Coresidential carers, however, spend significantly more time (between 4 and 5 hours more each week) on housekeeping chores than noncarers.

This difference is probably explained by the fact that household chores done for a dependent adult living in the community are counted as care because they occur outside the caregiver's home. In contrast, additional laundry, cooking, cleaning and so on occasioned by the presence of a dependent adult in the household are probably coded as general household work and not attributed to "care."

Detailed profiles

Figures 4.1–4.6 illustrate in more detail the substitution decisions of Canadian and Australian caregivers. As Figures 4.1 and 4.2 show, male and female caregivers both spend a good deal of that additional time on cooking and cleaning – this is

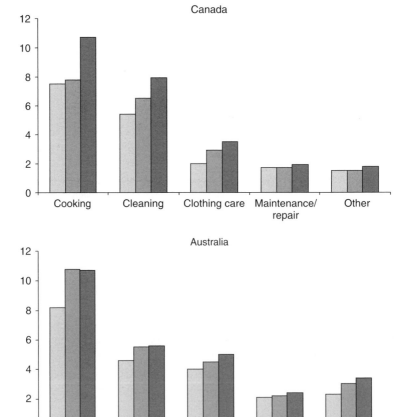

Figure 4.1 Domestic work time of female carers and noncarers.

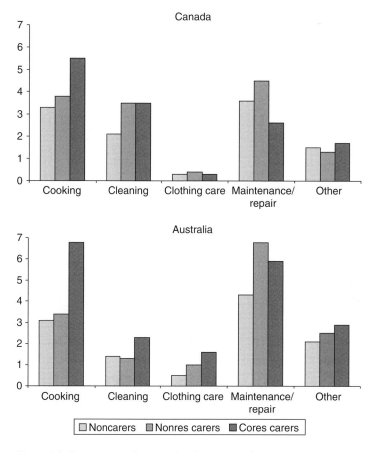

Figure 4.2 Domestic work time of male carers and noncarers.

especially true for coresidential caregivers. Women caregivers also spend more time on clothing care (washing, ironing, and mending clothes) than noncaregivers. Men caring for a nonhousehold adult spend more time on repairs and maintenance (probably maintaining the care recipient's property) in both Canada and Australia. Interestingly, Australian men who are coresidential caregivers also spend more time on maintenance and repairs than noncaregivers, while coresidential male caregivers in Canada spend less time maintaining their own homes.

Figures 4.3 and 4.4 help explain the differences in leisure time among noncaregivers, coresidential caregivers, and ex-residential caregivers. Men caring for a dependent adult spend less time attending sporting, arts and entertainment events, instead spending more time on such home-bound, sedentary pursuits as reading and writing. Women sacrifice different kinds of leisure activities, spending less time on active sports and watching television or listening to the radio. These patterns are fairly similar for Canadian and Australian respondents.

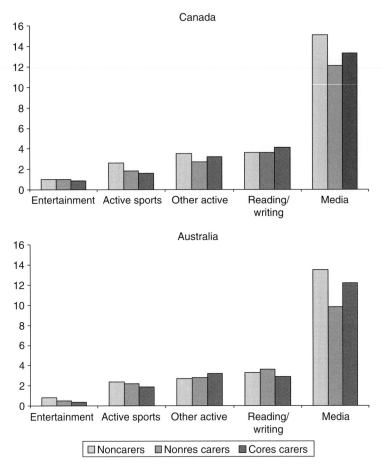

Figure 4.3 Recreation/leisure time of female carers and noncarers.

Figures 4.5 and 4.6 shed some light on why caregivers caring for a nonhousehold adult appear to be more involved in their communities and have more active social lives. A small part of this difference can be attributed to greater involvement in religious activities, which is consistent with the literature on volunteer work showing that both formal and informal volunteers have stronger religious affiliations. However, most of this extra time can be attributed to more socializing for both men and women. The patterns are similar for Canadians and Australians with two exceptions: Australian women who are coresidential caregivers spend a good deal more time socializing than their Canadian counterparts (more even than noncaregivers); and Canadian men caring for a nonhousehold adult spend more than twice as much time socializing as Australian men who care for someone outside their household.

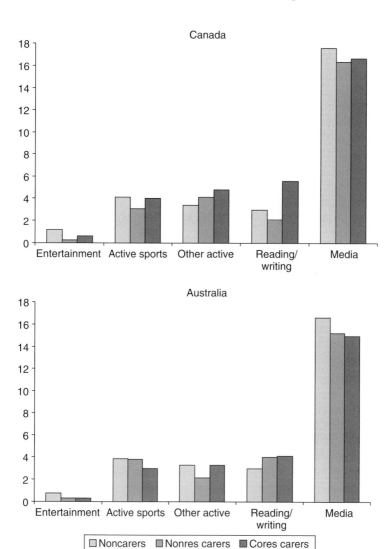

Figure 4.4 Recreation/leisure time of male carers and noncarers.

The broad similarities in the impact of caregiving on patterns of time-use are striking. The differences between caregivers and noncaregivers in others are significant and have the same sign, although the sizes of some effects differ. That such parallel patterns are evident in two countries with different public policies and service delivery arrangements provides support for the concept of time signatures, and holds out the prospect that these might be used to provide improved estimates of the cost of informal care.

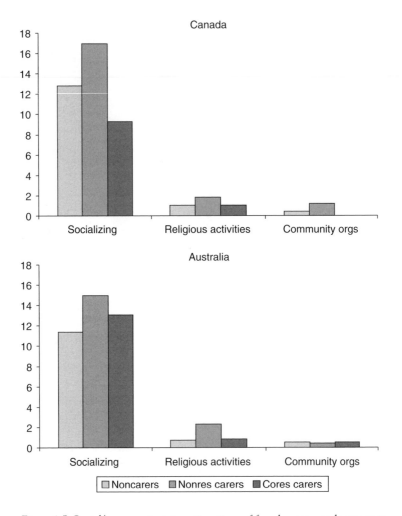

Figure 4.5 Social/community interaction time of female carers and noncarers.

Summary

Adult dependent care responsibilities affect the rhythm of daily life for care-givers. There are only 24 hours in a day: time for care must be found somewhere. At an aggregate level, much of the care time appears to be subtracted from the time available for paid work and leisure. Caregivers' care responsibilities appear to constrain out-of-home entertainment and participation in active sports. Women's caring responsibilities are more likely to keep them from active leisure.

At the same time, the day-to-day housekeeping load appears to be greater for caregivers, especially when the care recipient lives with them. Most of this

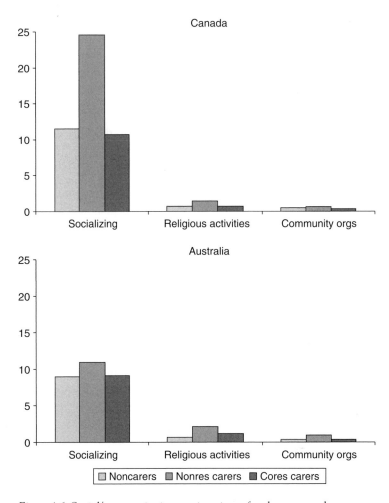

Figure 4.6 Social/community interaction time of male carers and noncarers.

additional domestic work seems to take the form of cooking and cleaning, as well as laundry for women, and home repair and maintenance for men. This contributes to the invisibility of coresidential caring, at times making it invisible even to the caregivers themselves.

Those caring for a nonhousehold member appear to have much more active social lives than even noncaregivers. Perhaps the association results from a selection effect, with those who care for others outside their own homes being predisposed to this form of civic participation. Alternatively, it may suggest that caring for someone living in the community provides exposure to a wider circle of friends, family, and acquaintances, drawing caregivers into civic participation. Or perhaps such care involves more social and emotional support and monitoring than physical care. More likely, the social and emotional support and monitoring dimensions of care are not well accounted for in time-diary data when the respondent is caring for someone in their own household.

Despite differences in the prevalence of coresidential and nonresidential caregiving situations in Canada and Australia, and in the overall amount of time spent on care tasks, the impact of caregiving on caregivers' lives seems remarkably similar, with a couple of notable exceptions. While caring for an adult living in another household is associated with substantial increases in the time men and women spend socializing in both Canada and Australia, the increases are especially large in Canada. In addition, regression results suggest that, unlike Australian men, Canadian men's domestic work time is unaffected by their caregiver status. The time signature data, however, suggest an explanation. Coresidential male caregivers seem to spend more time cooking, which is apparently offset by a reduction in time spent maintaining their home. Finally, in Australia coresidential care involves greater reductions in leisure time than nonresidential care for both men and women.

Among the most important findings are those that reveal the hidden nature of many care activities. The additional domestic workload borne by coresidential caregivers suggests one type of "hidden" care. As suggested earlier, it is likely that the presence of a physically or cognitively dependent adult in the household increases the caregiver's burden in ways not easily distinguished from his or her normal household responsibilities. It may also be that the time nonresidential caregivers spend commuting to the care recipient's residence is poorly captured in the data analyzed here. Perhaps most enlightening is the finding that nonresidential caregivers appear to spend substantially more time socializing than noncaregivers. The most likely explanation is that this represents yet another form of hidden care – social and emotional support and/or transporting or accompanying recipients to social and community activities such as religious services which get coded as social activities rather than care activities.

Acknowledgments

An Australian Research Council grant funded a collaborative research project between the Social Policy Research Centre and Carers NSW that serves as the focus of much of the discussion in this chapter.

Notes

1 In this chapter the North American term "caregiver" is used in preference to the terms "carer" and "care provider" (commonly used in the United Kingdom and Australia) to distinguish the care of the frail elderly or people with a disability from other forms of caring labor.
2 Member countries of OECD at the time of writing were Australia, Austria, Belgium, Canada, Czech Republic, Denmark, Finland, France, Germany, Greece, Hungary, Iceland, Ireland, Italy, Japan, Korea, Luxembourg, Mexico, Netherlands, New Zealand,

Norway, Poland, Portugal, Slovak Republic, Spain, Sweden, Switzerland, Turkey, United Kingdom, and United States.

3 Because time-use data are collected as a matter of course in many countries, they also provide an opportunity for cross-national comparisons that can be used to describe differences in life styles, living standards, and quality of life under different social, economic, and political conditions. It is easier to make cross-national comparisons of time-use than of income or expenditure. The day has 24 hours in all countries and is not subject to exchange rate fluctuations or variations in purchasing parity. Moreover, time-use researchers began standardising procedures for the collection of time-use data in the 1960s (Szalai 1972), and organizations including EUROSTAT and the International Association of Time Use Research have expanded this collaboration to refine data collection procedures and begin harmonizing data cleaning and analysis techniques. Methodological studies have shown that time-diaries are not particularly sensitive to whether the information is collected prospectively or retrospectively, in diaries with fixed intervals or with open intervals, provided respondents are not dealing with a period of more than 48 hours (Niemi 1993; Robinson and Godley 1997). Activity classifications also are fairly standardized ensuring good international data comparability. In recent years, the United Nations has played an active role in this area (e.g. see www.un.org/Depts/unsd/timeuse/index.htm).

4 All levels of government, federal, state, and local government.

5 It also shows that the majority of people caring for an older person look after more than one elderly person at the same time.

6 People living in institutions or in the Northern Territories were not sampled.

7 There is one feature of time-use data that readers should keep in mind when interpreting the data presented in this chapter. Not everyone engages in every activity every day. Since each record in the data file represents a single diary day, it will appear that some people never engage in some activities when, in fact, they simply did not engage in the activity on the diary day. That is, there will be many zero observations for some of the less frequent activities. When this "truncation" problem is severe, estimates of the relationships between the dependent and independent variables obtained from multivariate analyses, such as the regression analyses with which we began our analyses, may be biased. The most widely used empirical solution to the truncation problem is Tobit analysis. However, this technique turns out to have its own empirical problems (most notably heteroskedasticity, or non-normally distributed error terms) when applied to time-use data, especially when many of the independent variables are categorical. The best alternative is a two-stage estimation procedure which makes it difficult to interpret the relationship between the independent variables of interest and time spent on various activities. We have chosen to use OLS regression despite the noted limitations. Readers are advised, therefore, that regression coefficients presented in this volume may be biased, but their signs and significance levels are reliable. In cross-tabular analysis, the truncation problem raises the dilemma of whether to present mean times for all respondents or for only those respondents who reported engaging in the activity that day. In the first case, real averages may be underestimated; in the second, one risks overestimating the mean. We have chosen the more conservative alternative of estimating means for all respondents. Absolute values may thus be underestimated, but the impact will be minimal for the aggregate activity categories.

References

Andolsek, K. M., Clapp-Channing, N. E., Gehlbach, S. H., Moore, I., Proffitt, V. S., Sigmon, A., and Warshaw, G. A. (1988) "Caregivers and Elderly Relatives. The prevalence of Caregiving in a Family Practice," *Archives of Internal Medicine*, 148: 2177–80.

Arber, S. and Ginn, J. (1992) "In Sickness and in Health: Caregiving, Gender and the Independence of Elderly People," in C. March and S. Arber (eds), *Families and Households: Division and Change*, London: Macmillan.

Arber, S. and Ginn, J. (1997) "Informal Caregivers for Elderly People," in C. Ungerson and M. Kember (eds), *Women and Social Policy*, London: Macmillan, pp. 357–8.

Arno, P., Levine, C., and Memmnott, M. (1999) "The Economic Value of Informal Caregiving," *Health Affairs*, 18: 182–8.

Australian Bureau of Statistics (ABS) (1995) *A Focus on Families – Caring in Families: Support for Persons Who are Older or Who Have Disabilities*, Catalogue No. 4423.0. Canberra: Australian Bureau of Statistics.

—— (1997) *Time Use Survey*, Canberra: Australian Bureau of Statistics.

—— (1998a) *Disability, Ageing and Carers: Summary of Findings*, Catalogue No. 4430.0, Canberra: Australian Bureau of Statistics.

—— (1998b) *Time Use Survey Australia: User's guide 1997*, Catalogue No. 4150.0, Canberra: Australian Bureau of Statistics.

Australian Institute of Health and Welfare (2001) *Australia's Welfare 2001*, Canberra: AGPS.

Bittman, M. and Thomson, C. (2000) "Invisible Support," in J. Warburton and M. Oppenheimer (eds), *Volunteers and Volunteering*, Sydney: Federation Press, pp. 98–112.

Brody, E. (1981) "Women in the Middle and Family Help to Older People," *The Gerontologist*, 21(5): 471–9.

Casey, B. and Yamada, A. (2002) "Getting Older, Getting Poorer? A Study of the Earnings, Pensions, Assets and Living Arrangements of Older People in Nine Countries," Labour Market and Social Policy Occasional Paper No. 60, Paris: OECD.

Christopherson, S. (1997) "Childcare and Elderly Care: What Occupational Opportunities for Women?," Labour Market and Social Policy Occasional Papers No. 27, Paris: OECD.

Fast, J. E., Keating, N. C., and Forbes, D. A. (2000) "A Matter of Time: The True Cost of Eldercare," Paper presented at the Annual Scientific and Educational Meeting of the Canadian Association on Gerontology, Edmonton, Alberta, October.

Finch, J. and Groves, D. (1983) *A Labour of Love: Women Work and Caring*, London: Routledge & Kegan Paul.

Fine, M. and Thomson, C. (1995) "Three Years at Home: The Final Report of the Longitudinal Study of Community Support Services and Their Users," Report and Proceedings No. 121, Sydney: Social Policy Research Centre.

Fleming, R. and Spellerberg, A. (1999) *Using Time Use Data: A History of Time Use Surveys and Uses of Time Use Data*, Wellington: Statistics New Zealand.

Harris Interactive (2002) "Failure to Seek Medical Advice for the Early Symptoms of Alzheimer's Disease Results in Delayed Diagnosis and Treatment Which is Often Regretted Later," *Health Care News*, 12(4). www.harrisinteractive.com/news/newsletters/healthnews/ accessed on July14, 2003.

Hennessy, P. (1995) "Social Protection for Dependent Elderly People: Perspectives from a Review of OECD Countries," Labour Market and Social Policy Occasional Paper No. 16, Paris: OECD.

—— (1997) "The Growing Risk of Dependency in Old Age: What Role for Families and For Social Security?," *International Social Security Review*, 50(1): 23–39.

Henwood, M. (1998) "Ignored and Invisible? Carers Experience of the NHS," London: Carers National Association.

Jacobzone, S. (1999) "Ageing and Care for Frail Elderly Persons: An Overview of International Perspectives," Labour Market and Social Policy Occasional Paper No. 38, Paris: OECD.

Jenson, J. and Jacobzone, S. (2000) "Care Allowances for the Frail Elderly and Their Impact on Women Care-Givers," Labour Market and Social Policy Occasional Papers No. 41, Paris: OECD.

Keating, N., Fast, J., Frederick, J., Cranswick, K., and Perrier, C. (1999) "Eldercare in Canada: Context, Content and Consequences," Ottawa: Statistics Canada.

Land, H. (1978) "Who Cares for the Family?," *Journal of Social Policy*, 7(3): 357084.

Linsk, N. L., Keigher, S. M., Simon-Rusinowitz, L., and England, S. E. (1992) *Wages for Caring: Compensating Family Care for the Elderly*, New York: Praeger.

Merrill, D. M. (1997) *Caring for Elderly Parents: Juggling Work, Family, and Caregiving in Middle and Working Class Families*, West Port, CT: Auburn House.

Moss, M. S., Lawton, M. P., Kleban, M. H., and Duhamel, L. (1993) "Time Use of Caregivers of Impaired Elders Before and After Institutionalization," *Journal of Gerontology: Social Sciences*, 48(3): S102–11.

Neysmith, S. M. (2000) "Networking Across Difference: Connecting Restructuring and Caring Labour," in S. M. Neysmith (ed.), *Restructuring Caring Labour: Discourse, State Practice, and Everyday Life*, Ontario: Oxford University Press, pp. 1–28.

Niemi, I. (1993) "Systematic Error in Behavioural Measurement: Comparing Results from Interview and Time Budget Studies," *Social Indicators Research*, 30: 229–44.

Parker, G. (1992) "Counting Care: Numbers and Types of Informal Carers," in J. Twigg (ed.), *Carers: Research and Practice*, London: HMSO.

Robinson, J. and Godbey, G. (1997) *Time for Life: The Surprising Ways Americans Use their Time*, University Park: Pennsylvania State University Press.

Schofield, E., Bloch, S., Herrman, H., Murphy, B., Nankervis, J., and Singh, B. (eds) (1998) *Family Caregivers: Disability, Illness and Ageing*, London: Allen and Unwin.

Szalai, A. (ed.) (1972) *The Use of Time: Daily Activities of Urban and Suburban Populations in Twelve Countries*, The Hague: Mouton.

Twigg, J. (ed.) (1996) "Issues in Informal Care," in Organization for Economic Cooperation and Development, *Caring for Frail Elderly People: Policies in Evolution*, Number 19, London: OECD Social Policies Studies.

Ungerson, C. and Kember, M. (eds) (1997) *Women and Social Policy*, London: Macmillan.

Part III

Valuing childcare and elder care

5 Bringing up Bobby and Betty

The inputs and outputs of childcare time

Duncan Ironmonger

Raising a child to adulthood requires a significant expenditure of time as well as money. Expenditures on little Betty and Bobby represent investments in the future. If time and money devoted to children are not well spent, there are large negative consequences for society. In recent years, the care and well-being of children has become the focus of increased community concern in Australia (Cashmore 2001).

Many researchers have explored the monetary inputs into childrearing in terms of direct and indirect expenditures, including institutional childcare costs and foregone earnings of mothers. Some notable work in the United Kingdom and the United States includes Joshi (1990), Haveman and Wolfe (1995), Waldfogel (1997), Joshi *et al.* (1999), and Folbre *et al.* (2003). Recent research in Australia includes Valenzuela (1999), Australian Institute of Family Studies (2000), Richardson (2000), Gray and Chapman (2001), and Henman (2001). However, the total time devoted by family members, specifically by parents, to the care of children is rarely calculated.

Researchers often overlook the huge investment of time it takes to adequately raise children partly because caring for children offers parents "process benefits," or intrinsic satisfaction (Juster and Stafford 1991; Ironmonger 1996b: 40). Of course, for some parents these benefits may be negative. Regardless of levels of satisfaction, the parenting of young children is an obligation that remains in force twenty-four hours a day, seven days a week. We all know that the time devoted to children is large. But "How large?" is a matter of some confusion (Budig and Folbre, Chapter 3, this volume).

Australian time-use data provide a valuable opportunity to estimate the total time inputs provided by households, schools, and childcare services and compare their relative magnitudes. This chapter uses data from the Australian Time Use Survey of 1997 to estimate hours of care provided by the household sector of the economy, making a distinction between hours spent by adults in providing care and the hours of care received by children. This distinction is important because of potential overlaps both between care providers and between care recipients. In any caring situation, the input hours will equal the output hours only when the number of adult carers is the same as the number of children cared for. For example, if a grandmother cares for two grandchildren together for a 5-hour period, she has provided 5 hours of inputs, but 10 hours of total child-care have been received. Restricting the analysis to households with only one child, and making reasonable assumptions regarding other households, it is possible to estimate the total child hours of care received by all children.

This chapter begins with a review of the way in which childcare input time has been measured, with particular attention to the recording of time devoted to secondary or parallel activities in diary-based surveys. Next, it offers estimates of the amount of unpaid care received from household members by children of different ages, along with comparisons of the amount of care time received in paid childcare, school, and self-care. The final section provides an estimate of the relative size of labor inputs into household childcare compared to labor inputs into other household and market activities. The results clearly demonstrate the macroeconomic significance of household care to the economy as a whole.

Childcare provided by household members (adult input hours of care)

Time-use surveys provide researchers with detailed information on household childcare by eliciting data on how individuals spend every minute of the 1,440 minute day. These statistics can then be weighted and aggregated to provide estimates for time-use during a 168 hour week (Ironmonger 2000). The cross-national time budget studies in twelve countries conducted in the 1960s inspired many countries, like Australia, to conduct their own national time-use studies (Szalai 1972). In the past forty years, national statistical offices in many countries have followed the Szalai methodology collecting diary-based time-use surveys from national surveys of time-use from representative samples of households.

Table 5.1 provides international comparisons of time devoted to children in twelve countries in the late 1980s and early 1990s. Most of the differences in survey methodologies were overcome by tabulating data for common age ranges and standardizing assumptions (such as including travel time associated with childcare). A striking feature across all these countries is the relatively low level of average time devoted to children, only 3.8 hours per week (hpw) for all women and 1.4 hpw for all men. These estimates are small because they are limited to activities in which childcare was designated as the primary activity. A closer look at Australian data helps explain why this conventional definition of childcare time is misleading.

Household time devoted to childcare in Australia

The 1997 survey conducted by the Australian Bureau of Statistics (ABS) shows that, on average, Australian women spent 5.3 hpw in primary activities with children, while men spent 1.9 hpw. Figure 5.1(a) shows that adult time inputs vary considerably over the life course. Both women and men spend the greatest amount of time in activities with children while they are in their thirties.

Table 5.1 Childcare in twelve OECD countries (hours/adult/week)

Country	Women	Men	Average adult
Denmark, 1987	2.2	0.9	1.5
Netherlands, 1987	2.6	0.7	1.6
Italy, 1988–89	2.6	0.8	1.8
France, 1985–86	3.3	0.8	2.1
Austria, 1992	3.7	0.9	2.2
Finland, 1987–88	3.3	1.3	2.3
United States, 1985	4.1	2.0	2.7
Germany, 1991–92	3.7	1.4	2.7
Britain, 1983–87	4.2	1.4	2.8
Canada, 1992	4.2	1.6	3.0
Australia, 1992	5.7	1.6	3.7
Norway, 1990–91	5.6	2.7	4.4
Mean of 12	3.8	1.4	2.6

Source: Goldschmidt-Clermont and Pagnossin-Aligisakis (1995).

The Australian data make it possible to look beyond time spent in primary activities to secondary or simultaneous activities. In any interval of time, people often undertake several activities at once. When completing their time-use diaries, respondents in the Australian Time Use Surveys have to record not only their primary or main activity but also any simultaneous or secondary activity. These questions appeared at the top of each page of the diary heading the first two columns in the following form (ABS 1993: Appendix D Collection Instruments).

First Column of Diary
WHAT WAS YOUR <u>MAIN</u> ACTIVITY?
(Please record all activities, even if they only lasted a few minutes)

Second Column of Diary
WHAT ELSE WERE YOU DOING AT THE SAME TIME?
(e.g. childminding, watching television, listening to the radio)

Respondents were given little guidance about the distinction between what is primary (main activity) and what is secondary (else doing at the same time). They were given the following instructions to read before beginning the diary: "To fill in the diary: write down your main activity (e.g. at work, cooking etc., childminding, watching TV); write down anything else you did at the same time (e.g. childminding, nursing parents/grandparents, watching television, listening to the radio, talking to a neighbour)" (ABS 1993: Appendix D Collection Instruments).

In addition, respondents were asked to make sure they had read two pages of examples of a completed diary before beginning the recording of their own activities. These examples showed both columns filled out with entries for every five-minute period with the entry "Nothing" shown in the second column as an answer for times when nothing else was being done. Apart from these examples, respondents were given no indication of the criteria they should use to determine which of two simultaneous activities is the "main" or primary activity. The recording depends entirely on what each respondent understands by "main."

Many researchers have found it problematic to examine the time involved in secondary activities because of aggregation problems. For example, 1 hour an individual spends on cleaning (primary activity) and caring for children (secondary activity) could be considered 1 hour of cleaning plus 1 hour of child-care. Alternatively, the two activities could be split, with 30 minutes attributed to cleaning and 30 minutes to childcare. As a result of these apparent difficulties with dual activities, little systematic research has been undertaken on simultaneous time use.[1]

But consideration of the total time spent in caring for children is necessary, because evidence shows that this is far greater than the virtually arbitrary amount of this time recorded in diaries as main or primary activities. Estimates based on primary activity yield numbers that are dramatically lower than those reported by parents in stylized surveys that ask them to estimate how much time they devoted over the preceding week (Ironmonger 1996a; Budig and Folbre, Chapter 3, this volume). When secondary time is included, estimates of total time devoted to children increase substantially. The figure of unpaid childcare reported by households is multiplied four times with the inclusion of childcare carried out while doing something else (Ironmonger 1996a: 56). Bittman and Pixley (1997) similarly report that nearly 75 percent of all time spent in child-care in Australia is spent while performing another activity.

As can be seen from Figure 5.1(b) below, the total amount of time (primary and secondary) devoted to children is four times greater than primary time alone, but follows the same pattern over the adult life course.

One way to illustrate the significance of simultaneous activities is to use Australian data from 1997 to construct a two-way matrix table of average time spent on primary activities by time spent on secondary activities (see Tables 5.2 and 5.3). Because of space constraints, only secondary activities that sum to more than one hour per week are shown in these tables. The matrix approach does not entail double-counting; each minute of the day is recorded only once in the body of the table. Both the row totals and the column totals (the printed table does not show all columns) sum to a total of 168 hpw. The matrix shows how much each category of time-use is recorded both as a primary and as a secondary activity.

On average, over all ages and stages of life, women did 14.2 hpw of childcare while recording that they were "mainly" doing something else. Men, on average, spent an additional 6.2 hpw on childcare while "mainly" undertaking another activity. Most secondary childcare is done while women and men record in the first column of the diary that their "main" activity was sleep or doing domestic chores. That there is some overlap between primary and secondary childcare (1.56 hours for women and 0.37 hours for men) suggests that parents are often dealing with more than one child (and more than one activity) at any given time. Summing the total of both primary and secondary time in childcare, but counting this overlap only once, gives an unduplicated estimate of the total time spent in childcare.

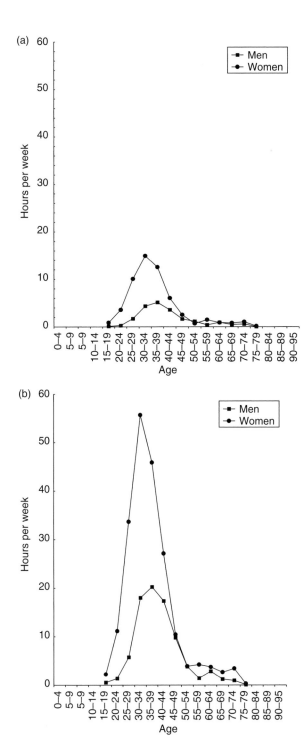

Figure 5.1 (a) Primary time on childcare in Australia, 1997; (b) total time on childcare in Australia, 1997.

Table 5.2 Matrix of primary by secondary activities of time-use, Australian women, 1997 (hpw; including only secondary activities summing to more than 1 hpw)

Primary activity	Secondary activity								
	No activity	Domestic activities	Childcare	Eating and drinking	Watching TV or videos	Listening to radio, compact discs etc.	Communication	Other passive leisure	Total (hpw)
No activity	0.21	—	—	—	—	—	—	—	0.21
Labor force	12.90	0.03	0.15	0.11	0.25	1.41	0.35	0.13	15.39
Domestic activities	10.94	0.44	2.49	0.08	2.27	2.75	1.72	0.22	20.97
Childcare	2.34	0.15	1.56	0.04	0.43	0.27	0.39	0.07	5.31
Purchasing goods and services	4.22	—	0.55	0.01	0.04	0.38	1.02	0.05	6.36
Sleeping	54.23	—	5.84	—	0.01	0.01	0.01	0.01	60.15
Personal care	4.39	0.02	0.39	0.01	0.22	0.63	0.18	0.09	5.94
Health care	0.65	—	0.02	—	0.08	0.05	0.03	0.03	0.87
Eating and drinking	4.25	0.08	0.82	0.02	1.86	0.78	2.52	0.64	11.09
Others: sleeping, eating, and personal care	0.07	—	0.01	—	0.01	0.01	0.01	—	0.11
Education	2.49	—	0.03	0.03	0.17	0.19	0.27	0.04	3.25
Voluntary work and community participation	2.11	0.04	0.32	0.09	0.47	0.28	0.73	0.03	4.45
Social life and entertainment	2.67	—	0.19	0.04	0.07	0.28	0.44	0.07	3.79
Active leisure	1.84	—	0.22	0.01	0.11	0.27	0.67	0.08	3.26
Watching TV or videos	9.00	0.23	0.73	0.36	0.03	0.05	1.39	0.99	12.86
Listening to radio, compact discs, etc.	0.68	0.01	0.02	0.01	0.01	—	0.04	0.04	0.81
Communication	3.55	0.10	0.44	0.26	0.48	0.25	0.03	0.19	5.36
Other passive leisure	4.54	0.04	0.38	0.12	1.09	0.68	0.61	0.29	7.82
Total (hpw)	121.08	1.14	14.16	1.19	7.59	8.26	10.39	2.97	168.00

Source: Australian Bureau of Statistics *Time Use Survey 1997*.

Table 5.3 Matrix of primary by secondary activities of time-use, Australian men, 1997 (hpw; including only secondary activities summing to more than 1 hpw)

Primary activity	Secondary activity								Total (hpw)
	No activity	Domestic activities	Childcare	Eating and drinking	Watching TV or videos	Listening to radio, compact discs, etc.	Communication	Other passive leisure	
No activity	0.38	—	—	—	—	—	—	—	0.38
Labor force	25.55	0.03	0.10	0.21	0.25	3.34	0.64	0.23	30.46
Domestic activities	7.14	0.14	0.53	0.05	0.81	1.48	0.90	0.17	11.27
Childcare	0.85	0.04	0.37	0.01	0.21	0.11	0.23	0.05	1.91
Purchasing goods and services	2.98	0.01	0.14	0.01	0.03	0.30	0.55	0.06	4.14
Sleeping	57.29	—	3.08	—	0.01	0.00	0.01	—	60.41
Personal care	4.01	0.01	0.14	0.01	0.16	0.39	0.15	0.10	4.97
Health care	0.50	—	0.01	0.00	0.06	0.04	0.01	0.01	0.65
Eating and drinking	4.67	0.04	0.35	0.03	1.79	0.81	2.20	0.69	10.66
Others: sleeping, eating, and personal care	0.08	—	0.01	—	0.01	0.02	0.01	—	0.12
Education	2.26	—	0.03	0.01	0.10	0.18	0.11	0.03	2.77
Voluntary work and community participation	1.84	0.13	0.06	0.05	0.30	0.30	0.44	0.26	3.54
Social life and entertainment	2.61	—	0.08	0.05	0.04	0.30	0.41	0.07	3.59
Active leisure	3.57	0.01	0.14	0.02	0.09	0.48	0.85	0.14	5.37
Watching TV or videos	11.82	0.10	0.62	0.38	0.04	0.07	1.56	1.07	15.76
Listening to radio, compact disc, etc.	0.78	0.01	0.01	0.01	0.01	—	0.03	0.08	0.93
Communication	2.14	0.04	0.16	0.15	0.35	0.13	0.01	0.24	3.26
Other passive leisure	4.54	0.04	0.38	0.12	1.09	0.68	0.61	0.29	7.82
Total (hpw)	133.00	0.61	6.21	1.11	5.34	8.64	8.74	3.50	168.00

Source: Australian Bureau of Statistics Time Use Survey 1997.

Table 5.4 Total childcare time, Australia 1992 and Canada 1992 (hpw)

| | Australia 1992 | | Canada 1992 | |
	Primary time	Total time (primary and secondary)	Primary time	Total time (stylized question)
Women	5.7	18.1	4.2	17.9
Men	1.6	6.9	1.7	6.4
Adults	3.7	12.5	3.0	12.3

Sources: Australian Bureau of Statistics Time Use Survey 1992 and Statistics Canada General Social Survey 1992.

As can be seen from Table 5.2, women report an unduplicated total of 17.9 hpw of time providing childcare of which 15.6 hours (87 percent) is done while they are doing something else. Table 5.3 reveals a similar, though slightly more pronounced pattern for men. Of the total unduplicated time of 7.8 hpw they spend in providing childcare, 89 percent is done while they are doing something else.

On average, then, Australian adults spent about 13 hpw in childcare activities. This is almost four times the average adult 3.6 hpw of primary time reported. Still, it falls far short of the amount that would result if parents of young children fully reported their total responsibility time, which approximates 24 hours a day.

In 1992, Statistics Canada collected data on childcare through a diary-based survey and also asked "Last week, how many hours did you spend looking after children who live in your household?" (Paille 1994: 24). Thus, Canadian data provide a basis for direct comparison between time in primary activities and responses to a more general, stylized question. Estimates based on stylized questions were much higher. As Paille explains "According to stylized data…men and women spend about 4 times as much time caring for children as compared to the primary activities reported in the diary. These differences are likely due to the fact that the 1992 General Social Survey diary obtains primary activities only" (Paille 1994: 12).

As can be seen from Table 5.4, the Australian diary-based total of primary and secondary childcare time for 1992 provides results that are highly consistent with results from the stylized question on childcare from Canada in the same year. This convergence supports the conclusion that parents' retrospective reports on childcare conform closely to the sum of primary and secondary time devoted to children reported in diary-based surveys.

Time-use researchers have apparently never considered "travel" or "traveling" to be a secondary activity. Travel is typically coded as to its purpose (to and from "work," to and from "shopping," etc.) but no minutes of travel are included as secondary activities in surveys where secondary activities are recorded. If a respondent reports "reading a newspaper" as a primary activity (in the first column of the diary) and "traveling to work by train" as the secondary activity (in the second column), travel is given priority. The survey statistician switches the reported priorities since getting to work is clearly the main purpose of this simultaneous activity. That is, travel is considered an *overriding activity*.

A case can be made that the care of young children or of disabled and frail adults should also be an overriding activity and always counted as primary, rather than secondary. A further argument for this treatment of recorded time-use data is that most countries legally mandate that someone must be responsible at all times for the care and supervision of children under specific ages.

Care received by children (output hours of care)

Children receive care outside the household as well as within it. Childcare provided by the market economy is measured not by the adult hours of input time but by the hours children spend in care, child output hours of care. Thus, in order to put the care provided by households in context with that provided by the market, we need to make estimates of the child hours of care provided by households.

Surveys of paid childcare services

As growing numbers of women enter paid employment, the size of the formal childcare industry is increasing. A number of countries regularly survey and monitor the provision of paid childcare services. For example, in the United Kingdom the various authorities responsible for education in England, Scotland, Wales, and Northern Ireland regularly collect data on registered childcare places (Holloway and Tamplin 2001). Since 1989, the ABS has tallied the number and characteristics of children and families who use various formal and informal childcare arrangements. From 1987 onwards, these surveys have been conducted at three-year intervals; the latest survey was conducted in 1999 (ABS 2000a).[2]

The ABS defines *formal* care as regulated care which takes place away from the child's home and includes attendance at preschool, a childcare center, family day care and occasional care. It does not include care through attendance at primary or secondary schools. *Informal* care is nonregulated and can take place in the child's home or elsewhere, including care by family members, friends, neighbors, and paid babysitters (but not by parents). The ABS Child Care Surveys "tell us nothing about the child care provided by the parents. By some strange twist ... 'child care' is seen as something provided by everyone else other than the parents!" (Ironmonger 1996a: 32).

In 1999 there were 3.12 million children aged 0 to 11 in Australia. In total, they received about 24 million hours per week (mhw) of care from sources other than their parents. About 23 percent of children spent some time in formal child-care, 37 percent of children spent time in informal childcare and 51 percent used formal and/or informal care. As can be seen from Table 5.5, children spent about 14 mhw in informal childcare. The majority of this care was provided at no cost. Only 3 percent of informal care time was provided by siblings or step-parents, and

Table 5.5 Formal and informal childcare, Australia, 1999 (number of childcare hours per week in thousands)

	Child hours '000	Percent at no cost, %	Paid hours '000
Informal care by			
sisters/brothers/step	414	95	20
other relatives	11,278	97	294
other persons	2,384	64	849
Total informal	14,076	89	1,163
Formal care by			
long day care	4,527	1	4,477
preschool	2,551	17	2,111
family day care	1,466	2	1,437
before and after school	1,064	4	1,020
occasional care	239	8	220
other formal	156	13	136
Total formal	10,003	6	9,402
Total	24,079	51	10,565

Source: Australian Bureau of Statistics *Child Care Australia June 1999*.

only 1.2 million were paid for. In contrast, children received 10 mhw of formal childcare; nearly all (94 percent) of this care was paid for.

How do these hours of nonparental and market care compare with those provided in the household? To answer this question, we can return to the ABS time-diaries of 1997.

Hours of care provided by household members in one-child households

Using diary-based data for a one-child household, the total *input* childcare hours recorded in the diaries by the surveyed adults can be used as a reasonable estimate of the child hours *received* by the child from the adult household members. For any particular household, this estimate requires that the survey collects data from all household adults. This is done in the Australian official time-use surveys conducted by the ABS in 1992 and 1997. This method of estimation also checks the assumption that only one adult (a person 15 or older) at any particular time records the responsibility for the care of the child, by reference to the micro data files containing the "episode" data on time use.

The one-child household was also chosen for this analysis because these households avoid the complication in multi-child households of the need to allocate recorded input times childcare to particular children (Ironmonger 1996a). The amount of childcare undertaken varies not only by the age of a woman or a man, but also the age of the children under care. The average times spent by women and men in one-child households were analyzed according to the age of the child. Data are not available for single ages but only for five age groups: 0–1 years, 2–4 years, 5–9 years, 10–12 years, and 13–14 years.

Table 5.6 Hours per week of childcare time given and received by children in one-child households, Australia, 1997

Age of child (years)	Input time (adult hours)	Output time (child hours)
	Hours per child per week	
0–1	91.2	84.0
2–4	82.4	78.0
5–9	70.8	68.1
10–12	37.9	35.8
13–14	30.4	29.3
0–14	63.8	60.5

Source: Australian Bureau of Statistics *Time Use Survey 1997*.

Estimates of the time per week spent on a single child of various ages were calculated on hours per adult per week, adjusting for the number of adults in the households and correcting for the overlap time when more than one adult reported childcare during any specific interval. These hours can be interpreted as the hours per child of childcare received.

In summary, a child less than 2-years old receives about 84 hpw of total childcare time from women and men in one-child households. A child between the ages of 2 and 4 years receives about 78 hpw. As children enter the school system at 5 years, this care time drops to 68 hpw. But, a child between the ages of 10 and 12 still receives about 36 hpw of childcare and one aged 13–14 years, 29 hpw.

Women provide 70 percent of total unpaid childcare. Overall, ages 0–14 year children in one-child households receive 60.5 hpw of childcare and this is recorded as 63.8 hpw of input time by adults – for only 5 percent of the time does more than one adult record giving childcare time at any moment (see Table 5.6).

All households

The estimate of average hours of care per child for one-child households can be used to calculate the average hours of care per child in all households. Children in multi-child households are assumed to receive the same amount of care (measured in child output hours) as children in one-child households. Economies of scale for child care in multi-child households imply that 1 hour of parental child care input can benefit more than one child, and therefore generate more than 1 hour of childcare "output." Whether multi-child household children receive more or less output hours of care than other children has not yet been investigated.

The number of children under the age of 15 years in Australia in 1997 was 3.93 million. Multiplying the average hours per week per child of 60.5 gives a total of 237.5 mhw (see Table 5.7). These are "output" hours, or hours that

Table 5.7 Total hours of childcare received by children in Australia, 1997

Age group (years)	Sleep time	Awake time	Care time provided by			
			Household	Market	School	Self
			Hours per child per week			
0–1	93	75	84.0	na		
2–4	79	89	78.0	na		
5–9	71	97	68.1	na	20	
10–14	67	101	33.2	na	25	42.8
0–14	74.1	93.9	60.5	2.6	15.1	14.3
			Millions of hours per week			
0–1	47.4	38.2	42.8	na		
2–4	62.1	70.0	61.4	na		
5–9	93.6	127.9	89.8	na	26.4	
10–14	87.9	132.5	43.5	na	32.8	56.1
0–14	291.0	368.6	237.5	10.2	59.2	56.1

Note: na, age group distribution not available (mostly 2–5 years).

children received. The total "input" hours, or hours provided by adults, average 12.9 hours per adult per week, or 188.3 million. On average, households provided 126 "output" hours for every 100 "input" hours.

Table 5.7 also shows the hours per week that children were awake and asleep. A variety of sources were used to make these estimates. The Australian time use surveys cover only those aged 15 years or more (adults). For the very young adults (aged 15–19 years) sleep time was just 63 hpw, 9 hours per night, compared with an overall adult average of 58 hpw, 8.3 hours per night. As there are 168 hpw, this means 15–19-year-olds are awake for 103 hpw, 15 hours per day. Thus, it is likely that oldest children, aged 10–14 years, sleep slightly more and are thus awake for slightly less, say 101 hpw.

Some surveys have collected data on time use from children's point of view. A US survey of 1981–82 included children aged 3–17 years (Trimmer *et al.* 1985). A Bulgarian survey of 1988 included children 0–6 years (Raikova 1993) and an Italian survey of 1989 enlisted children aged 3–13 years (Buratta and Sabbadini 1993). Survey results are consistent with the estimates of sleep time presented in Table 5.7.

Comparison of the household care time shown in the third data column in Table 5.7 with the awake time in the second data column shows that, overall, on average for children of ages 0–14 years, adults in the household report caring for only 60.5 hours of a child's 93.9 average hours awake each week. However, this calculation is based on the assumption that all childcare hours are hours when children are awake; for the youngest children, adults report caring while they are asleep. An alternative way of interpreting Table 5.7 would be to conclude that adults in the household care for children 93.9 hpw out of a total of 168 hours in the week. In any case, the table shows that as children grow older, the hours per child per week provided by adults in the household declines considerably.

Market, school, and self-care time

To fill out the full picture of childcare an account needs to be made of the paid childcare provided by the market and the "childcare" in effect provided by schools. Australian children begin attending school at age 5 or 6. Formal paid care, as reported in the ABS Child Care Surveys, is concentrated on ages 2–5 years. The 10.6 mhw of paid formal and informal care shown in Table 5.5 for 1999 is estimated to be 10.2 mhw in 1997.[3] This converts to only 2.6 hpw per child. In Australia, compulsory school starts at age 6. On the assumption that school provides care to a child for about 25–30 hpw, estimates for the care time provided by schools can be constructed. With an adjustment to take account of school holidays, this converts to about 25 hpw per school child.

Obviously, after the age of about 10 years, children take care of themselves for an increasing proportion of the time they are not at school. By the age of 11, childcare time reported by adults in the time-use survey is down to about 36 hpw (5 hours per day). By the age of 14, total reported childcare is under 30 hpw. For older children self care, not covered by others is thus estimated to be about 43 hpw.

The lower section of Table 5.7 converts the average hours per child into millions of hours per week for all children using official population estimates.[4] Of the total of 307 mhw of care received by children, 77 percent was provided by unpaid adults in households, 3 percent by paid child carers and 19 percent by schools. These relative percentages reveal the tremendous significance of the unpaid childcare that family members provide.

The macroeconomic dimensions of childcare

Let us now put the "childcare" sector of the economy into macroeconomic perspective. The 188 mhw of unpaid adult time devoted to childcare can be placed in the context of unpaid work in other household activities ("household industries") and the paid work involved in market industries.

Just over 560 million hours of labor time were devoted to household industries in 1997. In contrast, over the same period, about 300 mhw was required to operate all the market industries. The household industries absorbed about 240 mhw more labor time than the market industries. The household childcare industry absorbed 188 mhw of time, while community services used 57 mhw of paid labor time to operate education and health services in schools, universities, and hospitals.

When time spent in secondary activities is included, childcare becomes the largest industry in both the household and market economies. It absorbs more labor than any other paid or unpaid economic activity. The total amount of time Australians spent on caring for children in 1997 was equivalent to almost

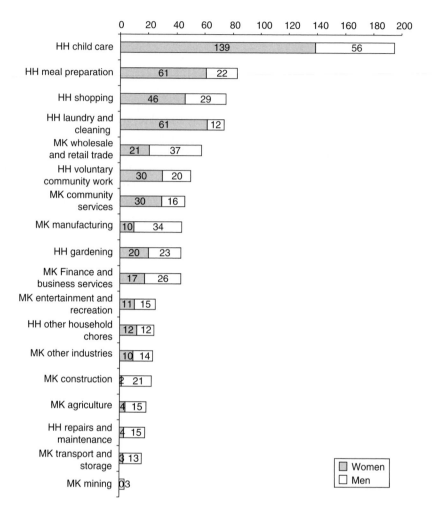

Figure 5.2 Work (expressed as mhw) in all household (HH) and market industries (MK) in Australia in 1997.

Sources: Australian Bureau of Statistics *Time Use Survey 1997* and *Labour Force Hours Worked and Average Hours Worked 2001.*

two-thirds (63 percent) of the entire labor time absorbed by the market economy, 300 mhw (see Figure 5.2).

Conclusion

Of all the activities necessary for the continuation of economic and social systems, the caring and nurturing of children clearly takes the most time. Time-use surveys, which give researchers detailed information on primary and secondary time, make it possible to construct a more accurate picture of exactly how much time it takes to care for children. Properly interpreted, the surveys show that 77 percent of the care of children is unpaid care undertaken by households.

Most research has focused on the 3 percent of childcare provided by the childcare industry of the market economy. The financial costs of childcare provided by the market sector have been recognized and well researched. Many governments now subsidize or provide financial rebates for the costs of paid childcare.

However, the cost of the childcare provided by households themselves is usually overlooked. A priority for researchers is to develop methods for estimating the dollar value of the care and nurture provided to children by households and there is an urgent need for a "thorough examination of the market and nonmarket costs of childcare and nurture" (Ironmonger 1996b: 60). Some preliminary output-based experimental estimates of the cost of childcare in Australia and the United Kingdom have recently been made by asking what it would cost to purchase unpaid childcare in the market (Holloway and Tamplin 2001; Soupourmas and Ironmonger 2002). The value of the output of household childcare in 1999 in Australia is estimated at AUD206 billion (37 percent of Gross Market Product, GMP) and in the United Kingdom UKP 224 billion (25 percent of GMP).

Understanding the cost of raising a child, in terms of money and time, is particularly important for development of social and economic policies related to children. The full cost of children should be taken into account when assessing the adequacy of benefits and services provided by governments to help parents in the crucial job of caring and nurturing children. The insights into the true micro and macro dimensions of childcare obtained from careful analysis of the Australian data would apply to many other countries. The research community should try to incorporate these insights into discussions of public policy.

Acknowledgments

An earlier paper on this topic with a similar title was presented to a conference on Investing in Children at the University of Otago, Dunedin, New Zealand, July 1996. This chapter represents an update and refinement of Ironmonger (1996a), perhaps the first paper to quantify the total amount of time provided to Australian children. The genesis of this chapter goes back to the invitation from Professor Anne B. Smith to take a careful look at the data on childcare for her inaugural conference at the Children's Issues Centre at the University of Otago, Dunedin, New Zealand. That 1996 "Bringing Up Betty and Bobby" paper depended on the careful tabulation by Glenys Harding of the 1992 data on the simultaneous use of time in Australian households. Since then Faye Soupourmas, Research Fellow in the Household Research Unit, University of Melbourne, has collaborated with me on all of our research on the care of children and specifically has been the principal researcher on the output-based estimates of the value of unpaid childcare. The editors of this volume, Nancy Folbre and Michael Bittman, have been a constant encouragement and have made many useful editorial suggestions. Any remaining obscurities and errors are of course my own fault.

Notes

1 An exception is the paper by Williams and Donath (1994).
2 The Child Care Surveys were conducted over a two-week period as a supplement to the ABS Monthly Population Survey. Data collected on the use of childcare referred to the week prior to the interview. Information on childcare arrangements was obtained from persons responsible for children under the age of 12 in the sample households.
3 Interpolating between 10.0 million hours in 1996 and 10.6 million hours in 1999.
4 Australian Bureau of Statistics (2000b) *Population By Age and Sex, Australian States and Territories* – table 9, Estimated Resident Population by Single Year of Age, Australia, June estimates.

References

Australian Bureau of Statistics (1993) *Time Use Survey Australia 1992 User's Guide*, Catalogue 4150.0, Australian Bureau of Statistics: Canberra.
—— (1998) *How Australians Use their Time, 1997*, Catalogue 4153.0, Australian Bureau of Statistics: Canberra.
—— (2000a) *Child Care Australia, June 1999*, Catalogue 4402.0, Australian Bureau of Statistics: Canberra.
—— (2000b) *Population By Age and Sex, Australian States and Territories*, Catalogue 3201.0, Australian Bureau of Statistics: Canberra.
—— (2001) *Labour Force Hours Worked and Average Hours Worked, Australia*, Catalogue 6291.0.40.001, Australian Bureau of Statistics: Canberra.
Australian Institute of Family Studies (2000) *A Guide to Calculating the Cost of Children*, AIFS: Melbourne.
Bittman, M. and Pixley, J. (1997) *The Double Life of the Family: Myth, Hope and Experience*, Sydney: Allen-Unwin.
Buratta, V. and Sabbadini, L. L. (1993) "Can Time Use Statistics Describe the Life of Children?," in *ISTAT Time Use Methodology: Toward Consensus*, Roma: Istituto Nazionale di Statistica, pp. 51–65.
Cashmore, J. (2001) "Child Protection in the New Millennium," *Social Policy Research Centre Newsletter*, 79: 1–5.
Folbre, N., Fuligni, A., Finoff, K., and Yoon, J. (2003) "By What Measure? Family Time Devoted to Children in the U.S." manuscript, Department of Economics, University of Massachusetts, Amherst, MA 01003.
Goldschmidt-Clermont, L. and Pagnossin-Aligisakis, E. (1995) *Measures of Unrecorded Economic Activities in Fourteen Countries*. New York: Human Development Report Office, United Nations Development Programme.
Gray, M. and Chapman, B. (2001) "Foregone Earnings for Child Rearing: Changes between 1986 and 1997," *Family Matters*, 58: 4–9.
Haveman, R. and Wolfe, B. (1995) "The Determinants of Children's Attainments: A Review of Methods and Findings," *Journal of Economic Literature*, XXXIII (December): 1829–78.
Henman, P. (2001) "Updating Australian Budget Standards Costs of Children Estimates," *Department of Family and Community Services Policy Research Paper No. 7*, Department of Family and Community Services: Canberra.
Holloway, S. and Tamplin, S. (2001) "Valuing Informal Childcare in the United Kindgom," *Economic Trends*, 574 London: Office of National Statistics (www.ons.gov.uk/hhsa/).

Ironmonger, D. S. (1996a) "Bringing Up Betty and Bobby: The Macro Time Dimensions of Investment in the Care and Nurture of Children," in N. J Taylor and A.B Smith (eds), *Investing in Children – Primary Prevention Strategies, Proceedings of the Children's Issues Centre Inaugural Child and Family Policy Conference, 10–13 July 1996*, Children's Issues Centre, University of Otago: Dunedin, New Zealand, pp. 27–42.

—— (1996b) "Counting Outputs, Capital Inputs and Caring Labor: Estimating Gross Household Product," *Feminist Economics* 2(3): 37–64.

—— (2000) "An Overview of Time Use Surveys," *International Seminar on Time Use Studies*, New Delhi: Central Statistical Organisation, Ministry of Statistics and Programme Implementation, Government of India.

Joshi, H. (1990) "The Cash Opportunity Costs of Childrearing: An Approach to Estimation Using British Data," *Population Studies*, 44(1): 41–60.

——, Paci, P., and Waldfogel, J. (1999) "The Wages of Motherhood: Better or Worse?," *Cambridge Journal of Economics*, 23: 543–64.

Juster, F. T. and Stafford, F. (1991) "The Allocation of Time: Empirical Findings, Behavioural Models and Problems of Measurement," *Journal of Economic Literature*, 29: 471–522.

Paille, B. (1994) *Estimating the Volume of Unpaid Work Activities in Canada, 1992: An Evaluation of Data from the General Social Survey*, General Social Survey Working Paper #10. Ottawa: Statistics Canada.

Raikova, M. (1993) "Methods and Approaches in Child Time Use Study," pp. 45–50 in ISTAT *Time Use Methodology: Toward Consensus* Roma: Istituto Nazionale di Statistica.

Richardson, S. (2000) "Society's Investment in Children," *National Institute of Labour Studies Working Paper No 151*, Flinders University: Adelaide.

Soupourmas, F. and Ironmonger, D. S. (2002) "Household National Accounts: Output Based Estimates of Child Care in Australia and the United Kingdom," Paper presented to the International Time Use Association for Time Use Research Annual Conference 2002, Technical University of Lisbon, Lisbon, 15–18 October.

Szalai, A. (ed.) (1972) *The Uses of Time: Daily Activities and Suburban Populations in Twelve Countries*, Mouton: The Hague.

Trimmer, S. G., Eccles, J., and O'Brien, K. (1985) "How Children Use Time," in F. T. Juster and F. P. Stafford (eds), *Time, Goods and Well-Being*, Ann Arbor: Institute of Social Research, University of Michigan, pp. 353–82.

Valenzuela, R. (1999) "Costs of Children in Australian Households: New Estimates from the ABS Household Expenditure Survey," *Family Matters*, 53: 71–6.

Waldfogel, J. (1997) "The Effect of Children on Women's Wages," *American Sociological Review*, 62(2), 209–17.

Williams, R. and Donath, S. (1994) "Simultaneous Uses of Time in Household Production," *Review of Income and Wealth*, 40(4): 433–40.

6 Valuing informal elder care

Douglas A. Wolf

Among the activities labeled "caring" or "care work," care provided to the disabled elderly population exhibits several distinctive features. Social norms as well as legal requirements dictate that parents provide care for their children, and all children require such care for at least part of their young lives. Furthermore, parents are expected to enjoy, on balance, the experience of providing that care, despite its occasional frustrating, exhausting, or otherwise unpleasant moments. In contrast, grown children may not anticipate providing personal-care services to their elderly parents, may hope not to find themselves facing such care needs, and may not face a legal requirement that they do so – or face a requirement that is not enforced. The children may not, in fact, ever face such needs because some percentage of the elderly reaches the end of life without developing personal-care needs. The need to care for a child is in nearly all cases a temporary situation, followed by a transition – a lengthy and gradual transition, to be sure – to the capacity for self-care associated with independent living as an adult. However, the transition into disability during old age may occur gradually or rapidly, and is likely to signal the onset of an irreversible state of dependency, one that will end only in death. Thus, for several reasons elder care merits, and receives, special attention.

Yet, elder care and other major types of care work, such as caring for young children, share many common elements: much of the care is provided in private households and is done so "informally" by family members; the care entails heavy use of time inputs; care is provided more often by women than by men; the care effort imposes costs in many intangible domains upon those who do it; and, the caring produces benefits for society at large. Both the costs and the benefits are hard to quantify, in principle and in practice.

This chapter addresses the problem of attaching a monetary value to informal elder care. I first provide new data that support a well-established fact, namely that family members constitute the principal source of care services to disabled elders. I then discuss reasons why it is important to try to assign a monetary value to informal elder care, reviewing several approaches that have been used for that purpose. Most attempts to establish a social value for informal care have used a "replacement cost" approach, which I argue produces inflated estimates of the social value of such care. I conclude with some suggestions about the role in public policy analysis of estimates of the social value of informal elder care. I use data from the United States to support my arguments, although those arguments apply, in varying degrees, to other national settings as well.

The importance of informal elder care

Although different countries exhibit considerable variation in the types and generosity of publicly funded programs with which to meet the care needs of older people (Giarchi 1996), the family remains "everywhere the most important provider..." of such care (Sundström 1994:15). There is a voluminous research literature concerned with the nature, extent, components, and consequences of informal care provided to disabled elders. Much of that work is based on small, local-area samples, but in recent years a number of national-level data sources have become available with which to study informal elder care.

One of the most detailed sources of national-level information on elder care in the United States is the National Long-Term Care Survey (NLTCS). This panel study includes interviews with persons 65 and older (or with proxy respondents on their behalf), conducted in 1982, 1984, 1989, 1994, and 1999. All sample members receive a brief screening interview intended to establish the presence of disability with respect to either Activities of Daily Living (ADLs) – eating, getting into and out of bed, getting around indoors, dressing, bathing, and using the toilet – or Instrumental Activities of Daily Living (IADLs) – doing housework or laundry, meal preparation, shopping, getting around outdoors, getting places beyond walking distance, money management, and taking medication. Those screening positively for such a disability receive a detailed follow-up interview, whether they live in a nursing home or in a community setting (nursing home residents were interviewed only in the beginning of 1984, however). One component of the follow-up interviews used with community-dwelling elders identifies all "helpers" – persons providing either hands-on or standby help with one or more of the ADL or IADL tasks listed here. I use the NLTCS's term "helpers" and the term "caregivers" interchangeably.

The NLTCS respondents are asked to indicate, for each listed helper, how many days in the past week the helper provided help, and how many hours of help were provided during the past week. One hours-of-help question pertains to all ADLs as a group, and another pertains to all IADLs as a group; time spent helping with individual tasks is not ascertained. The relationship of each helper to the respondent is also obtained. The relationship codes used distinguish among family members in considerable detail, as well as among friends, employees, and people from "helping organizations." Thus, the NLTCS data permit a very detailed study of the help received by dependent elders in the United States. It is possible to determine the number and types of individuals helping with each ADL or IADL task, as well as to identify all the tasks that each helper provides help with. The total volume of care hours expended on behalf of a care recipient, the division of these hours between ADLs and IADLs, and the distribution of those components over the set of helpers, can also be analyzed.

A weakness of the NLTCS data is the use of "last week" as a reference period. Other US-based studies have used a wide range of informal-care accounting periods, ranging from one day – either "yesterday" (Davis *et al.* 1997) or a "typical" or "average" day (e.g. the National Longitudinal Caregiver Study used by Moore *et al.* 2001) – to two weeks (the Disability Followback Survey used in LaPlante *et al.* 2002), one month (Rice *et al.* 1993), or even, in the case of the Health and Retirement Survey, a full year (Soldo and Hill 1995). The longer reference periods will presumably elicit a larger volume of care hours, at a likely cost of greater measurement error.

In the 1999 NLTCS data, a surprisingly large percentage of all identified helpers – about 41 percent – are reported to have spent zero hours helping during the past week. Informal helpers, particularly children and other relatives who may not live nearby, may help out only occasionally, or may regularly alternate with others in providing help with various tasks. Some tasks, such as money management, providing transportation, or even shopping, may not be performed as often as once a week. In my analysis of the NLTCS helpers data, I assume that all reported helpers, even those who apparently spent no time helping during the last week, are bona fide helpers. Moreover, I assume that the subset of helpers who are reported to have spent at least one hour helping during the past week are representative of what is done is a typical week.

The analysis of 1982 NLTCS data by Stone *et al.* (1987) presented the first descriptive profile of elder-care helpers based on nationally representative US data. Stone *et al.* described the characteristics of caregivers in great detail, pointing out that a majority (71.5 percent) were female, and that close family members (spouses and children) constituted a large majority (72.9 percent) of all helpers. Liu *et al.* (2000) discussed the mix of caregiver types found in the more recent 1989 and 1994 waves of NLTCS data.

I present new findings from the most recent round of NLTCS data collection, carried out in 1999. The findings are based on data provided by 2,947 community-dwelling respondents, who listed a total of 5,105 helpers (a few respondents, and a few of the helpers they identified, have been excluded from the analysis because of missing or inconsistent data items). Adjusted for differential sampling probabilities, this represents an average of 1.68 helpers per recipient of help. I have classified helpers by type (*spouse, child, other informal*, and *formal*) and coresidence status. The *other informal* category is mostly relatives (such as siblings and in-laws), but also includes nonrelatives ("friends") and a relationship category called "someone else" (which, lacking further information, I chose to include with the informal caregiver group). The *formal* category includes employees as well as anyone from a "helping organization." Coresidence status is noted only for children and other informal helpers, since nearly every spouse lives with the respondent, and nearly every formal helper does not.

Table 6.1 presents the distribution of helpers according to type, coresidence, and the nature of help provided. In comparison to 1982, spouses and children have diminished in relative importance among the pool of helpers: in 1999 they are 58.2 percent of all identified helpers, considerably less than the 72.9 percent

Table 6.1 Characteristics of helpers and help provided, 1999 NLTCS

| | Helpers, by type and coresidence status | | | | | | | |
| | Spouse | Children | | | Other informal | | | Formal |
		Coresident	Noncoresident	Total	Coresident	Noncoresident	Total	
Percent of all helpers	24.4	11.4	22.4	33.8	6.7	14.7	21.4	20.3
Percent of helpers of this type								
Female[a]	65.6	65.1	64.9	65.0	61.2	78.1	71.6	—
Providing ADL help only	3.4	2.8	8.6	6.6	8.5	8.8	8.7	7.9
Providing IADL help only	61.2	52.7	74.8	67.3	50.6	77.4	69.0	63.4
Providing ADL and IADL help	33.4	44.5	16.7	26.1	40.9	13.8	22.3	28.8
Average hours of help provided								
ADL help	22.0	20.9	11.0	16.1	18.5	18.7	18.6	17.3
IADL help	22.6	18.6	8.2	12.5	18.5	7.6	11.4	12.4
Percent of all hours supplied								
ADL hours	32.6	17.8	8.8	26.6	9.0	9.8	18.8	21.9
IADL hours	34.2	17.3	11.6	28.9	9.5	7.1	16.6	20.2
Unweighted n	1,094	579	1,205	1,784	343	790	1,133	1,094

a Excludes cases with gender not reported.

reported in Stone *et al.* (1987). Over half of the *other informal* helpers are also family members, however, and inasmuch as this type comprises another 21.4 percent of all helpers, it is evident that the family remains the principal source of help to dependent elders.

Table 6.1 also shows that among both children and other informal helpers, about twice as many live away from the person helped as those who live with the care recipient. About two-thirds of the helpers in the three informal-helper categories (spouse, child, other) are women (the gender of *formal* helpers was not recorded in the NLTCS data), illustrating the continuing overrepresentation of women among care workers. Among all helper categories, the most common form of help is with IADL tasks only, followed by ADL and IADL tasks in combination. It is also clear that coresidence and ADL assistance are closely linked: about 25 percent of noncoresident children helpers are involved in ADL assistance, while over 47 percent of coresident children help with ADL tasks. Similarly, striking differences appear among those classified as *other informal* helpers.

The hours of help data also display differences across both caregiver type and category of activity. In most cases, caregivers who help with ADLs spend more time doing those tasks, on average, than is spent by people helping with IADLs. Coresident children provide many more hours of help with each class of activities than do noncoresident children; this difference, however, does not hold among other informal caregivers. Finally, spouses tend to provide more hours of help on average than do any other caregiver type. As a result, spouses account for about 24 percent of all helpers but provide around 33 percent of all hours of help.

Rationale for valuing informal elder care

Because family members provide, without compensation, a majority of the help with tasks of everyday life that is received by disabled older people, it is natural to consider the problem of attaching an economic value to that help. Much of the large literature on the gendered nature of informal care argues that its social value should be explicitly recognized (Hooyman and Gonyea 1995). A related literature argues for including unpaid work in national income accounts (Ironmonger 1996).

There are several reasons to develop estimates of the implicit monetary value of informal care. Such estimates call attention to the full set of resources devoted to long-term care needs. They are especially important to the extent that public policy recognizes or interacts with informal care. Estimates of the economic value of informal care are also useful insofar as they illuminate the distribution within the population of this type of value-producing activity, particularly with respect to gender and race.

Having an estimate of the value of informal care also provides a yardstick against which to assess the coverage or "penetration" of existing policies that expend resources on elder care, or policy proposals that would extend the collective provision of care services. For example, in the United States, direct cash payments to those providing informal care to family members are permitted in a majority of states, generally through waivers to Medicaid home health program regulations (Stone 2000). Estimates of the social value of informal care are crucial to any distributional analysis of direct or indirect caregiver-payment schemes such as these.

Another US policy indirectly related to the valuation of informal care is the Family and Medical Leave Act of 1993, which permits eligible employees to take up to 12 weeks of unpaid leave per year for purposes of caring for relatives with serious medical conditions. Theoretically, this imposes costs on employers and employees (Ruhm 1997). Any such social costs, however, must be weighed against the social value of the care facilitated. More recently, the National Family Caregiver Support Program, begun in 2001, aims to "… help family members provide care for the elderly at home," explicitly underwriting social values with social costs (US Department of Health and Human Services 2001).

Proposals to expand compensation for informal caregiving through tax credits or direct payments implicitly recognize that such care is valuable to society. Such proposals are well within the scope of policy discussion in recent years. For example, in 1999 President Clinton proposed legislation that included income-tax credits of up to $1000 for caregivers of dependents with personal-care needs (Komisar and Feder 1999). In the following year the proposal was reintroduced with a higher tax-credit cap of $3000 (The White House 2000). In 2000, presidential candidate Gore incorporated such a credit into his long-term care proposals, while candidate Bush proposed adding a new income tax exemption for in-home caregivers (see the "Gore 2000" and "George W. Bush for President" websites). Legislation introduced in the 107th Congress also included tax credits for taxpayers who care for spouses or other dependents (S. 464, "A bill to amend the Internal Revenue Code of 1986 to allow a tax credit for long-term care givers," introduced March 6, 2001; S. 627, "A bill to amend the Internal Revenue Code of 1986 to allow … a credit for individuals with long-term care needs," introduced March 2, 2001). Less direct policy interventions have also been proposed: for example, one bill introduced in the House of Representatives in 2002 would give informal caregivers credits towards the determination of Social Security eligibility and benefits (H.R. 4743, "A bill to amend title II of the Social Security Act to credit prospectively individuals serving as caregivers of dependent relatives with deemed wages for up to five years of such service," introduced May 15, 2002).

Although estimates of the social value of informal care are, therefore, important for several reasons, excessively high estimates of the social value of informal care are likely to distort the policy debate with respect to public provision of long-term care, and might hinder the efforts of those who would advocate for improved societal coverage of long-term care benefits. An estimate that overstates the value of informally provided care will wrongly suggest that existing publicly funded efforts are doing a worse job than they really are, while inflating the estimated cost of achieving a more complete coverage of the target population. Thus, a critical examination of existing estimates is warranted.

Approaches to valuing informal care

If society has an interest in seeing that the care needs of the frail elderly are met, then society should be prepared to attach a value to informal care activities. The preceding statement is deceptively simple, however, because it is not clear whether the problem is to value the time *inputs* used in informal care – inputs that are by definition uncompensated – or to value the care produced by those inputs, in other words the *outputs* of informal care efforts.

An economist might approach this problem using the tools of cost–benefit analysis: the outputs produced by the "program" through which community-based elder care is delivered should be valued by adding together everyone's "willingness to pay" for those outputs – that is, the monetary value that corresponds to the well-being associated with the current array of informal elder-care services (Boardman *et al.* 1996). In computing the aggregate willingness to pay, it would be important to include assessments of the monetary-equivalent valuations of informal care by caregivers, care recipients, and all others who are neither providers nor recipients of this type of care.

In principle, the aggregate willingness-to-pay figure, properly developed, could serve as a measure of the social value of informal care. Yet, there are substantial methodological problems associated with eliciting honest and accurate information on willingness to pay (see Mitchell and Carson 1989): citizens not directly involved in the provision or receipt of informal elder care would have a legitimately hard time assessing the monetary value to them of a service which, so far as they can tell, is already provided and is provided at no tangible cost to them. Those who suspected that their tax payments might be used to underwrite a greater collective presence in elder care would have a clear incentive to understate their true preferences. A more serious critique of the willingness-to-pay approach, however, is pertinent even in the absence of these methodological and strategic considerations: the distribution of willingness to pay – that is, of demands – for a service depends crucially on the existing distribution of income and wealth, since each individual's demands are constrained by available resources. The inequities embedded in the wide dispersion of income presently found in the United States and elsewhere would simply be transferred to any social-valuation figure obtained through the willingness-to-pay approach. In the case of informal elder care, these inequities would be compounded by the fact that lower-income people – those whose circumstances dictate relatively low willingness-to-pay figures – are also at elevated risk of both experiencing disability in old age (Schoeni *et al.* 2001) and providing informal care to disabled family members (Couch *et al.* 1999).

Alternatively, one might attempt to measure the "opportunity costs" – that is, the monetary value of inputs used, if they were instead allocated to their next-best use – of the resources devoted to informal elder care. One could, in other words, try to value the inputs to rather than the outputs of informal care work. But, the opportunity-cost approach to valuing informal-care inputs is also problematic. The market wage is theoretically appropriate for valuing the marginal care hour supplied by an employed caregiver, but a large percentage of informal care providers is not employed. Furthermore, many informal care-givers are themselves well into retirement, and may face rather low potential labor market wages. In fact, discounted by the probability that a job could be found, the expected market wage for many older caregivers may be close to zero. In theory, the value of time for someone voluntarily unemployed exceeds the market wage, but this will lead to a low estimate of the opportunity cost of many caregivers' time. Some researchers have rejected the use of an imputed market wage as a measure of opportunity costs, arguing that discrim-inatory labor market practices systematically undervalue women's labor (Rice *et al.* 1993).

Reflecting these difficulties, most existing attempts to assign a monetary value to informal care have used a *replacement-cost* approach. Replacement-cost esti-mates of the social value of informal care are obtained by first determining the aggregate volume of care hours, then multiplying total hours by an appropriate hourly wage rate. The result is a monetary figure, which represents the cost of hiring paid helpers to supply the care hours otherwise supplied informally. There are obvious problems with both components of this calculation. First, there may be ambiguity regarding both what constitutes "care" and in reporting the hours spent in caring activities. Men and women, and also care providers and care recipients, often have different ideas about what constitutes care "beyond that required as part of normal everyday life" (Walker *et al.* 1995: 402). Second, there is a range of potential market prices appropriate to informal-care activities, lead-ing some researchers to use a range of wage rates to bound the "true" figure. One widely cited example of this approach is by Arno *et al.* (1999), whose midrange estimate of the total economic value of informal care in the United States in 1997 is US$196 billion, a number nearly twice that of formal nursing and home-care expenditures combined. The operational definitions of "caregiver" and care hours used in Arno *et al.* are rather broad. Among the many other examples of replacement-cost estimates of the value of informal care, some focused more nar-rowly on care triggered by specific conditions such as dementia, are Langa *et al.* (2001), Rice *et al.* (1993), Leon *et al.* (1998), and the Australian Institute of Health and Welfare (1997).

These past studies based on the replacement-cost approach have generally paid little attention to its theoretical foundations. One fruitful way to think about replacement-cost valuation of caring is to think of it as a collective-bargaining "threat point," that is, the amount of payment that informal care-givers could plausibly demand from society in return for continuing their care efforts. The replacement-cost valuation of informal care is, in other words, the costs of the paid care that society would have to provide if informal caregivers withdrew their services, or threatened a care workers' "strike" in the absence of societal compensation for their work.[1] Equivalently, it is the aggregate wage bill that informal care workers should demand, should society decide to "hire" them to perform their services, and as such properly calls attention to the *outputs* of informal care work.

Problems with the replacement-cost approach

There are several problems with the replacement-cost approach to valuing informal care, not the least of which is its encouragement of confusion concerning "costs" versus "benefits." The market wages of professional helpers typically used in the replacement-cost estimates are clearly not a measure of the self-assessed value that individuals attach to their own time: a paid helper's wage rate exceeds the value many caregivers would attach to their own time, and fall short of that value for many other caregivers. This would remain true whether market wages or "psychic" (or "reservation") wages are estimated for each informal caregiver.

Estimated replacement costs are, rather, an estimate of social "benefits" in the form of tangible costs that would otherwise be borne were society to pay for them; in other words, they represent cost *savings* rather than costs *expended*. In keeping with the "care workers' strike" image invoked earlier, the value to society of informal elder care is the amount of compensation the caregivers would be awarded following a successful negotiation for societal compensation of their work. As such, the benefits do not correspond to the conception of willingness-to-pay found in the cost–benefit analysis literature. Some authors (e.g. Arno *et al.* 1999) make explicit the equivalence between replacement costs and social benefits, while others (e.g. Rice *et al.* 1993; Leon *et al.* 1998; Moore *et al.* 2001) do not, leaving an impression that "replacement costs" are a form of expenditure.

There are two components to the replacement-cost approach: the first is the number of care hours to which a value is to be assigned, and the second is the price, or wage, with which those counted hours are to be valued. The difficult issues concerning the use of the informal caregiver's market wages, or their reservation wage, or a paid helper's wage, all pertain to the problem of determining the appropriate dollar value with which to value informal-care inputs. But there are several reasons to think that nominal reports of informal-care hours overstate the volume of socially valuable care. In the following section, I present several such arguments, many of which relate to the theme of *joint production* in caring.

Joint production of care for self and care for others

A key feature of much of what is counted as time spent in informal care is that it produces more than one identifiable output. For example, time spent shopping for items to be consumed by the care recipient may overlap fully with time spent shopping for items for the caregiver's use. The same may be true for time spent in meal preparation and, if the caregiver and care recipient live together, in doing housework and laundry. The care tasks with the greatest potential for this type of joint production tend to be IADL tasks, and the potential for joint production is further increased when the caregiver and care recipient live together. The role of joint production in informal care has been noted in earlier research, including Netten (1993) and Wolf (1999).

Table 6.2 shows the distribution of caregiver types across those caregivers helping with each identified ADL and IADL task in the 1999 NLTCS data.

Table 6.2 Percentage distribution by type and coresidence status of persons who help with each ADL and IADL tasks, by task

Helpers, by type and coresidence status

	Spouse	Children			Other informal			Formal
		Coresident	Noncoresident	Total	Coresident	Noncoresident	Total	
ADL tasks								
Eating	23.3	16.8	16.4	33.2	10.9	10.6	21.5	22.0
Get in/out of bed	29.9	16.9	13.8	30.7	9.2	9.1	18.2	21.2
Indoor mobility	26.7	18.0	17.5	35.5	9.3	8.7	17.9	19.9
Dressing	29.5	15.2	12.3	27.5	8.1	8.7	16.8	26.2
Bathing	27.2	15.4	11.4	26.8	8.4	10.1	18.5	27.5
Toileting	25.8	15.3	14.7	30.0	8.6	11.5	20.2	24.0
IADL tasks								
Housework/laundry	36.0	15.4	12.9	28.3	8.0	9.8	17.9	17.9
Meal preparation	34.7	15.7	10.4	26.1	10.7	9.1	19.9	19.4
Shopping	31.1	19.9	19.7	39.7	8.8	10.3	19.1	10.1
Get around outside	25.0	18.4	23.6	42.0	8.5	12.5	21.0	12.0
Travel	21.0	17.6	28.9	46.4	8.9	15.5	24.4	8.2
Money management	34.9	19.0	28.5	47.5	6.9	7.3	14.2	3.5
Taking medication	31.0	19.8	14.5	34.3	10.0	8.3	18.3	16.4

In this table, rows sum to 100 percent: for example, among all those who help the care recipients with eating, 23.2 percent are spouses, 33.2 percent are children (further subdivided into coresident children – 16.8 percent of all such helpers – and noncoresident children – 16.4 percent of all those helping with the eating task), 21.5 percent are other informal helpers, and 22 percent are formal helpers. The message of Table 6.2 is that the tasks with the greatest potential for joint production – production of "self care" along with elder care – are also the tasks with the greatest involvement of close family members, that is spouses and children.

Table 6.3 presents the same information, but in a different form: percentages should be read columnwise rather than by rows. Table 6.3 shows the percentage among each category of helper who provides help with each identified ADL or IADL task. For example, among all spouses who provide *any* help, 10 percent help with eating, 19.7 percent help with getting into or out of bed, 20 percent help the care recipient with getting around indoors, and so on. The column percentages add to more than 100 percent, because the typical helper is involved with more than one, and often many, care tasks. Table 6.3 again shows the strong involvement of close family members in care tasks with the greatest potential for joint production. Furthermore, joint production is facilitated by coresidence: spouses and coresident children are heavily involved in helping the care recipient with housework, meal preparation, and shopping, for example.

The presence of joint production in informal elder care leads to an argument that replacement-cost estimates of the social value of that care are inflated. In the extreme, joint production might be "complete." For example, an hour of a caregiver's time may be used to prepare a meal that will be consumed by both the caregiver and the care recipient. That same hour might be used to prepare a meal that is consumed by the care recipient only, or, it might be used to prepare a meal that is consumed by the caregiver only. In the case of perfect, or complete, joint production, caregivers can rightly demand as societal compensation the full cost of replacing the hour spent preparing the care recipient's meal, and society should be prepared to shoulder those costs. However, the hour of paid care that society hires to replace the informal hour will be used to prepare only the care recipient's meal; the (former) informal caregiver will still need to spend that same hour preparing her own meal, or make other arrangements that also entail costs of some sort. From a social perspective the new arrangement is inefficient, inasmuch as the former gains achieved through joint production are completely lost. There are potential gains to be realized, in the form of a sharing rule: Society will compensate the caregiver for some portion of the care hour, the caregiver will engage in the joint production of care for self and care for another, and the gains, or efficiencies, associated with joint production will be restored. Thus the caregiver's efforts are collectively rewarded, and both caregiver and society are better off than they otherwise would be.

One possible fair sharing rule is equal division, that is, valuing the informal care hour at half its replacement cost. But, a greater share to the caregiver – perhaps, a share equal to the aggregate ratio of informal to total care efforts – could

Table 6.3 Percentage of helpers who help with each ADL and IADL task, type and coresidence status

Helpers, by type and coresidence status

	Spouse	Children			Other informal			Formal
		Coresident	Noncoresident	Total	Coresident	Noncoresident	Total	
ADL Tasks								
Eating	10.0	15.5	7.7	10.3	17.0	7.5	10.5	11.4
Get in/out of bed	19.7	23.8	9.9	14.6	22.0	10.0	13.7	16.8
Indoor mobility	20.0	28.8	14.3	19.2	25.3	10.8	15.3	17.9
Dressing	18.9	20.8	8.6	12.7	18.9	9.3	12.3	20.2
Bathing	25.7	31.1	11.8	18.3	29.1	15.9	20.0	31.3
Toileting	15.0	19.0	9.3	12.6	18.3	11.2	13.4	16.7
IADL tasks								
Housework/laundry	68.7	62.8	26.9	39.0	55.9	31.2	38.9	41.0
Meal preparation	40.0	38.8	13.1	21.8	45.2	17.6	26.2	26.9
Shopping	51.2	70.1	35.4	47.1	52.8	28.1	35.8	19.9
Get around outside	20.4	32.1	20.9	24.7	25.2	17.0	19.6	11.7
Travel	27.9	50.0	41.9	44.7	43.1	34.4	37.1	13.1
Money management	33.8	39.5	30.2	33.3	24.6	11.7	15.7	4.0
Taking medication	27.0	36.9	13.8	21.6	31.8	12.0	18.2	17.2

be justified as well. Whatever sharing rule is adopted, it leads to a "discount" factor to be applied to a subset of care hours – those devoted to tasks in which the potential for joint production is greatest – prior to the calculation of their replacement-cost value.

Joint production of care and "normal exchange"

Another type of joint production occurs when close family members supply informal care services to spouses or parents unable to care for themselves. In particular, the time devoted to face-to-face care is not only care time, it is also social interaction time, reinforcing and nurturing the emotional, relational, affective ties that characterize most familial relationships (and that helps to prompt the helping behavior itself). Family members typically engage in some level of visits, phone calls, and other social interactions when all are healthy and independent, but the socio-emotional component of family interactions remains present to some degree when the contact is occasioned by care provision. Consequently, caregivers derive some satisfaction – they experience rewards – from their caring experiences (Kinney and Parris Stephens 1989; Lawton *et al.* 1991; Martire *et al.* 1997). The social-interaction element of intrafamilial caregiver–care recipient dyads is much less likely to arise in formal care situations. For this reason, family caregivers are likely to spend more time in their caring activities than would a paid caregiver, holding constant the assistance needs of the care recipient. Put somewhat differently, a family member's affective ties to the person they are helping motivates them to spend more time with the care recipient than would a paid helper hired to assist with the same task.

If the preceding assertion is correct, then the average time spent by an informal helper should exceed the average time spent by a formal helper, if the care needs of the persons helped are held constant. Table 6.4 attempts to establish whether this is true using the 1999 NLTCS data, which are unfortunately not ideal for this purpose. Table 6.4 presents the average of total hours of help per week received by care recipients whose helper group contains only formal, or only informal, helpers. The data are further disaggregated according to whether ADL help only, or IADL help only, or both types of help, are received. While this approach achieves a certain degree of homogeneity with care recipient groups, I cannot with much confidence claim that care needs are truly held constant across the rows of this table. And, there is relatively little that can be done to strengthen the analysis, because in the NLTCS data there are no uniform measures of the *need* for care independent of the *receipt* of care, across all respondents.

Bearing in mind these caveats, note that in almost every case, care recipients whose needs are met exclusively by informal caregivers receive more hours, on average, than care recipients whose needs are met exclusively by formal helpers. The differences are especially striking for those getting ADL assistance only: those relying exclusively on formal helpers (an admittedly small group of 11) receive, on average, 5.2 hours of help per week. Those helped by a spouse only get nearly twice this much, and those helped by children only over three times

Table 6.4 Average hours of help received, by composition of helper group

Help received	Composition of helper group				
	Informal helpers only				Formal helpers only
	All	Spouse only	Children only	Spouse and children	
ADL only					
Average ADL hours	28.0	9.1	16.5	50.7	5.2
(number of observations)	(58)	(17)	(21)	(7)	(11)
IADL only					
Average IADL hours	14.7	20.2	10.7	16.8	12.5
(number of observations)	(570)	(143)	(201)	(34)	(102)
ADL and IADL					
Average ADL hours	21.1	20.0	19.8	26.5	19.4
Average IADL hours	24.6	25.3	22.3	26.9	25.2
(number of observations)	(566)	(178)	(148)	(50)	(63)

this much. Again, there is some uncontrolled variation in care needs – that is in the severity of disability – across these groups, but the direction of bias is not obvious: past research indicates that as care needs grow, informal-only care networks tend to expand to include formal helpers, suggesting that the informal-only helper groups are faced with comparatively less-demanding care needs than are mixed formal–informal helper groups (Tennstedt *et al.* 1993; Freedman *et al.* 2002). If a more refined analysis were to confirm this "overprovision" of informal care relative to that supplied by paid helpers, this would further support the proposition that replacement-cost estimates of the social value of informal care are inflated. Fewer socially provided formal care inputs would be needed to produce an equivalent amount of functioning.

Joint production of multiple forms of assistance

Some approaches to the measurement of informal care time entail separate reports of time spent in various activities, without any attempt to net out overlapping time uses. For example, the Caregiver Activity Survey (Davis *et al.* 1997) asks caregivers to estimate the number of hours and minutes devoted to each of thirteen distinct types of care (including "communicating" and "supervision" in addition to the usual ADL and IADL tasks). Total care time is obtained by adding the thirteen individual components without regard to potential overlaps. As an indication of the substantial potential for such overlap, the maximum one-day total found in the sample was 75.33 hours of care! The supervision and communicating categories together represented over half of this total. A Swedish study (Wimo *et al.* 2002) also found that over half of measured care hours were spent in "supervision" or "surveillance." Rice *et al.* (1993) placed about 46 percent of the time spent by informal caregivers to Alzheimer's patients in "social/recreational" and "behavior management" categories, neither of which involves hands-on personal care. There is some indirect evidence of the presence of overlap in the hours-of-care reports contained in the NLTCS data: A handful (20) of the caregivers reportedly provided 168 hours of help – that is, 24 hours per day, every day – in the week preceding the survey.

The fact that task-specific reports of time used in informal elder care can add up to 24 or more hours per day suggests that two or more of the care tasks can, occasionally, be done at once. In fact, it seems quite likely that supervisory time overlaps fully with most of the other care tasks typically mentioned in studies of elder care. This reflects yet another manifestation of the potential for joint production in elder care. In addition to joint production of supervisory care and other types of care, there may also be a potential for joint production of supervisory care and other "goods" not counted as care, including leisure – an admittedly constrained, and limited, form of leisure – as well as sleep. And, the potential for joint production in elder care suggests, as I have argued before, a rationale for discounting some portion of reported informal-care hours prior to conducting replacement-cost calculations of value.

Koopmanschap and Brouwer (1998) suggest that when valuing informal dementia care hours, any leisure-time activities forgone should not be assigned any monetary value, but instead counted as a reduction in the quality of life. This reflects their tendency to view "costs" narrowly in terms of *production* (even of nontraded, abstract, household goods). In contrast, consider Folbre's (2002) distinction between "active" and "supervisory" time in parents' childcare activities. The former consists of "engaged" time, during which parent and child interact directly, or participate in shared activities, while the latter, as the label suggests, denotes supervisory constraints, such as the need to maintain a watchful, alert presence (even while a care recipient is asleep). Folbre, unlike Koopmanschap and Bouwer, assigns a monetary value to *all* the supervisory-care time, even that which comes from leisure rather than other "productive" activities. But, Folbre uses a lower cost figure for supervisory than for active time, arguing in part that there are economies of scale in substitute supervisory care. Folbre's use of a discounted replacement-care wage rate for supervisory time and my suggestion to discount supervisory care hours pertain to different elements of the replacement-cost calculation, but each has the same effect.

Put somewhat differently, although society is surely prepared to value supervisory care, it is not likely to be prepared to hire a separate supervisor for each disabled elder requiring one. Indeed, one reason to organize care in an institutional setting is to facilitate the economies of scale that can be achieved in supervisory care. Thus, the replacement-cost valuation of the supervisory component of informal elder-care services tends to overstate the social value of the services produced.

Is all care "needed"?

Some portion of the care that informal caregivers provide to close family members may not be "needed," in the sense that the care recipient could perform the tasks without difficulty in the absence of the care. Johnson and Lo Sasso (2000), who analyzed caregiving using data from a US survey, found that in 1994 3 percent of women who indicated that their parents did not need assistance with personal care actually provided such assistance. They also found that a more substantial number of women (24 percent) also provided help with household chores and errands when their parents could perform those tasks independently. Similarly, Bootsma-van der Wiel *et al.* (2001) studied differences between the concepts of *competence* (the ability to perform an activity without help, with or without difficulty) and the actual *performance* of ADL and IADL tasks in a sample of older Dutch persons. They found that 22 percent of women (and 10 percent of men) lacked the ability to perform one or more ADLs without assistance, yet 35 percent (22 percent among men) received help with one or more activities. In other words, a substantial proportion of men and women receiving ADL assistance could perform the ADL task[s] by themselves, albeit in some cases only "with difficulty." Receipt of assistance in these circumstances is not, of course, necessarily inappropriate and almost certainly improves the recipient's quality of life. However, given the finiteness of resources with which to address human needs, it is unlikely that society would place as high a value on informal help given to persons able to function without it, as to persons who cannot function without it.

Some offsetting biases

While there are several reasons to imagine that care recipients' reports of time spent in their care are inflated, there are also good reasons to suppose that some efforts on their behalf are underreported or completely unreported. For example, the time spent by a noncoresident child in preparing a meal that is brought to the care recipient's house may be overlooked by the care recipient, since it is not observed. Furthermore, time spent arranging for, monitoring, or otherwise interacting with formal care providers and other actors in the service-provision sector may go unreported by the care recipient. These types of reporting errors are more probable in the NLTCS data, in which care hours are reported by the care recipient, than in other surveys that elicit reports of care hours from those who provide them. Still, on balance, there seems to be considerably greater potential for overreporting than for underreporting of relevant hours of informal care for purposes of social valuation.

Replacement costs and public policy

I have argued that whatever wage rate one uses, a replacement-cost estimate of the social value of informal care based on nominal reports of informal care hours provided will produce inflated estimates. The data used to support these arguments cannot, however, provide any sense of how large the alleged overestimate might be. Moreover, I am not prepared to suggest appropriate discount rates to be applied to specific situations – whether to housework or other IADL help hours in which the potential for joint production is great, or to hours of supervisory or "on call" assistance – although research that employs a range of possible replacement-cost adjustments would seem to be in order.

Previously, I mentioned a number of policy areas in which estimates of the social value of informal care can play an important role. A recurring theme in this regard is the importance of distributional analyses. I know of no studies that attempt to characterize the distribution of informal care, expressed in replacement-cost terms, *within* the population, or across identifiable groups distinguished by age, race, gender, employment status, other familial responsibilities or any other socially relevant attribute. It seems safe to assume, nonetheless, that the contributions to social value produced by informal caregivers are quite unequally distributed within the population. It seems equally safe to assume that were society to compensate informal caregivers for the value they produce, and were the resources with which to provide such compensation to be collected in proportion to income (e.g. through broad-based taxation) the distribution of those levies would be unevenly distributed within the population. And, finally, it is likely that the two distributions – one of value produced, the other of expenditures avoided – would be quite dissimilar: those shouldering the costs of producing socially valuable informal care are probably not enjoying a comparable share of the social benefits they produce. Empirical research aimed at testing the preceding assertions should be given high priority. And, the sensitivity of these distributional analyses to alternative methods of accounting for the distinctively *public* value of informal caregiving should play a role in the research.

More generally, informal elder care provided by family members is but another instance of the positive social externalities of actions taken within, and at considerable cost to, families. Folbre (1994), among others, has argued that the privately borne costs of childbearing produce substantial uncompensated positive social benefits. Children, of course, ultimately become an important source of informal elder care, reinforcing the argument that they provide positive social externalities. Elementary principles of policy analysis indicate that societal well-being can be improved through interventions that equate private and public (i.e. external) costs and benefits. If childbearing produces positive externalities, then policies that "reward" childbearing (or, equivalently, that lower its costs) – such as tax reductions, child allowances, or low-cost childcare – may be warranted. Such policies already exist, of course, although many commentators argue that further reductions in the cost of childbearing are needed (England and Folbre 1999).

To invoke the social value of informal care as a rationale for differential tax treatment by parental status is to echo past calls to link Social Security benefits to fertility (Demeny 1987; Burggraf 1997). An interesting parallel has arisen in Germany, whose 1994 Dependency Insurance Act launched a universal long-term care insurance program funded through an earmarked payroll tax. In a 2001 decision issued by Germany's highest court, it was ruled unconstitutional to tax parents and the childless at the same rate; interestingly, the judge rejected, for lack of evidence, the argument that parents used fewer care resources, basing his decision instead on the fact that parents, through their childbearing, produce the future workers needed to keep the system solvent while the childless do not (Schneider 2002). Research aimed at quantifying the social value of informal care, accompanied by distributional analyses as described here, would go some distance towards providing the evidence that Germany's high-court judge failed to find.

Note

1 I am grateful to Nancy Folbre for suggesting the "care workers' strike" imagery.

References

Arno, P., Levine, C., and Memmnott, M. (1999) "The Economic Value of Informal Caregiving," *Health Affairs*, 18: 182–8.

Australian Institute of Health and Welfare (1997) *Australia's Welfare 1997: Services and Assistance*, Canberra: AIHW.

Boardman, A. E., Greenberg, D. H., Vining, A. R., and Weimer, D. L. (1996) *Cost–Benefit Analysis: Concepts and Practice*. Englewood-Cliffs, NJ: Prentice-Hall.

Bootsma-van der Weil, A., Gussekloo, J., and de Creen, A. J. M. (2001) "Disability in the Oldest-old: 'Can Do' or 'Do Do'?," *Journal of the American Geriatrics Society*, 49: 909–14.

Burggraf, S. (1997) *The Feminine Economy and Economic Man*, Reading, MA: Addison-Wesley.

Couch, K. A., Daly, M. C., and Wolf, D. A. (1999) "Time? Money? Both? The Allocation of Resources to Older Parents," *Demography*, 36: 219–32.

Davis, K. L., Marin, D. B., Kane, R., Patrick, D., Peskind, E. R., Raskind, M. A., and Puder, K. L. (1997) "The Caregiver Activity Survey (CAS): Development and Validation of a New Measure for Caregivers of Persons with Alzheimer's Disease," *International Journal of Geriatric Psychiatry*, 12: 978–88.

Demeny, P. (1987) "Re-Linking Fertility Behavior and Economic Security in Old Age: A Pronatalist Reform," *Population and Development Review*, 13: 128–32.

England, P. and Folbre, N. (1999) "Who Should Pay for the Kids?," *Annals of the American Academy of Political and Social Sciences*, 563: 194–207.

Folbre, N. (1994) "Children as Public Goods," *American Economic Review*, 84: 86–90.

—— (2002) "Valuing Parental Time: New Estimates of Expenditures on Children in the United States," Presented at the meetings of the Allied Social Science Association, January 2–5, Atlanta, Georgia.

Freedman, V. A., Aykan, H., Wolf, D. A., and Marcotte, J. E. (2002) "Disability and Home Care Dynamics Among Older Unmarried Americans," Revision of paper presented at the annual meetings of the Population Association of America, Washington, DC, 2001.

George W. Bush for President (webpage) (2000) "Bush Proposes Long-Term Care Proposal." http://georgebush.com/news/2000/may/pr051000_ltc.asp (accessed 6/8/2000).

Giarchi, George Ciacinto (1996) *Caring for Older Europeans: Comparative Studies in 29 Countries*. Aldershot: Arena.

Gore 2000 (webpage) (2000) "Gore Would Help Families and Friends Meet Long-Term Care Needs of Loved Ones," www.algore2000.com/briefingroom/releases/pr_0606_CA_1.html (accessed 6/8/2000).

Hooyman, N. and Gonyea, J. (1995) *Feminist Perspectives on Family Care*. Sage.

Ironmonger, D. (1996) "Counting Outputs, Capital Inputs, and Caring Labor: Estimating Gross Household Product," *Feminist Economics*, 2: 37–64.

Johnson, R. W. and Lo Sasso, A. T. (2000) "Parental Care at Midlife: Balancing Work and Family Responsibilities Near Retirement," The Retirement Project. Urban Institute. Brief Series, No. 9, March 2000. Available at www.urban.org/retirement.

Kinney, J. M. and Parris Stephens, M. A. (1989) "Hassles and Uplifts of Giving Care to a Family Member with Dementia," *Psychology and Aging*, 4, 402–8.

Komisar, H. and Feder, J. (1999) "The President's Proposed Long-Term Care Initiative: Background and Issues," Commonwealth Fund Policy Brief (July).

Koopmanschap, M. A. and Brouwer, W. B. F. (1998) "Indirect Costs and Costing Informal Care" in A. Wimo, B. Jönsson, G. Karlsson, and B. Winblad (eds), *Health Economics of Dementia*, New York: John Wiley and Sons, pp. 245–56.

Langa, K., Chernew, M. E., Kabeto, M. U., Herzog, A. R., Ofstedel, M. B., Willis, R. J., Wallace, R. B., Mucha, L. M., Straus, W. L., and Fendrick, A. M. (2001) "National Estimates of the Quantity and Cost of Informal Caregiving for the Elderly with Dementia," *Journal of General Internal Medicine*, 16: 770–8.

LaPlante, M. P., Harrington, C., and Kang, T. (2002) "Estimating Paid and Unpaid Hours of Personal Assistance Services in Activities of Daily Living Provided to Adults Living at Home," *Health Services Research*, 37: 397–415.

Lawton, P. M., Moss, M., Kleban, M. H., Glicksman, A., and Rovine, M. (1991) "A Two-Factor Model of Caregiving Appraisal and Psychological Well-Being," *Journal of Gerontology: Psychological Sciences*, 4: 181–9.

Leon, J. Cheng, C., and Newmann, P. J. (1998) "Alzheimer's Disease and Care: Costs and Potential Savings," *Health Affairs*, 17: 206–16.

Liu, K., Manton, K. G., and Aragon, C. (2000) "Changes in Home Care Use by Disabled Elderly Persons: 1982–1994." *Journal of Gerontology: Social Sciences*, 55B: S245–53.

Martire, L. M., Parris Stephens, M. A., and Atienza, A. A. (1997) "The Interplay of Work and Caregiving: Relationships Between Role Satisfaction, Role Involvement, and Caregivers' Well-Being," *Journal of Gerontology: Social Sciences*, 52B: 279–89.

Mitchell, R. C. and Carson, R. T. (1989) *Using Surveys to Value Public Goods*. Washington, DC: Resources for the Future.

Moore, M. J., Zhu, C. W., and Clipp, E. C. (2001) "Informal Costs of Dementia Care: Estimates from the National Longitudinal Caregiver Study," *Journal of Gerontology: Social Sciences*, 56B: S219–28.

Netten, A. (1993) "Costing Informal Care," in A. Netten and J. Beecham (eds), *Costing Community Care: Theory and Practice*, Cambridge: Ashgate, pp. 43–57.

Rice, D. P., Fox, P. J., Max, W., Webber, P. A., Lindeman, D. A., Hauck, W. W., and Segura, E. (1993) "The Economic Burden of Alzheimer's Disease Care," *Health Affairs*, 12: 165–76.

Ruhm, C. (1997) "Policy Watch: The Family and Medical Leave Act," *Journal of Economic Perspectives*, 11: 175–86.

Schneider, U. (2002) "Recent Developments in Long-Term Care in Germany," Presented at the FAMSUP meeting, Strasbourg, July 11–12.

Schoeni, R. F., Freedman, V. A., and Wallace, R. B. (2001) "Persistent, Consistent, Widespread, and Robust? Another Look at Recent Trends in Old-Age Disability," *Journal of Gerontology: Social Sciences*, 56B: S206–18.

Soldo, B. J. and Hill, M. S. (1995) "Family Structure and Transfer Measures in the Health and Retirement Study: Background and Overview," *The Journal of Human Resources*, 30 (Supplement): S108–37.

Stone, R. (2000) *Long-Term Care for the Elderly with Disabilities: Current Policy, Emerging Trends, and Implications for the Twenty-First Century*, Milbank Memorial Fund.

——, Cafferata, G. L., and Sangl, J. (1987) "Caregivers of the Frail Elderly: A National Profile," *The Gerontologist*, 27: 616–26.

Sundström, G. (1994) "Care by Families: An Overview of Trends" in Organization for Economic Co-operation and Development, *Caring for Frail Elderly People: New Directions in Care* (OECD Social Policy Studies No. 14), pp. 15–55.

Tennstedt, S. L., Crawford, S. L., and McKinlay, J. B. (1993) "Is Family Care on the Decline? A Longitudinal Investigation of the Substitution of Formal Long-Term Care Services for Informal Care," *The Milbank Quarterly*, 71: 601–24.

US Department of Health and Human Services (2001) "HHS Launches National Family Caregiver Program," HHS News release of 2/15/2001, www.hhs.gov/news/press/2001pres/20020215.html (accessed 1/9/2002).

Walker, A., Pratt, C., and Eddy, L. (1995) "Informal Caregiving to Aging Family Members: A Critical Review," *Family Relations*, 44: 402–11.

The White House (2000) "The president triples his long-term care tax credit and urges Congress to pass a long-term care initiative in 2000," Press release dated January 19, 2000.

Wimo, A., von Strauss, E., Nordberg, G., Sassi, F., and Johansson, L., (2002) "Time Spent on Informal and Formal Care Giving for Persons with Dementia in Sweden," *Health Policy*, 61:255–68.

Wolf, D. (1999) "The Family as Provider of Long-Term Care: Efficiency, Equity, and Externalities," *Journal of Aging and Health*, 11: 360–82.

Part IV

Parenting, employment, and the pressures of care

7 Packaging care

What happens when children receive nonparental care?

Michael Bittman, Lyn Craig, and Nancy Folbre

Families in the advanced industrial countries organize childcare very differently now than they did in the past. Fertility levels have declined and levels of maternal employment outside the home have increased. Many parents depend on a variety of nonparental childcare services ranging from day care centers to informal assistance provided by friends or relatives. A significant proportion of families with children are headed by mothers on their own, who often rely heavily on nonparental care.

Yet evidence from the United States indicates increasing amounts of parental time spent in activities with children. When mothers increase their hours of paid employment, they do not seem to reduce time spent in activities with children by an equal amount, but rather to reduce the time devoted to housework and sleep (Bianchi 2000). Moreover, rising levels of maternal employment appear to have been counteracted by fertility decline. Although mothers' time is more limited, it is spread among fewer children. Evidence also suggests that married coresident fathers have increased the amount of time they spend with children (Bianchi 2000). Single mothers apparently spend more time with their children than mothers with a cohabiting father or partner, perhaps in an effort to compensate for the absence of another parent (Sandberg and Hofferth 2001).

These are all important parts of the story of changing care provision. However, the level of utilization of nonparental care is also likely to affect parental decisions and market work and care. Furthermore, the cost, quality, and supply of nonparental care are directly influenced by public policies. Public provision and/or subsidies that lower the costs imposed on parents have become a prominent issue in many countries.

Time-use data offer a new window into the factors influencing the level and composition of parental time with children. Yet few, if any, studies examine the interaction between parental and nonparental care time. Most studies focus on the impact of fertility, maternal employment, and household structure on parenting time (Bryant and Zick 1996a,b; Bianchi 2000; Hofferth 2001; Sandberg and Hofferth 2001). In this chapter, we use Australian time-use data from 1997 to examine the relationship between the use of nonparental care and the level and quality of parental time in activities with children. In order to assess quality, we develop a typology of parental care activity time, ranging from "developmental" activities such as reading aloud, to "low intensity" activities such as supervising a toddler who is watching television.

We begin with a brief review of the empirical and theoretical literature that motivates our typology of parental care activities. We then describe the Australian context, offering a descriptive picture of parental and nonparental care. Next, we outline several hypotheses regarding their interaction and present the results of a multivariate analysis. The results suggest that nonparental care does not reduce parental time spent in "developmental" activities with children, and that it is associated with a more egalitarian sharing of parental care time between mothers and fathers.

Parental time in activities with children

The emerging empirical picture of parental time-use deserves close consideration because it raises important questions about parental decision-making. Changes in maternal employment do not represent an exogenous change, but the result of couples' own decisions about many factors, including the availability, cost, and quality of nonparental care. Parents in general, and mothers in particular, may target a certain minimum level of interaction time with their children, and make other decisions in order to meet that target. One way to explore this possibility is to move beyond an emphasis on *quantities* of parental time with children to some typology of the *quality* of time.

Empirical patterns

As a society, we have a tendency to romanticize the past, and to conclude that families were once more child-oriented than they are today. Evidence from time-use diaries, however, challenges that view. While the time children spend at home has declined, the time that parents spend in activities with children has shown remarkably little change. Bryant and Zick (1996a,b) report similar levels of parental activity time in the United States in the 1920s and the 1970s, on the basis of retrospective reporting of primary activities by white, two-parent families. Using a more representative sample, Bianchi reports similar findings over the period from 1965 to 1998 for time spent with children under the age of 18. While these results should be interpreted with caution (Budig and Folbre, Chapter 3, this volume), they clearly suggest that maternal employment has smaller effects than previously assumed.

Cross-sectional data from time-diary studies do show that the amount of time that mothers spend in activities with children is lower among employed than non-employed women (Pleck 1981; Nock and Kingston 1988; Robinson 1989; Bryant and Zick 1996a,b; Robinson and Godbey 1997). However, employed mothers prioritize activity time over low intensity time. In their analysis of time-diary data collected from two-parent families in the United States in the early

1980s, Nock and Kingston (1988) find that non-employed mothers spend more time with their children than employed mothers do, but the bulk of this additional time is not spent in direct interaction with the children. While employed mothers spent 4 hours a day in the company of preschoolers and non-employed mothers spent 9 hours a day, the difference in time spent in direct interaction with preschoolers by employed and by nonemployed mothers was less than an hour (Nock and Kingston 1988).

Because employed mothers prioritize high quality time with their children, employment time does not reduce time in activities with children on an hour-for-hour basis. Zick and Bryant estimate that, over a lifetime, mothers who begin employment when their children reach school age spend about 92 percent of the time in childcare activities that "stay-at-home" mothers do. Mothers in the paid workforce throughout their children's lives reach about 82 percent of the same standard (Bryant and Zick 1996b; Zick and Bryant 1996). Sandberg and Hofferth examine the same issue from the children's rather than the parents' point of view. They estimate that, in both 1981 and 1997, the child of an employed mother spent with her about 86 percent of the time that the child of a "stay-at-home" mother did (Sandberg and Hofferth 2001).

Using data from the Child Time Use Supplement of the Panel Study of Income Dynamics for 1997, Hofferth provides an especially robust analysis of the effect of maternal employment, distinguishing its effect on the time that parents and children are participating in activities together from the time in which parents are listed as available. She finds that maternal employment diminishes the time the mother is available to the child by 5 hours a week, but the time spent participating in activities by only 2.4 hours a week. Multiple regression analysis confirms that maternal employment has a significant effect on available time, but not on participation in activities (Hofferth 2001). Hofferth also examines the effect of family structure on time spent with children. She finds that children's time (both available and participating) spent with parents is significantly lower in single parent households. Single mothers are apparently unable to fully compensate for the reduction in paternal time.

Less attention has been devoted to the analysis of fathers' time, because it is both quantitatively less important and shows less variation. Several studies in the United States show that co-resident fathers with wives in paid employment spend slightly more time with their children than men with "stay-at-home" wives (Gershuny and Robinson 1988; Sandberg and Hofferth 1999). However, in the cross-section, fathers' time allocation does not seem to be closely linked to maternal employment. Nock and Kingston (1988) find no difference in fathers' time with children according to whether or not their wives worked. Hofferth finds that longer female working hours are associated with slightly higher levels of both the engaged and the available time of fathers (Hofferth 2001). No studies to date have examined the time-use of fathers who are not coresident with their children, even though this group represents a growing proportion of all fathers.

Theoretical models

Most studies of parental time allocation take a descriptive approach, rather than explicitly testing hypotheses derived from theoretical models. Yet, a number of different theoretical perspectives offer some insights into the empirical patterns described earlier, including neoclassical approaches based on individual utility maximization, sociological theories of cultural norms and "doing gender," and bargaining perspectives that draw from both economics and sociology. While it is difficult to distinguish among them for predictions of parental time allocation, all these approaches call attention to the need for better measures of the quality of parental time.

Neoclassical economists, following Becker (1981), tend to emphasize the dictates of efficiency in the household, hypothesizing that individuals allocate their time to the most efficient use. As women's potential market earnings go up, they should reallocate time from unpaid to paid work. Even within the realm of unpaid work, they should take efficiency into account, choosing to allocate their time to activities they consider most valuable and productive. Mothers may consider the time they spend in activities with children their highest priority, both because it provides them with direct utility, and also because they believe it will benefit their children. This would help explain why the time they devote to such activities declines less with maternal employment than do hours of housework. This reasoning does not, however, explain why fathers' time allocation seems relatively insensitive to changes in maternal employment.

Moreover, it is difficult to ascertain to what extent parents make decisions based on their individual circumstances, and to what extent they simply conform to evolving social norms and expectations of their social role. The social meaning of "being a parent" is constructed through a complex cultural process that places a high priority on the participation of parents themselves, mothers in particular. Indeed, women who engage in long hours of employment during the week may feel a need to compensate for their lack of conformity with traditional gender roles by putting in more hours of activity time with children on the weekends. Such a pattern would be consistent with the impact of "doing gender" on the allocation of time to housework (Brines 1994). It would also help explain why fathers' time allocation to parenting activities has not increased more noticeably as mothers' hours of paid work have increased.

Mothers and fathers may, of course, have differing preferences and priorities. Bargaining approaches suggest that factors affecting their relative power or influence should be relevant to the allocation of time (Bittman *et al.* 2003). Women may choose to work longer hours in paid employment because this increases their economic independence or offers them more control over consumption decisions, such as decisions to purchase childcare. If women are constrained by the high priority they set on their children's welfare, then the cost and availability of high quality purchased childcare is likely to increase their bargaining power in the home.

It is important to note that all three theoretical perspectives challenge the often implicit assumption that increases in maternal employment are imposed on households from without, as an exogenous change. Upon reflection, it hardly seems surprising that increases in maternal employment have only small effects on maternal activity time with children – many mothers who cannot ensure that this will be the case probably choose to limit their hours of employment. In other words, maternal employment is an endogenous factor, the outcome of a process of household decision-making that may include elements of individual calculation, "doing gender," and bargaining. It seems quite likely that the cost and availability of nonparental childcare is one of several factors affecting such decisions.

However, utilization of nonparental care and maternal employment do not necessarily go hand in hand. Many families in both the United States and Australia utilize nonparental care for pre-school children even when the mother is not employed. Likewise, in many families, both parents engage in paid employment, but do not purchase any nonparental care. Both types of decisions are shaped by a complex causality, but all the theoretical perspectives summarized here suggest that desire to reach or maintain some minimum target of parental activity time with children may play a role. Hence, it seems important to look more closely at the *composition* of parental time spent in activities with children.

A typology of care activities

Parental interaction with children ranges from passive, supervisory care to highly demanding forms of interaction that have important consequences for the development of their personal capabilities. Most studies simply tally childcare in terms of total minutes of parental time. But the activity codes available in most time-use surveys can be used to create a typology of categories ranging from the most to the least intense interactions. We define four categories as follows:

1   Developmental childcare: Face-to-face parent–child interaction that involves activities believed to be critical for the development of children's linguistic, cognitive, and social capacities. Examples of developmental childcare activities are teaching, helping children learn, reading, telling stories, playing games, listening to children, talking with, and reprimanding children.[1]
2   High contact childcare: Face-to-face parent–child interaction that revolves around physical care of children. Feeding, bathing, dressing, putting children to sleep, carrying, holding, cuddling, hugging, soothing, are all examples of high contact childcare. This type of care fosters children's health, security, and emotional well-being.[2]
3   Travel and communication: Travel can be associated with transportation to school, visits, sports training, music and ballet lessons, parent and teacher nights. In addition to the time spent in motion, travel time includes time spent waiting, and meeting trains or buses. Communication (in person, by

telephone or written) includes discussions with a spouse, other family members, friends, teachers, and childcare workers when the conversation is about the child. Although these activities are not usually active interactions with children, they require a parent's full attention and represent an important component of care.[3]

4   Low intensity childcare: Time that involves activities with children in which parents play a background role, but provide more effort and attention than the purely supervisory responsibilities that are not captured by activity-based measures (Budig and Folbre, Chapter 3, this volume). These activities include supervising games and recreational activities such as swimming, being an adult presence for children to turn to, maintaining a safe environment, monitoring children playing outside the home, and keeping an eye on sleeping children.[4] Australian Time Use Surveys offer a particularly broad definition of this activity, although it still falls far short of the inclusion of all of children's sleep time (Ironmonger, Chapter 5, this volume).

Parental and nonparental childcare in Australia

The 1997 Australian Bureau of Statistics' (ABS) time-use survey collected excellent household-level data on both parental activities and the time children spent in formal and informal care outside the home. A description of the empirical patterns offers a fascinating picture of parental efforts and sets the stage for multivariate analysis.

Parental activities with children

Much of the time parents spend in activities with children is not captured as a "primary" activity. It often takes the form of a "secondary" activity, performed simultaneously with another activity (Ironmonger, Chapter 5, this volume). Table 7.1 illustrates this point. It presents the mean times spent by fathers and mothers in families with at least one child under 5 in each of the childcare activity categories, first when only primary activity, and second when both primary and secondary activity is counted.[5]

Apart from travel and communication, a sizeable proportion of all parental activities with children represents secondary time-use. This is particularly true for women, who average 62 percent of their developmental care, and over 92 percent of their low intensity care as secondary activities. Fathers with children under 5, on average, spend 88 percent of their low intensity care time and 45 percent of their developmental care time as a secondary activity. It is hardly surprising that low intensity care is often a secondary activity, but it is worth noting that a high proportion of developmental care also falls in this category, perhaps because it is less physically salient than high contact care or travel/communication.

Table 7.1 also shows that mothers spend far more time than fathers in activities with children, and use that time in different ways. Mothers seem to take primary

Table 7.1 Mean minutes a day in each category of childcare

Childcare activity category	Father			Mother		
	Primary	Primary and secondary	Proportion secondary (%)	Primary	Primary and secondary	Proportion secondary (%)
Developmental care	29	53	45	40	105	62
High contact care	27	30	10	114	125	9
Travel/ communication	7	8	13	26	27	4
Low intensity care	11	92	88	21	251	92
Total mean childcare	74	168	56	201	447	55

Source: ABS Time Use Survey 1997.

responsibility for high contact care, spending four times as long as men do in this activity. Although mothers spend longer than fathers in developmental activities, these represent a larger share of fathers' overall time spent in activities with children.

Nonparental care in Australia

In Australia, "formal childcare" refers to regulated care away from the child's home. It includes before and after school care centers, long day care centers, family day care (in which registered providers care for up to five preschool children in their own homes), nursery school and kindergarten centers, and occasional care centers. "Informal childcare" refers to nonregulated care in either the child's home or elsewhere. Informal care includes care provided by the child's siblings, the child's grandparents, another relative of the child, or any other person (ABS 1998b). It may be paid or unpaid.

Australian regulations require monitoring of the *quality* of formal childcare and the enforcement of standards. The Quality Improvement and Accreditation Scheme licenses long day care centers for one, two, or three year periods according to their compliance with 52 criteria.[6] The Federal Government makes Child Care Assistance payments to parents who use accredited centers. State governments monitor preschools, kindergartens, and occasional care centers. Family day care is also a state responsibility. Local groups apply for a state government license to administer the service. They must demonstrate how they would address 156 items on a risk assessment list. Once licensed, the organization assumes responsibility for recruiting, assessing, and monitoring caregivers. The quality of informal childcare is unknown and there is no enforcement of minimum standards.

Table 7.2 Utilization of nonparental childcare by household structure (as a percentage of all households with children under age 5)

Type of nonparental childcare	Married/cohabiting parents	Single parents
None	42	21
Formal care	33	34
Informal care	12	16
Both formal and informal care	13	29
Total	100	100

Source: ABS Time Use Survey 1997.

Table 7.3 Utilization of informal childcare by household structure (as a percentage of all families using informal care)

Type of informal childcare used	Married/cohabiting parents	Single parents
Grandparents	80	80
Other relatives	14	43
Other people	25	18

Source: ABS Time Use Survey 1997.

Australian families with children under the age of 5 make use of all the varieties of nonparental care. As can be seen from Table 7.2, more than half of all couples utilize formal or informal care: 33 percent use formal care, 12 percent informal care and nearly 13 percent of all married parents combine both types.[7] Single mothers differ from couples in two ways – a higher incidence of nonparental care (79 percent), and a greater reliance on mixing formal and informal arrangements.

Grandparents provide the bulk of informal care, and married/cohabiting parents and single parents are about equally likely to take advantage of their assistance. Single parents, however, are more likely to enjoy help from other relatives (see Table 7.3).

Parents who rely on both formal and informal care utilize the highest total amounts of nonparental care: 20 hours a week for married/cohabiting households and 27 hours for single-parent households. Married/cohabiting households who use only formal care consume, on average, 12 hours per week of this service, whereas single parents consume, on average, 18 hours per week. Families drawing only on informal care consume the lowest amount of nonparental care, an average of 8 and 9 hours per week for partnered and single parents, respectively (see Table 7.4). This pattern suggests that parents are likely to draw on informal care first and use formal care only beyond some threshold. If their demand for

Table 7.4 Average hours per week in nonparental childcare by type of care

Type of nonparental childcare	Couple household (h/w)	Single parent households (h/w)	Total number of users
Formal	12	18	550
Informal	8	9	212
Mixed formal and informal	20	27	230

Source: ABS Time Use Survey 1997.

nonparental care exceeds the supply of informal care, they are more likely to purchase formal care.

For a better understanding of the interaction between utilization of different types of care, we turn to a multivariate analysis.

Multivariate analysis

How does the use of nonparental care affect the quantity and quality of parental time in activities with children? Our exploration of this question is motivated by four hypotheses:

1   Parents who make use of nonparental care are mindful of the potential implications and seek to compensate by protecting particularly high quality components of their time with children. We expect reductions in time devoted to "developmental" activities to be lower than time in other, less interactively intensive activities.
2   Mothers take more responsibility than fathers for the quality of care. Therefore, we expect fathers to vary the developmental time they spend with children more than mothers do.
3   Fathers spend less time than mothers in activities with children, and their time inputs vary considerably less. Therefore, we expect utilization of non-parental childcare to reduce mothers' time with children more than fathers'. As hours of nonparental care increase, the gender division of labor in activities with children should become more equal.
4   Single mothers, like their married/cohabiting counterparts, resist reductions in time devoted to developmental activities. However, they are unable to provide sufficient additional time to compensate for the absence of another parent.

Data and model specification

We test these hypotheses on a sample of families with at least one child under the age of 5 in the 1997 ABS survey (1,690 person days). Both married/cohabiting and single-parent families are included. However, since the data set includes only four single fathers, the analysis of single parents is based on mothers only

(90 person days).[8] The dependent variables in our regression analyses are the minutes per day spent in four types of parental childcare activity – developmental activities, high contact activities, low intensity activities, and travel and communication associated with childcare. For the reasons discussed here, all the dependent variables include time recorded as either a primary or a secondary activity, since we believe this provides a more accurate measure than primary activity time alone.

The independent variables are the type of nonparental childcare utilized, the duration of nonparental care, and family type (married/cohabiting parents versus single parents). The model controls for the age of the youngest child in the household, the number of children in the household, hours of market work of each parent, parental educational level, household income, whether there is a disabled person in the household, and day of the week.[9] The latter item is an essential control when analyzing information collected from daily diaries, since the pattern of activities varies by day even for the same individual. We include hours of market work in the regression model because this not strongly correlated with hours of nonparental care.[10] For a complete specification of the model, see the Appendix at the end of this chapter.

Results

This model provides results that are easy to interpret, and we report the significant coefficients in Tables 7.5 and 7.6 for fathers and mothers respectively.[11] The constant terms in the first rows of each table represent time spent during the specified activity on a weekday by a 35–44-year-old, non-employed, married parent of one child under 3, who uses no nonparental care, has no tertiary educational qualifications, and does not live with a disabled household member. The coefficients in the remaining rows represent the impact of the indicated independent variable on minutes per day of the indicated type of parental activity (which can be positive or negative).

Developmental activities

As predicted by our first hypothesis, parents do seem to defend the time they spend in developmental activities with children. Neither the type nor the quantity of nonparental care utilized is associated with significant variation. For both mothers and fathers, the use of nonparental care neither increases nor reduces the time spent in activities thought to enhance their children's cognitive and social development (see Tables 7.5 and 7.6). Its effect on this aspect of parent–child interaction is neutral.

As predicted by our second hypothesis, fathers' developmental activity time is slightly more responsive to variations in personal circumstance than is mothers'. Hours of market work are associated with a reduction in paternal developmental time at the rate of half a minute a day for every hour of paid work. This yields a loss of 17.5 minutes per day over a standard 35-hour working week. Men spend

Table 7.5 Determinants of fathers' time in activities with children (minutes per day)

Variable	Developmental	High contact	Travel and communication	Low intensity
Constant	60	23	4	100
Mixed NP care	4	0.2	−0.5	26
Formal NP care only	−4	8	−1.7	36*
Informal NP care only	0.6	−7	3.2	42
Duration NP care (h/w)	−0.3	−0.3	0.2	−2**
Child >2 years	−10	−10*	3.7	−23
2 children	−0.9	6	3	16
3+ children	−10	1.7	6**	+11
Market work (h/w)	−0.5*	−0.3	−0.0009	−2***
Spouses' market work (h/w)	0.01	0.5*	0.09	1*
Household income	0.0017*	−0.009	−0.003	0.02
Disabled person in household	3	8	3	15
Parent is aged 25–34	0.7	−0.9	−0.4	−19
Parent is aged 45–54	−15	−8	−4	27
Parent has university qualifications	7	11*	0.6	52***
Parent has vocational qualifications	−8	7	−1.5	27*
Diary day is Saturday	15	12	−0.04	61***
Diary day is Sunday	37***	13*	−5*	68***

Notes: $* P<0.05$; $** P<0.01$; $***P<0.0005$.

37 minutes a day longer in developmental care activities on Sundays than on weekdays. There is a shallow positive association with household income, which predicts an increase of less than 2 minutes in fathers' developmental care time for every extra $1,000 weekly income earned.

As predicted by our fourth hypothesis, being a single parent is not associated with any significant impact on time spent in developmental activities. None of the loss of total childcare time associated with extra-household care identified earlier is taken from parental time allocated to developmental care. Parents preserve time in the developmental activities such as talking, reading to and playing with their children across variations in both childcare usage and family type.

All else equal, mothers' time in developmental care is impervious to variations in all the independent variables except the number of children. A woman with two or more children spends about half an hour a day longer in developmental activities than a mother of one. In results not shown, we found that this extra time allocation to additional children consists of secondary activities. Mothers of more than one child seem to be accepting greater task density (doing more things at once) in order to protect time in developmental activities.[12]

Table 7.6 Determinants of mothers' time in activities with children (minutes per day)

Variable	Developmental	High contact	Travel and communication	Low intensity
Constant	77	128	10	244
Mixed NP care	−20	−34*	12*	−50
Formal NP care only	−14	−25**	7	−14
Informal NP care only	−26	−39**	3	−95**
Duration NP care (h/w)	−0.5	−0.74	0.09	0.3
Single parent	17.2	17.2	6	28
Child >2 years	4	−75***	10**	11
2 children	28**	28**	10**	−3
3+ children	30**	−1.8	21***	−31
Market work (h/w)	−0.4	−0.9**	−0.3**	−3.5***
Spouses' market work (h/w)	0.3	0.02	0.3**	0.2
Household income	0.02	0.07	0.003	0.003
Disabled person in household	−6.5	−1.6	−0.7	1.7
Parent is aged 25–34	0.4	23**	−3	15
Parent is aged 45–54	42	−75	−15	53
Parent has university qualifications	8.9	33**	−1.7	92***
Parent has vocational qualifications	13.4	33**	−12**	72**
Diary day is Saturday	−6	−5	−20***	40
Diary day is Sunday	−4	−9	−28***	60*

Notes: * $P<0.05$; ** $P<0.01$; *** $P<0.0005$.

High contact care

Nonparental care does seem to replace some of mothers' time in high contact (physical) care of their children. The use of formal care is associated with a reduction of 25 minutes, the use of informal care with a reduction of nearly 40 minutes, and the use of mixed care with a reduction of 33 minutes from the constant term of 128 minutes (just over 2 hours) a day for maternal physical care of children under 3 years of age. This loss of high contact care time accounts for a large proportion of the reduction in total time in activities with children described here.

Single mothers do not spend a significantly different amount of time than partnered mothers in high contact care. Mothers' time in physical care is not further affected by the duration of nonparental childcare, but hours of paid work do have a downward impact on mothers' time in these activities. For every weekly hour worked, mothers reduce their high contact care time by 0.9 minutes a day, with an estimated loss of just over half an hour a day associated with standard 35-hour-per-week employment.

Maternal high contact time is also affected by some of the other control variables in the model. Mothers aged 25–34 spend 22 minutes a day longer than other mothers in physical care, and having either university or vocational qualifications is associated with just over half an hour a day of additional high contact time. Mothers of two-year-olds spend about half an hour more than other mothers performing high contact care, and if the youngest child is three or older, maternal physical care time is reduced by an hour and 25 minutes.

Consistent with our third hypothesis, fathers' time in high contact activities with children (for which the constant term is only 12 minutes per day) is completely unaffected by utilization of nonparental care. Nor does fathers' time in paid work affect their time in high contact activities. Several control variables, however, predict a change in paternal time. Fathers' high contact activity time is increased by 0.4 minutes a day for every hour his spouse spends in paid employment, yielding a gain of 13.5 minutes a day if the wife works a standard 35-hour week. Men with a university education average 11 minutes a day longer in physical care of children than other men, and fathers spend 13 minutes longer in physical care on a Sunday than on a weekday. As with mothers, physical care time is less with a child of three or older. The model predicts that, in the case of fathers, the reduction is just over 10 minutes a day.

Travel and communication

Fathers devote an average of 4 minutes a day to child-related travel and communication. This allocation of time is not affected by the use of extra-household childcare. Indeed, the only variables in the model that affect male time in these activities is the diary day falling on a Sunday, which is associated with a reduction of 5 minutes, and having three or more children, which is associated with an increase of 6 minutes a day in travel and communication to do with children.

Child-related travel and communication is a more time consuming activity for women, for whom the constant term is 10 minutes a day. However, as with fathers, the use of formal or informal nonparental childcare is not associated with either an increase or a decrease in travel and communication time for mothers.

The model does, however, predict that the use of a mixture of both care types increases maternal time in these activities by 12 minutes a day. A multiplicity of care arrangements requires more travel between venues, and more communication with others. Single parents' time allocation to these activities does not differ significantly from that of married mothers. This analysis shows how time-consuming an activity child-related travel and communication is for women, particularly as their youngest child matures. Mothers with a youngest child of 3 or older spend just over 20 minutes a day in child-related travel.

Travel time appears immune to economies of scale, and is the only childcare activity that increases steadily with each additional child. Mothers' travel time goes up by 10 minutes when they have two kids and by 21 minutes when they have three or more children. This means that a woman whose youngest child is no longer an infant spends increasing amounts of time, with each extra child, chauffeuring offspring around, up to a maximum of nearly 40 minutes a day. In results not shown, we found that this effect continues as the children mature beyond school entry age. By the time a woman's youngest child is aged 5–11, almost the largest proportion of her childcare time is allocated to child-related travel.

Several control variables are associated with a reduction in female travel and communication time. On weekends it is reduced by 20 (Saturday) to 28 (Sunday) minutes a day. Women with vocational qualifications spend nearly 12 minutes a day less than other women in these activities. A woman's hours of market work and her spouse's hours of market work have opposite effects on her time in child-related travel and communication. Her own market hours predict a reduction in child-related travel and communication of 0.3 minutes a day for every hour she works per week (0–35-hour change results in 10 minutes a day loss). Her spouse's weekly hours of market work predict an increase in a woman's travel and communication of 0.3 minutes a day for every hour he works (0–35-hour change results in a 12-minute gain).

Low intensity care

Passive childcare is a very time consuming activity, particularly for mothers. The constant term (representing time spent on a weekday by a mother of one child under 3, who uses no extra-household care, does no paid work, has no tertiary qualifications, is aged 35–44, and has no disabled household member) is 4 hours a day. Most of this is conducted as a secondary activity while undertaking other tasks. The model predicts no change in this time with the use of formal childcare, or the use of mixed care, but it does predict that women who use informal care only will reduce their passive care time by an hour and a half a day.

No effect upon maternal low intensity care is associated with the duration of care. The use of nonparental care reduces maternal time in low intensity care only in the case of those mothers who use informal care. As we showed earlier, this is a minority of mothers, a disproportionate number of whom are single parents enjoying the assistance of family members (mostly grandparents). Mothers' time in low intensity care is reduced by time spent in paid work. The model predicts that maternal time in passive care will decline by 3.5 minutes a day for every hour worked a week, yielding a loss of just over 2 hours (122 minutes) a day when a standard 35-hour week is worked. This is the largest impact on any aspect of a parent's time spent in activities with children, showing that low intensity care is disproportionately diminished by maternal absence, although only when that absence is caused by paid employment.

Some of the independent variables in the model predict increases in low intensity care time. Mothers spend nearly an hour longer in passive care on a

Sunday than on a weekday. Higher levels of education are associated with longer passive care time, with women who have university qualifications spending an additional hour and a half, and women with vocational qualifications spending an additional hour and fifteen minutes longer compared to women with lower levels of education.

Male low intensity activity time is affected by the use of nonparental care. Mixed care and informal care do not affect male low intensity activity time, but the use of formal care is associated with an increase of 36 minutes a day. This suggests that men are more likely to be involved in low intensity activities with their children if formal nonparental care is used. However, this effect is countered if the duration of care is over about 20 hours a week. Male low intensity care time declines by 2 minutes a day for each hour the child spends in care (30 hours in nonparental care yields a daily loss of 57 minutes a day). Paid work time also reduces paternal low intensity care, although the effect is not as pronounced as for women. Male low intensity care time declines by 2 minutes a day for every hour worked a week (a change from 0 to 35 hours yields a 70 minute a day loss). This suggests that it is only men who are working less than standard hours who have a net increase of low intensity childcare associated with the use of nonparental care.

Spouses' hours of paid work have an opposite impact, predicting an increase in fathers' time in low intensity activities of nearly a minute a day for every hour his wife works. Having a spouse who works a 35-hour week would therefore increase fathers' low intensity care time by 35 minutes a day. Men also spend more time in low intensity care on Saturdays (61 minutes) and Sundays (68 minutes). The model also predicts that men with a university education will spend 52 minutes a day longer, and that men with vocational qualifications will spend 27 minutes a day longer in low intensity childcare activities than men with no tertiary qualifications.

Discussion

Obviously, childcare remains predominantly women's work. The expenditure of time by mothers in nearly all activities with children is three to four times greater than that of fathers. Therefore, it comes as no surprise that the type of non-parental care utilized significantly affects the composition of mothers' time. Hours of market work amplify this effect. As our first two hypotheses suggest, mothers protect developmental activities while substantially reducing low intensity, child-minding activities. Some physical care of children seems to be transferred to nonparental caregivers.

Fathers' time in developmental childcare activities is less resistant to change and seems inversely related to their own hours of market work. However, both fathers' high contact and their low intensity activity time seem to increase slightly along with spouses' hours of market work. Nonparental childcare has an effect independent of hours of maternal employment, decreasing maternal high contact time and increasing the proportion of high contact care undertaken by fathers. As our third hypothesis suggests, the gender division of labor in activities with children becomes somewhat more equal. Developmental activities represent an exception to this pattern, since mothers and fathers devote nearly the same amount of time to these (as a result, it comprises a much greater proportion of fathers' than mothers' total time in activities with children).

Although care outside the home does not alter the gender balance in developmental care, travel and communication, or high contact care, it does affect the gender balance of low intensity care. Longer hours of care outside the home reduce mothers' time spent in high contact childcare activities, but increase fathers' involvement in low intensity care activities. It seems that nonparental care replaces some of the physical aspects of maternal parenting, and that the use of childcare, especially formal childcare, is associated with significant increases in paternal low intensity time. Thus, the distribution of childcare time between mothers and fathers becomes more equal as hours of nonparental care increase. Although men are not taking over the high contact care, they are spending longer in children's company and fulfilling a supervisory role.

Like previous results derived from US data, these findings reveal a trade-off between time in market work and time in activities with children (Pleck 1981; Nock and Kingston 1988; Bryant and Zick 1996a,b; Robinson and Godbey 1997; Bianchi 2000; Sandberg and Hofferth 2001). But the trade-off is very small, amounting to only about 3 minutes reduction per day in time in activities with children per additional weekly hour of maternal employment. Time with children is shifted to accommodate other commitments. Nonparental care may be used to facilitate this shifting rather than as a direct substitute for parental time.

Regardless of the weekly hours children spend in care outside the home, or the type of care used, children enjoy the same amount of time in developmental activities with their parents. Nonparental care substitutes for low intensity activities, and a higher proportion of time that parents do spend with children is spent in developmental and high contact activities. Parents do not always maintain other forms of "quality time." Mothers reduce time in high contact activities, which consist largely of physical care such as feeding and changing diapers. These are less amendable to rescheduling the talking and playing activities that comprise developmental care. Some physical care activities, such as bathing a child, or putting a child to bed, are more easily performed at the end of a traditional paid work day. These activities are probably less susceptible to reduction and may acquire greater symbolic importance.

Australian children living with single mothers spend more time in nonparental care than those living with married/cohabiting parents. Yet, as our fourth hypothesis predicts, they spend no less – and no more – time with their mothers in any category of activity. While the descriptive results in the previous section indicate that single mothers try to compensate for the absence of a second parent, the regression analysis indicates that their behavioral response to the independent variables is not significantly different from that of married mothers. Single mothers do benefit from higher levels of informal care, suggesting that their children may have more interaction with family members such as grandmothers.

Conclusion

The results presented here testify to the resilience and flexibility of parental commitments to child rearing. Parents prioritize certain types of activities with their children and rearrange their schedules to accommodate these. As a result, increased hours of maternal employment and increased utilization of nonparental care lead to only small reductions of parental time in activities with children. A shift toward higher quality care also occurs, as developmental activities come to represent a larger proportion of time parents spend interacting with children.

Individual calculation, social norms, and gender bargaining probably all play an important role in the reconfiguration of parental time. Cross-sectional differences suggest that movement away from gender specialization in parenting is taking place, albeit at a very gradual pace. The provision of nonparental care seems to encourage this movement toward reduced specialization, allowing mothers to delegate some of their routine responsibilities to paid care providers. Mothers are moving toward a pattern of time allocation that fathers have traditionally enjoyed, in which the most rewarding activities play a more prominent role.

Appendix

Table 7A.1 Model specification

Independent variables	
Uses both formal and informal care	Both formal and informal (yes = 1)
Uses formal care only	Formal (yes = 1)
Uses informal care only	Informal (yes = 1)
Total hours per week of nonparental childcare[†]	Midpoint of ranges, yields values 0–60
Family type	Single parent household (yes = 1)
Controls	
Age of youngest child	Child is 3–5 (yes = 1)
Number of children in household	Two children (yes = 1)
	Three or more children (yes = 1)
Hours per week in paid work	Midpoint of ranges, yields values 0–50
Spouse's hours per week in paid work	Midpoint of ranges, yields values 0–50
Household income	Midpoint of ranges, yields values 0–2,300
Disabled person in household	Disabled person (yes = 1)
Age of parent	Aged 25–34 (yes = 1)
	Aged 45–54 (yes = 1)
Qualifications of parent	Has university qualification (yes = 1)
	Has vocational qualification (yes = 1)
Diary day is Saturday	Saturday (yes = 1)
Diary day is Sunday	Sunday (yes = 1)

Source: ABS Time Use Survey 1997.

Note
† Only entered in model of mothers' time spent in childcare.

Notes

1 Based on Australian Bureau of Statistics (ABS) activity codes 521 and 531.
2 Based on ABS code 511 and 512.
3 Based on ABS code 57 and 58.
4 Based on ABS code 54.
5 Excluding the time in which childcare was recorded as a secondary activity to sleep.
6 The initial assessment is self-administered, and is validated by peer review. If the center fails to meet minimum standards, it is given time to improve. In extreme cases, the license is revoked, which triggers an effective withdrawal of government funding because parents can no longer claim Child Care Assistance in respect of that center.
7 The ABS treats legally married and de facto married couples alike, reflecting their treatment in the Australian legal system. Moreover the unit of the sample – a household – is defined by coresidence. In this chapter, the term "married" applies to de jure and de facto partnerships and the term "married" is used interchangeably with "cohabiting." The term "two-parent household" applies to both de jure and de facto relationships.
8 Although Australian time-use data are of exceptionally high quality, they suffer from some limitations where assessment of childcare is concerned. In families with more than one child, there is insufficient information to determine the relationship between parental time and nonparental time. The relevant variables record only the total nonparental care time and not the time for each individual child. For example, a family may have one child in formal care, and another child at home in parental care. Limiting the universe to families with only one preschool child drastically reduces the sample size. There were insufficient numbers of single-child families, whose child was of preschool age to permit a statistically robust analysis. Initially, we sought to resolve this problem by pooling data from two surveys (1992 and 1997). However, because each of the surveys contained slightly different information about the use of nonparental care some detail was lost in the processes of pooling. Following some sensitivity testing, we discovered that restricting the sample to families with at least one child under the age of 5 (the age at which Australian children begin schooling) produces very similar results. Consequently, we have chosen to analyze a larger subsample of families with at least one child under the age of 5 drawn from the most recent survey. Both two-parent and single-parent families are included, in order to investigate the effect of family structure.
9 Australian educational attainment categories are generally an ordinal set – incomplete schooling, completed highest level of secondary education available, university degree or post-graduate qualification. However, the category vocational qualification is anomalous because it is a post-school accreditation to work a specific vocation, recognized trade or craft often involving a combination of study and apprenticeship. Entry to vocational study is based on the completion of middle-school rather the highest level of secondary education available.
10 "Hours of paid work" and "hours of nonparental care" have a correlation of only 0.47 for partnered women and 0.35 for single mothers. This indicates that nonparental childcare is being used for other purposes than allowing mothers to work more hours in paid employment. Likewise, we find some women not using nonparental childcare when they are employed. In 111 cases (diary days), mothers who were in the paid work force used no nonparental care. In 50 cases (diary days), women who performed paid work on the diary days used no nonparental care. A close examination of individual case records reveals plausible circumstances explaining the discrepancy between women's hours of work and use of nonparental care. Some are doing shift work, but a more common situation is employment at home. Most of these women are working part-time, doing clerical work in the private sector, although some work in agriculture. An examination of their husband's records suggests that some of the women are farmers' wives

who participate in farm work while supervising children, and others are doing clerical work for their husbands' businesses while supervising children. These results increase our confidence that "hours of nonparental care" and "hours of paid work" can be included as separate independent variables in the regression model.

11 A complete set of results including all coefficients and standard errors is available from the authors on request.

12 We also find (in results not shown) that the use of informal care is associated with a reduction in maternal time in developmental care as a primary activity; this time is made up through secondary activity.

References

Australian Bureau of Statistics (1998a) *How Australians Use Their Time 1997*, Catalogue No. 4153.0, Canberra, Australia.

—— (1998b) *Time Use Survey Australia: User's Guide*, Catalogue No. 4150.0, Canberra, Australia.

Becker, G. (1981) *A Treatise on the Family*, Cambridge, MA: Harvard University Press.

Bianchi, S. (2000) "Maternal Employment and Time with Children: Dramatic Change or Surprising Continuity?" *Demography*, 37, 401–14.

Bittman, M., England, P., Sayer, L., Folbre, N., and Matheson, G. (2003) "When Does Gender Trump Money? Bargaining and Time in Household Work," *American Journal of Sociology*, 109: 186–214.

Brines, J. (1994) "Economic Dependency, Gender, and the Division of Labor at Home," *American Journal of Sociology*, 100: 652–88.

Bryant, W. K. and Zick, C. D. (1996a) "Are We Investing Less in the Next Generation? Historical Trends in the Time Spent Caring for Children," *Journal of Family and Economic Issues*, 17: 365–91.

—— and —— (1996b) "An Examination of Parent–Child Shared Time," *Journal of Marriage and the Family*, February 58: 227–37.

Fisher, K., McCulloch, A. and Gershuny, J. (1999) "British Fathers and Children," *Working Paper*, Institute for Social and Economic Research, Essex University (December).

Gershuny, J. and Robinson, J. (1988) "Historical Changes in the Household Division of Labor," *Demography*, 25: 537–52.

Hofferth, S. (2001) "Women's Employment and Care of Children in the United States," in T. Van der Lippe and L. Van Dijk (eds), *Women's Employment in a Comparative Perspective*. New York: Aldine de Gruyter.

Nock, S. and Kingston, P. (1988) "Time with Children: The Impact of Couples Work-Time Commitments," *Social Forces*, 67: 59–85.

Pleck, J. H. (1981) *Wives' Employment, Role Demands and Adjustment: Final Report*. Wellesley, MA: Wellesley College Center for Research on Women.

Robinson, J. P. (1989) "Caring for Kids," *American Demographics*, 11: 52.

—— and Godbey, G. (1997) *Time for Life. The Surprising Ways Americans Use Their Time*. Pennsylvania: Pennsylvania State University Press.

Sandberg, J. F. and Hofferth, S. L. (2001) "Changes in Children's Time with Parents: United States, 1981–1997," *Demography*, 38: 423–36.

Zick, C. D. and Bryant, W. K. (1996) "A New Look at Parent's Time Spent in Child Care: Primary and Secondary Time Use," *Social Science Research*, 25: 260–80.

8 Parenting and employment

What time-use surveys show

Michael Bittman

For over a decade controversy has raged about whether economic progress and the advancement of women have led to a perverse result – resulting in more work and less leisure (Schor 1991; Robinson and Godbey 1997; Gershuny 2000; Jacobs and Gerson 2001). It seems entirely possible that new constraints and pressures have neutralized the benefits of increased prosperity. Against the background of an increasing perception of time-pressure, there have been a variety of claims and counter-claims made about changes in paid working hours and in the amount of leisure time available. Let us look at the evidence for the increase in perceived time-pressure and then examine each of these claims and counter-claims in a little more detail.

Perceptions of time-pressure

Perhaps the strongest indication that time-pressures are increasing is the growing proportion of the population reporting the feeling of being short of time. Since 1965, the US time-use researcher John P. Robinson and his collaborators have been asking respondents: "Would you say you always feel rushed, even to do the things you have to do, only sometimes feel rushed, or almost never feel rushed?" The proportion of 18–64-year olds who report always feeling rushed rises from 24 percent in 1965 to 28 percent in 1975, leaps to 35 percent in 1985 and "reaches its peak of 38 percent in 1992, before declining slightly in 1995" (Robinson and Godbey 1997: 231). Zuzanek (2000) also notes indications of an increased perception of time-pressure in Canada. In 1992, 51.7 percent of all employed Canadian respondents felt rushed every day, and 56.2 percent said that they were more rushed than five years ago. In 1998, these figures rose to 53.5 percent and 59.2 percent, respectively.

Equivalent trends in Australia are difficult to interpret because the data for different years are not comparable. Although at least one question about perceived time-pressure have been included in some Australian time-use surveys, the response categories have been different and changed each time the question was asked. The questions which are most comparable are those which were asked in 1974 and 1997.[1] Although there are significant differences in the populations covered by the survey – the 1974 sample is composed of two subsamples, one urban (Melbourne)

Table 8.1 Feelings of time-pressure among prime-working-age population (25–54 years)

	Men (as %)	Women (as %)
1974, Melbourne/Albury-Wodonga	N = 420	N = 547
Always feel rushed	29.8	24.9
Only sometimes feel rushed	51.7	58.0
Almost never feel rushed	18.6	17.2
1997, Australia	N = 1875	N = 2110
Always feels rushed or pressed for time	12.4	16.7
Often feels rushed or pressed for time	32.2	35.0
Sometimes feels rushed or pressed for time	38.3	32.6
Rarely feels rushed or pressed for time	14.1	10.6
Never feels rushed or pressed for time	3.0	1.7

Sources: Cities Commission Time Use Survey, 1975; ABS Time Use Survey 1997.

and a less urbanized regional growth center (Albury-Wodonga), while the 1997 sample is national – an analysis of the national data revealed no significant relation between region and perceived levels of time-pressure (see Table 8.1).

Bearing in mind the difficulties of translating the older three-point scale into the newer five-point scale, it does seem as though the proportion of those reporting feeling relatively free of time-pressures is dwindling. In 1974, 17 percent of women reported that they "almost never feel rushed"; by 1997, the proportion feeling they had escaped time-pressure because they "rarely" or "never" felt rushed, had fallen to 12 percent.

Further confirmation of the extent and significance of the experience of time-pressure comes from the Women's Health Australia Project. In the first wave of this large longitudinal study of women's health, approximately 60 percent of young and middle-aged respondents said they had experienced feeling pressed for time "every day" or "often" (more than once a week).[2] Less than 20 percent reported feeling relatively free from pressures of time (that is, feeling pressured at infrequent intervals: "monthly or never"). The survey reveals an inverse relationship between feeling "rushed, pressured, or too busy" and health assessment; the more "rushed" an individual felt, the greater the likelihood that she would assess her health as poor. Among the mid-aged cohort of Australian women, there was a greater likelihood of reports of feeling "constant tiredness" as hours of paid work increased. Evidence from Finland also suggests health effects. According to the 1997 Finnish Time Use and Quality of Working Life Survey (QWLS), 69 percent of employees reporting high levels of time-pressure frequently experienced fatigue, 50 percent complained of exhaustion, 45 percent had sleeping problems, and 19 percent felt depressed. For respondents experiencing low levels of time-pressure, corresponding figures were considerably smaller. However, this kind of cross-sectional analysis can only establish the association between self-rated health and perceived time-pressure, so it is also possible that people who are less physically and emotionally healthy are more likely to report feeling time-pressure.

From the evidence available, it seems that most of the working-age population in these countries feel that they are under mounting time-pressure. This widely held perception probably helps explain the enthusiastic reception given to Schor's (1991) claim that in recent decades escalating hours of work in the United States have caused a decline in leisure in that country.

An unexpected decline in leisure?

Although Schor's claims resonated with many people's perceptions, they also provoked a spirited reaction from specialists in work and leisure. Among specialists the term "free time" is defined as the remaining time after the time spent in market and nonmarket work and meeting physiological needs (sleeping, eating, attending to personal hygiene, and grooming) is deducted. It represents the time potentially available for leisure pursuits. Using data from time-diaries – the most direct and reliable method of measuring free time – Robinson and Godbey have produced evidence contradicting any claim that the quantity of free time available to people in the United States has declined between 1965 and 1985 (1997: 131–3).

Robinson and Godbey's finding that free-time has increased over the last three decades has been replicated in thirty-six surveys across nineteen separate countries, including Australia (Gershuny 1992; Bittman 1998; Gershuny 2000). An analysis of 128,931 working-age people, drawn from the pooled Multinational Time Use database, shows how more free time became steadily available to both men and women from 1961 to 1983. It fell in the 1980s, but it then recovered in the early 1990s to resume a historical pattern of increase. The net increase in free time between the early 1960s and the early 1990s was more than 7 hours for women and 5 and one half hours for men (Bittman 1998: 372; Gershuny 2000).

It is difficult to escape the conclusion that, in aggregate, the time available for leisure for the working-age population is indeed increasing. The claim that leisure is declining is not supported by the best data available. This makes the perception of inescapably mounting time-pressure somewhat bewildering. This situation has produced some interesting speculation about this paradox. Robinson and Godbey (1997), following Linder (1970), have suggested that the perception of time famine is an illusion based on the growth of choices about what to do with their free-time. Jacobs and Gerson (2001), paying close attention to the detail of Schor's claims, argued that, far from being an illusion, the subjective impression of time famine is based on the objective changes among employed prime-working-age family households. I shall return to question of the origins of perceived time famine after first examining the claim that over recent decades the (paid) working hours have increased.

Overwork and the distribution of paid working hours

The answer to the question of whether the paid work-week has, on average, been getting longer over the last few decades depends to a large extent on the source of the data analyzed and how it is analyzed. Those relying on employers' estimates argue that the average US workweek is shorter now than it was in 1947 (Bluestone and Rose 2000: 22). Most estimates based on the official labor force surveys find that, while the average workweek has barely changed over the last few decades, the dispersion has increased markedly (Jacobs and Gerson 1998; ABS 1999).[3] This increased dispersion means that the proportion of those working long hours, say, more than 45 hours per week, has grown.

Time-use diaries are used less often than official labor force surveys to measure changes in the workweek. Nonetheless, they do provide some information on time spent in paid work. Robinson and Godbey argue that the per capita time devoted to paid work by American men and women of age 18–64 has fallen (1997: 94). Among prime-age Australian workers over the last quarter of a century, per capita employment hours have remained remarkably steady, but the numbers of unemployed have risen and the working day is getting longer for those who are in paid employment. Moreover, standard working hours are now less typical for both men and women, while work at unsociable times of the day (such as late in the evening when most other people are having leisure or during daylight hours on weekends) has also increased over the course of this period (Bittman and Rice 2002). Such changes in working-time affect the time available for other activities.

This suggests a potential solution to the riddle of why people report feelings of being pressed for time, while at the same time surveys show that free-time is increasingly available (and that the length of the average workweek has hardly changed). It could be that hours of paid employment are distributed differently, so that the proportion reporting long hours of market work and high levels of time-pressure has increased while the unemployed report having more leisure available.

A new resolution: balancing work and family?

Jacobs and Gerson propose an alternative solution to the riddle (1998, 2001). They suggest, following on from Bluestone and Rose (1997), that what has been fuelling the increasing sense of time-pressure is the spread of the dual-earner household. Regardless of changes in averages when individuals are counted, households as a whole are now likely to be supplying more labor to the market than in the days when it was only the male provider who specialized in market work. The sense of increased time-pressure, they speculate, may reflect the dual-earner household's need to manage a greater load of work, both paid and *unpaid*, than the specialized division of labor practised by their parents. The increase in free-time is presumably the result of higher levels of unemployment and earlier retirement.

In a recently published article, these authors analyzed working hours in the US Current Population Survey (CPS) in terms of household labor supply. They find that, on average, dual-earner couples supply 81.3 hours per week to the labor market (husbands 44.9 and wives 36.4) compared with the male breadwinner household's 44.7 hours per week (Jacobs and Gerson 2001: 51). On the basis of this analysis, they conclude that it is the increase in the proportion of households that are now dual-earner households, rather than any secular increase in the workload of this type of household since 1970, that provides the objective basis for increase in feelings of being pressured (Jacobs and Gerson 2001: 53).

Since they rely on CPS data, Jacobs and Gerson are limited to discussing hours of market work and to conjecture about the *combined paid and unpaid* workload of family households. Fortunately, Australian time-use data, which collects information about all the daily activities by adults in a household, provides a good window on combined market and nonmarket work of households.

How Australian time-use data might help solve the mystery

The Australian Bureau of Statistics' Time Use Survey has collected time-diaries from every person in the household over 15 years on three occasions – 1987, 1992, and 1997. To improve comparability, only the data on the primary activities of metropolitan heads of household and their spouses (where applicable) were analyzed.[4]

Table 8.2 shows how the average combined market hours of Australian couples have changed between 1987 and 1997, holding age constant. It is clear that, where the head of household is below 54 years of age, the hours households have, on average, been supplying to the labor market have increased significantly. For households whose head is above 54 years of age, the reverse is true. These findings are broadly consistent with the reasons advanced by Jacobs and Gerson for the loss of the leisurely feeling.

Table 8.3 shows the time spent in paid work and unpaid domestic work for a variety of household types for each of the three survey years.[5] As was the case in the analysis of the supply of market hours in the United States by Jacobs and Gerson, Australian dual-earning households where both husband and wife worked full-time supplied nearly twice as many hours (more than 90 hours per week) to the labor market as did those households where only the husband worked full-time and the wife was not employed (close to 50 hours per week).[6] Households where the husband is in full-time work and his partner does part-time market work are common in Australia. As might be expected their

Table 8.2 Average combined weekly hours of market work: metropolitan couples (with and without children)

Age group[a] (in years)	1987	1992	1997
25–39	50.50	56.72	56.37
40–54	56.08	54.87	58.03
55–64	36.45	32.43	30.48
65 or more	7.35	5.58	2.95

Sources: ABS Time Use Surveys 1987, 1992, 1997.

Note
a Based on the age of the reference person.

Table 8.3 Total hours per week spent in paid market work and unpaid housework, and childcare by prime-age,[a] metropolitan married or de facto couples in Australia

	Husband full-time, wife full-time	Husband full-time, wife part-time	Husband full-time, wife not employed	Husband not full-time	All couples
Paid market work					
1987	92	69	54	20	64
1992	91	68	47	33	64
1997	92	70	52	30	67
Unpaid housework and childcare					
1987	45	60	71	70	61
1992	44	63	67	64	58
1997	46	64	72	66	60
Total paid and unpaid work					
1987	137	128	125	90	126
1992	135	131	114	97	123
1997	138	134	123	97	128

Sources: ABS Time Use Surveys 1987, 1992, 1997.

Note
a "Prime-age" means household reference person is aged 25–54 years.

household supply of market work (roughly 70 hours per week) represents an intermediate position between dual career and traditional families.

Adding the information about nonmarket labour, it is clear that, as Jacobs and Gerson surmise, the domestic workloads of dual-earner households are not reduced sufficiently to compensate for the extra hours supplied to the labor market, and in consequence they have the highest "total" workloads. As can be seen in Table 8.3, between 1987 and 1997 dual-career couples spent around 137 hours per week in paid work and unpaid work.[7] This was 10 hours a week more than traditional couples, but only five hours a week more than couples where the husband worked full-time and the wife part-time. Traditional households allocate, on average, the highest hours to non-market work. However, in households in which the husband is employed full-time but the wife only part-time, these wives supply so many hours of unpaid work (over 60 hours per week) that their total hours are only slightly lower than in full-time dual-earner households. Indeed, their unpaid workload is closer to that of the households with a single male provider than it is to the full-time dual-career households. The lowest total workloads are found in households where, for some reason, a prime-working-age husband does not work full-time. These households supply on average less than a third of the hours of market work supplied by dual-career households, and exhibit slightly lower labor inputs in nonmarket work than in male-breadwinner households.

Table 8.4 Employment status among prime-age, metropolitan married or cohabiting couples (%)

	1987	1992	1997
Husband full-time, wife full-time	25.5	29.8	32.5
Husband full-time, wife part-time	27.4	30.6	29.9
Husband full-time, wife not employed	37.6	25.2	23.4
Husband not full-time	9.5	14.4	14.2
All couples	100.0	100.0	100.0

Sources: ABS Time Use Surveys 1987, 1992, 1997.

One remarkable feature of Table 8.3 is the relative stability of workloads of all household types over the 10-year period. Over the decade for which this data is available there is no statistically reliable indication of change, workloads at the end of the period are almost identical with workloads at the beginning of the period. This stability is also consistent with the argument advanced by Jacobs and Gerson in the US context, that is, the change is not in the typical work-load of a one-family type but the result of the rising proportion of couples in the hardest pressed type (dual-career families). The dual-career household is the predominant form of couple household found in the United States, and as Table 8.4 shows, in the short space of a single decade it has displaced the traditional family household and become the model type in Australia.

Children and changes in household labor supply

The biggest influences on women's time-use are employment and transitions between different life course phases, such as marriage, birth, retirement, or loss of a spouse. Australian households vary their paid and unpaid workload considerably in response to children and schooling.

Australian childless couple households allocate on average more than 70 hours per week to market work, or nearly two-thirds of their total work time. In contrast, households whose youngest child is preschool-age devote over 70 hours to nonmarket work, reducing their market hours to less than 60 per week (see Table 8.5). In couple households where the youngest child is at school, average weekly market and nonmarket work are almost equal.

The households with the longest hours of total work, paid and unpaid, are those with preschool-age children, while those with the shortest are childless couples. Couple households with children at school occupy an intermediate position. These total hours, however, mask the fact that a large quantity of time is devoted to childcare as a simultaneous activity accompanying another "main" or primary activity. It is important to note that these calculations, based on hours of primary activity alone, seriously understate the amount of time and effort

Table 8.5 Household supply of market and nonmarket labor by parental status of household (hours per week)

	Married, no children	Married, youngest 0–4 years	Married, youngest 5–14 years
1987			
Paid work	71.4	56.3	66.5
Unpaid work	43.2	76.8	60.7
Total work	114.6	133.1	127.2
1992			
Paid work	73.0	55.7	63.1
Unpaid work	46.0	75.8	56.3
Total work	119.0	131.6	119.3
1997			
Paid work	76.1	58.0	65.2
Unpaid work	43.1	76.7	62.8
Total work	119.3	134.7	128.0

Source: ABS 1997.

devoted to childcare (see Bittman *et al.*, Chapter 4, this volume; Ironmonger, Chapter 5, this volume).

Once again, these differences between households show remarkable stability over time. There are no significant trends in the household supply of either market or nonmarket work over this period. However, a growing proportion of Australians are childless and the age composition of those with children is changing, suggesting that there may be links between fertility decisions, the market labor supply and total workloads. Therefore, over the decade, the change in distribution of the population between categories is far more important than changing workloads for particular household types.

Lone parent households

Australian lone mothers' total hours of labor are greater than those of single women without children, by about same ratio as couples with children differ from couples without children.[8] However, the transfer of labor from market to non-market work in female single adult hours associated with the presence of children is even more pronounced than in couple households. Among single women without children, market work accounts for two-thirds of the total weekly work hours, whereas among lone mothers it accounts for one-eighth. Lone mothers with children attending school devote one-quarter of their total working hours to market work.

Lone mothers' weekly hours of total work are lower than might be expected. In couple households, two-thirds of the hours of nonmarket work are supplied by women. In both childless households and those with children, single women's

Table 8.6 Lone adult supply of market and nonmarket labor by parental status of household, 1997 (hours per week)

	Single, no children	Single, youngest 0–4 years	Single, youngest 5–14 years
Paid work	36.6	7.9	15.8
Unpaid work	18.4	56.7	41.4
Total work	55.0	64.6	57.1

Source: ABS 1997.

total hours of work are roughly half those supplied by both partners in couple households.

There is also an interesting pattern of total workload by age of the youngest child. The total workload of lone mothers whose youngest child is preschool age is on average almost 10 hours a week more than that of comparable childless women, whereas the total workload of lone mothers whose children are school age is barely above that of comparable childless women (see Table 8.6).

Australian lone mother's ability to control their total workload by switching their time allocation from market work to nonmarket work may partly be explained by their eligibility for income support. Lone mothers are eligible for an income support, up to the equivalent of 45 percent of average female full-time, ordinary time earnings, until their child is 12 years of age. There is no obligation to meet a job search or other activity testing criteria. While this support might appear generous in comparison with many of the other English-speaking countries, Australian lone mothers are nevertheless over-represented among the poor, with close to a quarter falling below the poverty line (Harding and Szukalska 2000).

Time spent caring for children

The time-use surveys show that mothers contribute disproportionately to the engaged time spent with children, although there has been some redistribution to fathers between 1974 and 1997. The time parents spend in activities with their preschool-age children has risen significantly over this time period (from 21 to 30 hours per week), but the average time a father spends in activities with preschoolers has doubled since 1974; and fathers' share of household time devoted to activities with children has risen from one-fifth to one-third (see Table 8.7).[9]

Parents and perceived time-pressure

Perceptions of time-pressure vary by household composition, and this effect is stronger for women than for men. Both women who live alone and men in

Table 8.7 Average weekly hours spent by married parents of a preschool child in activities with children as a primary activity

	1974	1987	1992	1997
Men	4.2	7.0	7.2	9.6
Women	17.1	23.6	24.3	19.6

Source: ABS 1997.

Table 8.8 Perceived time-pressure by marital status and age of youngest child

	Alone, no child	Married, no child	Married, youngest 0–4 years	Lone parent, youngest 0–4 years
Always feels rushed or pressed for time	5.1	14.6	20.2	34.4
Often feels rushed or pressed for time	26.1	32.5	41.7	25.0
Sometimes feels rushed or pressed for time	44.6	34.0	29.5	34.4
Rarely feels rushed or pressed for time	14.0	13.5	4.6	3.1
Never feels rushed or pressed for time	5.1	1.7	0.3	3.1
Not stated	5.1	3.7	3.6	0.0

Source: ABS 1998.

general, cluster around the mid-point of the scale of being rushed – they "sometimes feel rushed or pressed for time." But married women, mothers of preschool-age children, and lone parents, tend towards the extreme of "always being rushed or pressed for time," with a low proportion reporting that they "rarely" or "never" felt rushed (see Table 8.8).

Only a small proportion of men, regardless their marital and parental status, fall in the most extreme categories of perceived time-pressure, either saying they "always felt rushed or pressed for time" or at the opposite extreme, saying "never felt rushed or pressed for time". However, compared to men living alone, there is a substantial decline in the proportions of husbands and especially fathers who "rarely" feel rushed, and a corresponding increase in the number of those who say they "often" do (see Table 8.9).

Nevertheless, there can be little doubt that husbands and wives feel under greater time-pressure than single men and women, and that parents feel under greater time-pressure than couples without children. Lone mothers are the group that feels under the greatest time-pressure. This perception applies despite the fact that lone mothers spend less time in total work than mothers in couple households. Perhaps this reflects the fact that lone mothers have more constant responsibility for children and less opportunity for respite.

Table 8.9 Men's[a] perceptions of being rushed

	Alone, no child	Married, no child	Married, youngest 0–4 years
Always feels rushed or pressed for time	6.7	11.3	11.7
Often feels rushed or pressed for time	21.2	30.3	38.8
Sometimes feels rushed or pressed for time	37.8	34.0	36.3
Rarely feels rushed or pressed for time	28.0	16.2	6.3
Never feels rushed or pressed for time	3.1	2.5	2.2
Not stated	3.1	5.7	4.7

Source: ABS 1998.

Note
a Lone fathers are excluded from the analysis because estimates based on this very small sample cell size would be unreliable.

Parents and leisure-time poverty

Parents' perception of laboring under greater time-pressure is rooted in objective circumstances. Parents, especially mothers, are at the greatest risk of leisure-time poverty. Since the 1960s, the topics of poverty and deprivation have been linked. Increasingly, income poverty has been viewed as just one aspect of deprivation. Income poverty is considered damaging because exclusion from the consumption of basic goods and services is seen to limit a person's capabilities, and prevent them from fully participating in society. It follows from this social exclusion framework that people can be deprived of recreation, or leisure (Townsend 1979; Atkinson 1998; de Haan 1998).

Leisure is a peculiar thing. It is not itself a commodity, although participation in leisure activities may require the consumption of commodities. Leisure also requires time. Indeed, the very definition of leisure is based on time. In popular discourse, leisure is conceived as time at one's own disposal. The concept of leisure is usually defined by contrast with constrained activities. In labor economics, leisure is treated as the opposite of paid work. Leisure is often thought of as a residual. It is the "free" time that remains after maintaining one's body in a healthy and socially acceptable state, contracting time to the market, and meeting domestic and family responsibilities. From the standpoint of social exclusion, one can be "shut out of leisure" by lack of money or lack of time. More discussion about gender and leisure deprivation can be found in Chapter 9 in this volume by Bittman and Wajcman.

A common standard used internationally to benchmark (income) poverty is 50 percent of the median.[10] Households with incomes lower than 50 percent of the median are judged to be "poor." Applying an analogous standard (50 percent of the median leisure time) to a standard adult, we can get some idea of what social situation produces the most severe kinds of time poverty. Half-median leisure time for the whole adult population is 19 hours 15 minutes per week.

Experience with analyzing the time spent in leisure has shown that a variety of factors influence the time spent in leisure. The influence of gender on leisure time is the subject of a whole chapter (see Bittman and Wajcman, Chapter 9, this volume). Obviously, most men and women engage in more leisure pursuits on weekend days. Full-time employed adults have less time available than those in part-time employment and therefore devote less time to leisure activities. In contrast, people with a high probability of being retired (that is, aged 60 years or more) spent much more of the day in leisure pastimes, than those of a younger age. However, even at younger ages, the older an individual the higher the time allocated to leisure. Household or family circumstances also determine the time spent in leisure activities. The presence, age, and employment status of a spouse might all be expected to impact on time spent in leisure activities. Finally, labor economists expect that as the economic resources available to households rise, time to enjoy leisure will be preferred to extra income generated by devoting this time to market work. The net effect of each of these characteristics on time men and women spend in leisure has been modeled using Ordinary Least Squares multiple regression (see Tables 8A.1 and 8A.2 in Appendix). The predictions derived from this model can be used to examine how characteristics, or combinations of characteristics, affect the likely time spent in leisure. Table 8.10 expresses the predicted leisure time of people in these categories relative to the half-median standard and shows how far above or below the leisure-time poverty line they fall.

The major causes of leisure-time poverty are being female, having family responsibilities and longer hours of work. Those most at risk of leisure-time poverty, therefore, are those who have combinations of disadvantageous characteristics.

Mothers of very young children who are employed full-time are most at risk. This risk is greatest when they have a partner who also works full-time. Indeed, the mothers in couples where both adults work full-time suffer from the most severe leisure-time poverty as long as their children are aged younger than 15 years, although this becomes less so as the child matures.

The empirical findings suggest three options that might relieve this situation, especially since even high amounts of nonparental care do not completely substitute for mother's time spent relating to their child (see Bittman *et al.*, Chapter 7, this volume). The first – part-time work – is the one commonly chosen by Australian women and, according to Wolcott and Glezer (1995), is the most frequently preferred. Reducing weekly hours of paid work raises all women above the leisure-time poverty line, except for women with a youngest child below the age of 2 and a partner in full-time work. However, this option is not without associated risks, especially in the event of divorce, as studies have demonstrated how severely withdrawals from paid employment reduce women's lifetime earnings and increase their economic vulnerability (Gray and Chapman 2001).

The second option is to encourage fathers to take greater responsibility. Table 8.10 illustrates a case where the mother continues to be employed full-time while her partner is not in the labor force, the woman escapes. According to the

Table 8.10 Parents and time poverty

Parent	Woman 35 years in couple			Sole adult		Man 40 years in couple
Work status	Full-time	Full-time	Part-time	Full-time	Part-time	Full-time
Work status of partner	Full-time	Not in labor force	Full-time	—	—	Full-time
	Leisure hours per week, relative to half-median leisure time					
Youngest child <2 yrs	-6.88	0.06	-0.36	-1.20	5.33	1.88
Youngest child <5 yrs	-4.24	2.70	2.28	1.45	7.97	2.17
Youngest child <9 yrs	-2.74	4.20	3.78	2.94	9.47	4.36
Youngest child <15 yrs	-1.17	5.77	5.35	4.52	11.04	3.96
No children	4.38	4.38	10.90	10.07	16.59	8.94

predictions of the regression model developed in this chapter, the presence of stay-at-home fathers would raise the leisure time of their full-time working partners above the leisure-time poverty line. Research on marital bargaining over housework, however, shows that unconventional wife-as-predominant earner arrangements seem likely to invoke significant hyper-feminine displays aimed at neutralizing gender role deviance (Bittman *et al.* 2003).

A third option is divorce. Compared with their partnered counterparts in similar employment situations, lone mothers have significantly more leisure time. Lone mothers are less likely to be exposed to leisure-time poverty. However, in addition to having to cope with lower equivalent household incomes, they may experience more constrained leisure (see Bittman and Wajcman, Chapter 9, this volume), and therefore higher levels of perceived time-pressure.

Although all fathers are relatively deprived of leisure in comparison with men without children, they do not fall below the leisure-time poverty line, even when their children are very young. Wives' dissatisfaction with the fact that they are exposed to leisure-time poverty while their husbands are not may even become a motive for divorce, especially in situations where wives are unable to bargain for a redistribution of family responsibilities.

Conclusion

Having examined the evidence accumulated by this source of time-diary research spanning a quarter of a century, we can go some way towards resolving the paradox of how growth in available time for leisure could be combined with widespread perception of increased time-pressure. The hours available for leisure per capita have, indeed, increased slightly over the last twenty-three years. However, the roots of the perception of increased time-pressure over these decades lie in the unequal distribution of market and nonmarket work. The distribution of workloads between households and between the genders has become increasingly unequal. These feelings of increased time-pressure have an objective foundation for an increasing proportion of the population. The perception of being time-pressured is grounded in the actual demographic and social changes over these decades – more training and "early retirement" have resulted in a reduction in the span of working life, dual-career families have displaced male breadwinner families as the norm, the number of sole parents is rising steadily, and all parents are devoting more time to activities with their children than ever before.

By the end of the twentieth century, prime-working-age couple households were supplying more hours to the labor market than in the decade before, while those aged 55 years or more are increasingly spending less time in market work. The weekly hours dual-career families devote to market and nonmarket work are significantly higher than in any other kind of couple household. Even though dual-career couples appear to find ways to squeeze their weekly hours of nonmarket work, their combined market and nonmarket workloads exceeds that of other couples. Having this data on hours of nonmarket work allow us to see this plainly for the first time.

Needless to say, the transition from male breadwinner couple to dual-earner couple is the result of wives' increasing their hours of market work. Married people report more time-pressure than single people, and parents report more time pressure than childless people. Given the inequitable division of domestic labor by gender, it does not come as a surprise that women, especially mothers' report much higher levels of time-pressure than men. What, for more than a decade, has been taken to be a controversy about overwork (i.e. trends in individual hours), Jacobs and Gerson (2001) have correctly noted, is actually a manifestation of the difficulties of reconciling (paid) work and family responsibilities following the historical demise of the male breadwinner model.

Ignoring for the moment time devoted to childcare as a "secondary" activity or time spent as the parent "on call," Australian lone mothers spend more time in market and nonmarket work than comparable single women but less time than comparable mothers who live with the child's father. With their economic security underpinned by modest income transfers paid by the federal government, Australian lone mothers manage their total workload by switching their labor from market work to nonmarket work. However, being the only parent "on call" cannot, realistically, be ignored and the true constraints imposed by their family responsibilities surface in the more frequent than expected reports of extreme time-pressure.

All this means that explaining the paradox of increasing average per capita leisure combined with increased perception of time poverty does not require any presumption that respondents are in some way mistaken or deluded. While Linder's (1970) and Robinson and Godbey's (1997) speculations about how increased choice could lead to a perception of greater time-pressure are very interesting, the resolution of this paradox does not require this presumption. It is possible to devise objective measures of leisure-time poverty and to describe its distribution. Analysis as to which categories of people are most at risk of leisure-time poverty confirms the explanation developed so far. Those most vulnerable to leisure-time poverty have combinations of disadvantageous characteristics – they have full-time hours of market work, they have family responsibilities and they are women.

All this points to difficulties facing contemporary women as they seek to balance market work and family. The options currently available to women are either unattractive to women or have unpalatable consequences for all of us. Women could achieve a better balance if they reduced their market work but this seems, historically, to have been rejected by women themselves, perhaps because lack of an independent income is a vulnerable condition in an era of high divorce rates. Alternatively, women could further control their fertility, with more one-child families and higher proportion of women remaining childless. However, there is already something of a "moral panic" about fertility, which has already declined well below replacement rates in most of the countries of the West. A better balance could be achieved if *both* parents shared family responsibility. Although recently men have shown a willingness to spend more time with their children (and when their children are at a younger age), change has been very slow and the proportion of men assuming equal responsibility is currently very small. Such a gender distribution would still not eliminate the difference in combined market and nonmarket workloads between childless couples and couples with children. New solutions to this dilemma are urgently required, either by ensuring income security without long hours of market work for parents or ensuring population replacement through immigration.

Appendix

The regression model, applied separately to both employed men's and employed women's weekly hours of leisure, uses the following independent variables as proxies to capture the net effect of known influences on leisure.

Concept	Proxy
Effect of weekend	Saturday (Yes = 1)
	Sunday (Yes = 1)
Part-time employment	Part-time employment (Yes = 1)
Retired	Aged 60 years or more (Yes = 1)
Age	Age in years
Spouse's age	Spouse (Yes = 1) × age in years
Spouse's employment	Spouse employed f/t (1 = yes)
	Spouse employed p/t (1 = yes)
	Spouse unemployed (1 = yes)
	Spouse NILF
Age of youngest child	Youngest child 10–14 years (1 = yes)
	Youngest child less than 2 years (1 = yes)
	Youngest child 2–4 years (1 = yes)
	Youngest child 5–9 years (1 = yes)
Household resources	Equivalent disposable income($)

Table 8A.1 Multiple regression of male weekly hours of leisure time by life course, employment and income

Variable	B	SE B	Beta	T	Sig T
Age	0.0512	0.0243	0.0342	2.1030	0.0355
Spouse × spouse's age	−0.0421	0.0408	−0.0384	−1.0300	0.3030
Employed p/t	8.3257	1.0386	0.0877	8.0160	0.0000
Sole parent (1 = yes)	17.2221	1.0264	0.1912	16.7800	0.0000
Reference person aged 60 years or more (1 = yes)	19.0881	0.8537	0.3078	22.3580	0.0000
Spouse employed f/t (1 = yes)	−1.7241	1.8558	−0.0243	−0.9290	0.3529
Spouse employed p/t (1 = yes)	0.8160	2.0461	0.0117	0.3990	0.6901
Spouse unemployed (1 = yes)	2.4222	2.3834	0.0156	1.0160	0.3095

(*Table 8A.1 continued*)

Table 8A.1 Continued

Variable	B	SE B	Beta	T	Sig T
Spouse NILF	4.3167	2.1059	0.0739	2.0500	0.0404
Saturday	20.3509	0.7855	0.2729	25.9080	0.0000
Sunday	24.3030	0.8163	0.3139	29.7710	0.0000
Youngest child 10–14 years (1 = yes)	−4.9767	1.1107	−0.0511	−4.4810	0.0000
Youngest child less than 2 years (1 = yes)	−7.0562	1.2886	−0.0711	−5.4760	0.0000
Youngest child 2–4 years (1 = yes)	−6.7664	1.3421	−0.0623	−5.0420	0.0000
Youngest child 5–9 years (1 = yes)	−4.5771	1.1741	−0.0462	−3.8990	0.0001
Equivalent disposable income ($)	−0.0006	0.0006	−0.0131	−1.0870	0.2769
(Constant)	30.1194	1.0397		28.9690	0.0000
Adjusted R-squared	0.3103				

Source: ABS Time Use Survey 1992.

Table 8A.2 Multiple regression of female weekly hours of leisure time by life course, employment and income

Variable	B	SE B	Beta	T	Sig T
Age	0.1519	0.0191	0.1122	7.9670	0.0000
Spouse × spouse's age	−0.1422	0.0364	−0.1555	−3.9090	0.0001
Employed p/t	6.5235	0.7192	0.1189	9.0700	0.0000
Sole parent (1 = yes)	14.7163	1.1061	0.1567	13.3050	0.0000
Reference person aged 60 years or more (1 = yes)	12.7950	0.7168	0.2703	17.8500	0.0000
Spouse employed f/t (1 = yes)	2.2082	1.6956	0.0459	1.3020	0.1929
Spouse employed p/t (1 = yes)	3.2650	2.2826	0.0242	1.4300	0.1526
Spouse unemployed (1 = yes)	2.9133	2.0735	0.0232	1.4050	0.1601
Spouse NILF	6.9422	2.3621	0.0975	2.9390	0.0033
Saturday	15.7577	0.6984	0.2382	22.5620	0.0000
Sunday	18.0059	0.7176	0.2652	25.0910	0.0000
Youngest child 10–14 years (1 = yes)	−5.5461	0.9261	−0.0665	−5.9890	0.0000
Youngest child less than 2 years (1 = yes)	−11.2610	1.0474	−0.1307	−10.7510	0.0000
Youngest child 2–4 years (1 = yes)	−8.6179	1.0613	−0.0946	−8.1200	0.0000
Youngest child 5–9 years (1 = yes)	−7.1205	0.9459	−0.0851	−7.5270	0.0000
Equivalent disposable income ($)	0.0000	0.0006	0.0000	0.0040	0.9969
(Constant)	26.8442	0.9647		27.8260	0.9969
Adjusted R-squared	0.2308				

Source: ABS Time Use Survey 1992.

Notes

1 In 1974 respondents were asked "In general how do you feel about your time? Would you say you – Always feel rushed even to do the things you have to do? or Only sometimes feel rushed? or Almost never feel rushed?" In 1997 respondents asked "How often do you feel rushed or pressed for time?" were requested to choose among the following response categories " always", "often", "sometimes", "rarely", "never."
2 Lois Bryson, of the Women's Health Australia Project at the University of Newcastle, kindly made these preliminary findings available.
3 To produce the claim that Americans are working longer hours, both Schor (1991) and Mishel *et al.* (1999) concentrate on annual hours worked, relying more on increases in the number of workweeks in the year than on any sizeable increase in the average workweek.
4 The ABS 1987 Pilot Survey of Time Use was conducted exclusively in the Sydney Statistical Division, but subsequent analysis of the two national surveys shows that while time-use (not perceived time-pressure) is different in rural and urban areas, differences between metropolitan centers are negligible. In many instances, the analysis is limited to those of prime-working-age (25–54 years) to avoid the confounding effects of longer education and earlier retirement from the analysis.
5 In all jobs. It includes breaks and travel to and from work. This definition is broader than that used in the CPS and would be expected to produce higher estimated hours.
6 In both Australia and the United States, full-time is defined as 35 or more hours per week.
7 Ignoring the unpaid work that accompanies another activity which the respondent characterizes as their main activity. Time spent in these secondary unpaid work activities is often very substantial and is unevenly distributed by sex (see Bittman and Wajcman, Chapter 9, this volume).
8 The small proportion of lone fathers in the sample precludes any meaningful statistical analysis, so this section concentrates on the time-use of lone mothers.
9 Sole parents have been excluded from this analysis because of the small number in the metropolitan sample 1974 time-use survey.
10 The half-median standard of poverty is used widely by specialists analyzing data in the Luxembourg Income Study and by NATSEM in Australia (Saunders 1994: 116, 140). The idea of treating time-poverty on analogy to income poverty was first suggested to me by Robert E. Goodin (Bittman and Goodin 1998).

References

Atkinson, A. B. (1998) "Social Exclusion, Poverty and Unemployment," in A. B. Atkinson and J. Hills (eds), *Exclusion, Employment and Opportunity*, CASE/4, Centre for the Analysis of Social Exclusion, London School of Economics, London.
Australian Bureau of Statistics (1999) *Australian Social Trends*, Catalogue No. 4102.0, Canberra: ABS.
Bittman, M. (1998) "Land of the Lost Long Weekend – Trends in Free Time Among Working Age Australians 1974–1992," *Loisir et Société/Society and Leisure*, 21: 353–78.
—— and Goodin, R. E. (1998) *An Equivalence Scale for Time*, Discussion Paper No. 85, Sydney: Social Policy Research Centre, University of New South Wales.
—— and Rice, J. M. (2002) "The Spectre of Overwork: An Analysis of Trends between 1974 and 1997 Using Australian Time-Use Diaries," *Labour and Industry*, 12: 5–25.
——, England, P., Sayer, L., Folbre, N., and Matheson, G. (2003) "When Does Gender Trump Money? Bargaining and Time in Household Work," *American Journal of Sociology*, 109: 186–214.

Bluestone, B. and Rose, S. (1997) "Overwork and Underemployed: Unravelling an Economic Enigma," *The American Prospect*, 31: 58–69.

—— and —— (2000) "The Enigma of Working Time Trends," in L. Golden and D. M. Figart (eds), *Working Time: International Trends, Theory and Policy Perspectives*, London: Routledge.

de Haan, A. (1998) *"Social Exclusion": An Alternative Concept for the Study of Deprivation?*, Institute for Development Studies Bulletin, 29, 10–49.

Gershuny, J. I. (1992) "Are We Running Out of Time?," *Futures*, 24(1): 3–22.

—— (2000) *Changing Times: Work and Leisure in Postindustrial Society*, Oxford: Oxford University Press.

Gray, M. and Chapman, B. (2001) "Foregone Earnings from Child Rearing: Changes Between 1986 and 1997," *Family Matters*, 58: 4–9.

Harding, A. and Szukalska, A. (2000) "Making a Difference: The Impact of Government Policy on Child Poverty in Australia, 1982 to 1997–98," NATSEM, Canberra.

Jacobs, J. A. and Gerson, K. (1998) "Who are the Overworked Americans?," *Review of Social Economy*, 56: 442–59.

—— and ——(2001) "Overworked Individuals or Overworked Families? Explaining Trends in Work, Leisure and Family Time," *Work and Occupations*, 28: 40–63.

Linder, S. (1970) *The Harried Leisure Class*, New York: Columbia University Press.

Mishel, L., Bernstein, J., and Schmitt, J. (1999) *The State of Working America 1998–1999*, Washington, DC: Economic Policy Institute.

Robinson, J. P. and Godbey, G. (1997) *Time for Life: The Surprising Ways Americans Use Their Time*, University Park: Pennsylvania State University Press.

Saunder, P. (1994) *Welfare & Inequality: National & International Perspectives on the Australian Welfare State*, Melbourne: Cambridge University Press.

Schor, J. (1991) *The Overworked American: The Unexpected Decline of Leisure*, New York: Basic Books.

Townsend, P. (1979) *Poverty in the United Kingdom. A Study of Household Resources and Living Standards*, Harmondsworth: Penguin.

Wolcott, I. and Glezer, H. (1995) *Work and Family Life: Achieving Integration*, Melbourne: Australian Institute of Family Studies and the Commonwealth Government.

Zuzanek, J. (2000) "Time Pressure, Stress, and Health: Some New Evidence," Centre for Applied Health Research News, Online. Available at www.ahs.uwaterloo.ca/~cahr/news/vol20/time.html

9 The rush hour

The quality of leisure time and gender equity

Michael Bittman and Judy Wajcman

Time scarcity and the paucity of leisure time are at the center of discussions about the quality of contemporary life (Schor 1991; Nowotny 1994; Adam 1995; Hochschild 1997; Robinson and Godbey 1997). A number of recent developments contribute to this concern. Standard working hours, which assumed a forty-hour week over five working days, are no longer the norm. The increasing incidence of dual-earner families has spawned a vast literature on the "dual burden" or the "second shift." Working patterns are increasingly dominated by a drive for "flexibility" that can create severe difficulties for those seeking to combine work and family life.

All these developments appear to be placing increased pressure on leisure time. According to most evidence, people feel leisure time has become scarcer and more harried (Linder 1970; Frederick 1995; Robinson and Godbey 1997). This is especially the case for women, who juggle work, family, and leisure (Bryant and Zick 1996). Indeed, it has been suggested that women are suffering from time poverty (Vickery 1977; Hochschild and Machung 1989; Schor 1991; Hochschild 1997). The fear has been that, following the emergence of the dual-earner family as the norm, women will simply add a shift of paid employment to their existing responsibilities for housework and childcare. This problem has come to be known by various names – the "dual burden," the "double burden," the "double day," and the "second shift." There is now talk of a gender gap in leisure.

The emergence of the dual-earner family and the potential problem of the double burden are in tension with contemporary expectations governing the modern intimate relationship. A standard assumption of current sociology is that modern Western personal relationships are based on the central value of egalitarianism (Cheal 1991; Giddens 1992; Beck and Beck-Gernsheim 1995). However, the uneven distribution of unpaid work (housework, childcare, and shopping) allocated according to gender creates theoretical difficulties for this claim (Lopata 1971; Oakley 1974; Coverman and Sheley 1986). A way of recovering the claim about equality is through an emphasis on the idea of partnership and a concentration on the quantities of "total work" – that is, the combination of paid and unpaid working time (Becker 1985; Berk 1985). In order for the thesis about the dominance of the modern egalitarian family to be credible, an important corollary of the argument for gender equity in total work time would be gender equity in free time.

Indeed, in a recent article, Nancy Fraser (1997: 26) has argued that gender equity needs to be reconceptualized as a "complex notion comprising a plurality of distinct normative principles." One of the seven key principles that she proposes as crucial to gender equity concerns the distribution of leisure time. We agree that this is an important dimension of equality and consider that an empirical investigation of the issue is overdue.

This chapter presents evidence for the existence of a gender gap in free time. We do this by drawing on data from time-use surveys worldwide. First, we assess gender equity in relation to total work time and, second, we explore gender equity in "primary" free time. We then go on to present innovative measures of the quality of leisure. This will enable us to re-evaluate the issue of gender equity in leisure. In doing this, we hope to add a new dimension to the appraisal of progress towards equality between the sexes in contemporary society.

Mixed blessings: pure and constrained leisure

The time-use literature distinguishes between various classes of time-use, which are believed to be fundamentally different in character. Typically, it is argued that time must be allocated between four categories: paid work, unpaid work, self-care, and free time (Åas 1982; Robinson and Godbey 1997: 11–16).

Paid work-time is time committed to income producing activities in the market place, such as working for a wage or the time spent by self-employed persons in their business activities. In its broadest sense, it also includes the time spent commuting to work, breaks at work and, more controversially, voluntary work such as time spent in formal study. The label "unpaid work time" reflects the obligatory character of unpaid work. It includes childcare, food preparation, house cleaning, laundry, household management, gardening, house maintenance and repairs, car care, and shopping. Self-care or "personal" time is associated with the maintenance of bodily functions – sleeping, eating, washing, grooming, dressing, and medical treatment. Free time is a residual category. It is the time that remains after maintaining one's body in a healthy and socially acceptable state, contracting time to the market, and meeting domestic and family responsibilities. Free time encompasses both time devoted to activities undertaken explicitly for leisure, and discretionary uses of available time such as religious and civic activities. The emerging standard is to assign traveling time to its associated purpose.

In practice, most sociological interest has focused on the distribution of paid work, unpaid work, and leisure time. The concept of total work time combines the time spent in paid and unpaid work. It has been well established that there is a sexual division of labor in relation to these two types of work. There are competing interpretations of this sexual division of labor; one interpretation is that the sexes complement each other and another interpretation argues for noncomplementarity. Becker (1985) has proposed a theory of comparative advantage to explain why men "specialize" in paid work and women in unpaid work. Feminists have contested this interpretation, asserting that the sexual division of labor is rooted in a system of unequal power between men and women (England 1982; Berk 1985; Connell 1987; Pateman 1988; Oppenheimer 1997). According to feminists, unpaid work is assigned according to gender and not by the operation of some rational allocation of resources.

The rise of the dual-earner family has disturbed the traditional pattern of specialization (Oppenheimer 1994). Women are increasingly assuming what has hitherto been regarded as the male role, that of provider. Given the assignment of family responsibilities by gender, this raises the specter of a dual burden, or "second shift" for women, especially mothers, as men are not assuming a corresponding increase in domestic labor (Hartmann 1981; Hochschild and Machung 1989).

The difficulty with the concept of the "second shift," despite the large literature on the subject, is that it has been used ambiguously. Many authors have treated this concept in a very literal manner, assuming that women's increased hours of paid employment would simply be added to an undiminished quantity of time spent in unpaid work – practically a quantitative doubling (Meissner *et al.* 1975). Others argue that the typical decrease in average time spent in unpaid work is not sufficient to compensate women for the increased hours of paid work. The result is an unfair excess burden on women compared to men.[1] A strong test of these two hypotheses about the dual burden is to use "total work" time as an indicator of equity. If the first hypothesis is correct, there should be a large difference between the average total work time of men and women. If the second hypothesis is correct, there should still be a significant difference between the average total work time of men and women, although one would expect the difference to be relatively small. Surprisingly, little research has been published on the quantity of "total work" time undertaken by men and women. We will present a systematic analysis of total work time drawing on time-use data from advanced societies around the world.

It is often assumed that the obverse of total work time is leisure time. Focusing on the idea of leisure illuminates from a different angle the issue of time equity between the sexes. Since sleeping, eating, and grooming – the activities categorized under self-care – are practically constant, it makes sense to talk about a choice between work (both paid and unpaid) and leisure.

There is mounting evidence that an increasing proportion of Americans perceive their lives as "rushed" and feel that they do not have enough time to fit everything in. A related finding is that Americans report feeling subject to more "stress" from time constraints. To complete the picture of increasing time poverty, people agree with the proposition that they have "less free time than in the past" (Robinson and Godbey 1997: 230).

Women's specialized responsibility for childcare suggests that women have a distinctive experience of time, one that is fundamentally different from men's. Historians have drawn our attention to the link between the development of clock time and the industrial organization of labor (Thompson 1967; Landes

1983). Since men "specialize" in paid employment, it has been argued that their subjective lives are ruled by linear clock time. Feminist social scientists have conceptualized women's time as predominantly cyclical or task oriented (Kristeva 1981; Forman and Sowton 1989; Nowotny 1994; Adam 1995; Glucksmann 1998). The working times of women as wives and mothers, it is argued, cannot be captured by perspectives that "separate work from leisure, public from private time, subjective from objective time, and task from clock time" (Davies 1990). Research on women's caring and emotional work in particular has shown the limits of a linear conception of time (Gilligan 1982; Hochschild 1983; Larson and Richards 1994). Women's work typically involves coordinating multiple activities, "sequencing and prioritizing of certain times" (Adam 1995: 95). The implication of this perspective is, therefore, that women's experience of leisure is also distinctive and is difficult to disentangle from multiple and overlapping activities. Emphasizing the quality of women's leisure time, then, suggests a reformulation of the concept of a gender gap in leisure. The crucial issue is not just that women may have less primary leisure time, but that women's leisure time may be qualitatively "less leisurely" than men's (Deem 1988).

Much of the writing about women's experience of time has been philosophical in orientation and, in so far as it has drawn on empirical research, this has been of a qualitative nature. Evidence typically comes from small-scale studies, research designs that emphasize depth and are not intended to be statistically representative (Wimbush and Talbot 1988; Morris 1990; Rubin 1995; Glucksman 1998). Indeed, it is often claimed that it is impossible to capture the specificity of women's relationship to time using mass survey techniques. This article examines these propositions about women's distinctive experience of time. Its original contribution lies in demonstrating how quantitative information, gathered by mass survey techniques, can be used to investigate the lived experience of free time.

Data

The data for the analysis in this chapter comes from two sources – the Multinational Time Budget Data Archive and the Australian Bureau of Statistics 1992 Time Use Survey (Australian Bureau of Statistics 1993). All the data analyzed here are collected by the time-diary method. Thirty years of research has shown that the highest validity and reliability in the measurement of time spent in all activities is achieved by using time-diaries, which are now used around the world (Hill and Stafford 1985; Niemi 1993; Pallié 1993; Robinson and Gershuny 1994; Baxter and Bittman 1995; Goldschmidt-Clermont and Pagnossin-Aligisakis 1995; Robinson and Godbey 1997).

The evaluation of hypotheses about gender equity in total work and free time rests on an analysis of the Multinational Time Budget Data Archive (Gershuny 1990), with later Australian surveys added in a comparable form.[2] The entire Multinational Archive produces a pooled data set containing 128,931 cases drawn from thirty-six surveys conducted in nineteen countries and covering the period

Table 9.1 Component surveys of the modern Western subset Multinational Time Budget Archive

Survey	N	
	All men and women	Married and employed full-time
Australia 1992	9,602	3,801
Canada 1992	6,347	2,560
Denmark 1987	2,389	1,079
Finland 1987	10,276	6,001
Italy 1980	2,118	—
Netherlands 1985	2,348	769
Norway 1981	3,410	1,483
Sweden 1991	6,178	3,601
United Kingdom 1985	1,996	770
United States 1985	2,270	931
Total	46,933	20,995

from 1961 to 1992. In this chapter, we use a subset of this archive, restricted to the most recent surveys conducted in ten OECD countries, yielding a pooled database of 46,933 respondents, 20,995 of whom are married and employed full-time. Table 9.1 sets out the information about nation, date, and sample size for each component survey of Multinational Time Budget Data Archive.

The multinational archive is restricted to the age range 20–59 years and contains information about twenty categories of primary activities (Gershuny 1990), which are derived from the Szalai standardized activity classification. This standardized activity classification, originally developed for the comparative study of time-use in thirteen nations and conducted under the directorship of the Hungarian statistician Alexander Szalai, has become the basis of all contemporary activity classifications (Szalai *et al.* 1972).

A test of the claims made about women's distinctive experience of leisure time requires a data set which contains high quality information about simultaneous activities, the number of activity episodes, and the existence of background family care responsibilities. This information is not available in the pooled Multinational data set.[3] Only some surveys collect information about simultaneous activities and fewer still make any claims for the reliability of this information. The exception is the 1992 Australian Time Use Survey.

Details of methods used in the first full-scale Australian national time-use survey are given in the Note at the end of this volume. Experience has shown that the average of the number of episodes is a good indicator of the quality of diary data (Juster 1985; Robinson 1985). The mean number of episodes per day is 31.8 on Day One and 30.2 on Day Two. The high average number of episodes per day (over 30) indicates higher than usual data quality (Australian Bureau of Statistics 1993).

Measures

To test the competing propositions about women's dual burden and its detrimental effects on the available quantity of free time, we draw on diary information about the respondent's main, so-called primary, activity in ten OECD countries. The measures used cover average weekly hours spent by men and women in both paid and unpaid work activities (i.e. total work hours); the average share of unpaid work hours undertaken by women; and average amount of free time available to both men and women. These averages are calculated for the whole sample population and for a subsample of married men and women in full-time employment.

Characteristics of leisure

The concept of leisure is usually defined by contrast with constrained activities. In labor economics leisure is treated as the opposite of paid work. In popular discourse, leisure is conceived of as free time, time at one's own disposal, or "pure leisure." The difficulty with relying on *quantitative* measures of primary leisure is that it presumes all leisure is homogeneous, that is, *pure leisure*. All the measures presented so far rely on this basic assumption. Therefore, the findings we present about gender equity in primary total work time and in primary leisure time are subject to this qualification. We have been provoked into considering alternative, more sophisticated measures of time spent in leisure.

Combined activities

As we noted before, people frequently engage in more than a single activity at the same time – that is, there are simultaneous activities. The point here is that a leisure activity, with no distracting accompanying activities to constrain it, is different from a leisure activity that is accompanied by a constraining activity. Constraining activities do violence to the very concept of leisure (Henderson 1991).

Pure leisure can be differentiated from varying degrees of constrained or contaminated leisure. What we are attempting to do by distinguishing degrees of leisure is to capture variations in how leisure is experienced. It is precisely these aspects of the leisure experience that lie at the heart of feminist commentary on the gendered nature of leisure. Women's distinctive experience of leisure is said to result from an unequal responsibility for the care of others, including socio-emotional work. These responsibilities involve coordinating multiple and overlapping activities that contaminate pure leisure. To date, such discussion has run ahead of the facts. Our contribution to this debate is to show the way that large survey data can be employed to capture these qualitative dimensions of leisure.

Time-use surveys typically collect information about a primary activity (which the respondent describes as their "main" activity) and a secondary activity (that is, a simultaneous activity accompanying the primary activity). This provides the

Table 9.2 Possible combinations of leisure activities and other major activity groups

Primary activity	Secondary activity
Leisure	No activity
Leisure	Leisure
Leisure	Paid work
Leisure	Unpaid work
Leisure	With self-care

opportunity to consider activity combinations. For the purpose of this analysis, we have grouped all activities into four broad classes – paid work, unpaid work, self-care, and leisure. Each primary activity, therefore, can be of four kinds. Sometimes there is no secondary activity. Otherwise, each kind of primary activity can be combined with a secondary activity drawn from one of these four major groups (see Table 9.2).

Interrupted leisure

The experience of leisure changes substantially according to its fragmentation. The often reported finding that people feel their leisure time is not only scarce but more harried implies leisure has become more fragmented. Two people can experience the same aggregate of leisure time but those with more fragmented leisure, consisting of a greater number of leisure episodes of shorter duration, may justifiably feel more rushed.

In this study, we use duration of the longest leisure episode as one indicator of fragmentation. Highly fragmented leisure is indicated by short duration for the longest episode while, conversely, unbroken periods of leisure indicate a higher quality of leisure. Another indicator of the fragmentation of leisure time, aside from the *length* of the longest episode of leisure activity, is the sheer *number* of leisure activity episodes. Once again, concentrating on similar total leisure times may divert attention from significant differences in the nature of leisure. Leisure time, which is unceasingly disrupted by the intercession of a great number of externally generated nonleisure activities beyond the control of the actor is of lower quality than uninterrupted leisure (Smith 1979). A higher number of leisure episodes to achieve a comparable total of leisure indicates leisure of a lower quality. Once again, an increase in the number of separate leisure episodes may provide an explanation for the high proportion of the population reporting feelings of being "rushed."

Adult leisure

The proportion of adult leisure time devoted to adult leisure activities is another key indicator of the quality of leisure.[4] This measure is related to our measure of pure leisure – that is, leisure, properly understood, is activity free of constraints. In our second measure, we were concerned with how pure leisure could be contaminated by combination with simultaneous activities involving constraint. Here, we are concentrating on a different aspect of the leisure activity situation – that is, the presence or absence of children for whom one is responsible. For the purpose of this study, background responsibilities have major significance for our conceptualization of the quality of leisure.

Responsibility for the welfare of children involves an obligation to respond to their physical needs and demands. There is also increasing emphasis in Western culture on spending "quality time" with children, that is, devoting undivided attention to their activities. This means that parents are under a more or less permanent injunction to modify their own leisure preferences in order to focus on activities that are desirable for children. On this basis, a measure of the amount of leisure time spent with children present in the background indicates an important aspect of the adult quality of leisure experienced by women and men who are parents.

One could argue that leisure activity without children in the background indicates a purer quality of adult leisure. This is the most contentious of our three measures of the quality of leisure as, from another point of view, it might be argued that the best leisure is achieved when playing with one's own children. However, the fact that parents derive considerable pleasure from attending to their children's needs does not detract from the argument that they may, at the same time, be experiencing an adult leisure deficit.

Results

Total work hours

Two sets of findings are discussed in this section – those for all women and all men in the selected countries and those for married, full-time employed men and women in these same countries. The latter category approximates, as closely as this data set allows, the situation of men and women in dual-earner couples.

Considering the results for all men and all women, women continue to be responsible for the majority of hours devoted to unpaid work (see Table 9.3). Their share of unpaid work hours ranges from 70 percent in gender equity conscious Sweden to 88 percent in "familistically" oriented Italy (Esping-Anderson 1990; Sainsbury 1996). Women's mean share of unpaid work hours across the pooled sample drawn from surveys in ten different nations is 76 percent. Despite the highly gender-specialized nature of unpaid work, the difference in men's and women's primary total work hours is surprisingly small. Given the large sample size, these small differences are statistically significant but not substantially divergent.

Across the pooled data set the mean hours of work, both paid and unpaid, fall marginally above or below 50 hours per week, for all women and all men, respectively. The fifth column in Table 9.3 shows the difference between women's and

Table 9.3 Comparison of men's and women's mean total paid and unpaid work burden (based on primary activity only)

Survey	All men and all women				Married Employed full-time			
	Female share of unpaid work time (%)	Total paid and unpaid work (hours:minutes per week)		Unmatched dual burden (hours:minutes per week)	Female share of unpaid work time (%)	Total paid and unpaid work (hours:minutes per week)		Unmatched dual burden (hours: minutes per week)
		Female	Male			Female	Male	
Australia 1992	77	49:38	50:03	–0:25	73	59:50	57:32	2:18*
Canada 1992	75	52:25	50:15	2:09*	70	63:08	56:34	6:34*
Denmark 1987	72	50:20	52:24	–2:03	74	56:45	56:56	–0:11
Finland 1987	74	50:48	46:22	4:26*	74	56:52	51:41	5:11*
Italy 1980	88	56:13	51:22	4:51*	—	—	—	—
Netherlands 1985	77	42:04	44:52	–2:47*	77	49:19	49:40	–0:22
Norway 1981	77	50:12	49:01	1:10	74	59:22	51:26	7:57*
UK 1985	76	47:19	46:17	1:02	71	58:17	51:20	6:58*
United States 1985	74	52:34	54:48	–2:14	72	61:32	60:47	0:44
Sweden 1991	70	56:20	55:10	1:09	67	58:42	58:18	0:24
For pooled database	76	51:12	49:50	1:21*	72	58:37	55:00	3:37*

Note
* Difference between the men's and women's hours significant at the 0.05 level.

men's mean hours of total work, indicating the extent to which women's hours of total work are in excess of men's. In six countries, women's mean hours of total work are greater than those of men. The gender difference in total work hours ranges from a maximum of less than 5 hours in Italy to 1 hour 2 minutes in the United Kingdom. In Australia, Denmark, the Netherlands, and the United States, women's mean primary weekly hours of total work are actually less than those of men. Australia represents the point of near parity between the total work hours of the sexes, with a male excess of 25 minutes per week, while in the Netherlands men work an extra 2 hour 48 minutes per week. Across all the data in the pooled sample women spend on average 1 hour 22 minutes longer in a combination of paid and unpaid work than men. This difference is smaller than might have been predicted (Figure 9.1).

Consistent with the prediction of an emerging "dual burden" for employed women, when only married men and women who are employed full-time (more than 30 hours per week) are considered, the gender difference in hours of total work is larger. The results for Italy cannot be calculated owing to the lack of comparable information about marital and employment status. However, in the remaining nine countries, women in this situation are still responsible for the greater part of unpaid work. Indeed their share (72 percent) is only slightly lower than that for all women (76 percent). Restricting the analysis to this group increases the mean difference in total paid and unpaid work hours by an increment of 2 hours 16 minutes. This restriction also increases the number of countries in which there is a statistically significant gender difference in average hours of total work from 3 to 5. With the exception of the Netherlands, gender inequity is perceptibly exacerbated in those countries where significant differences are found in the whole population, namely, Canada, Finland, and the United Kingdom. In Norway and Australia, gender inequity emerges as a phenomenon specific to cohabitating and being full-time employed, rather than for the whole population. On the other hand, in nearly half the countries represented in the database, there are no significant gender differences in total work hours, even among those full-time employees with a spouse.

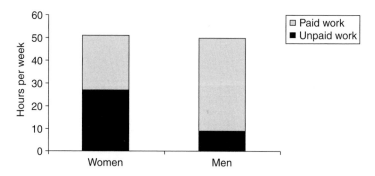

Figure 9.1 Mean hours of paid and unpaid work by gender.

Weekly hours of primary free time

Since the empirical referent for the competing propositions of gender specializa-tion and the dual-burden thesis are different, once again findings for all women and all men and for a restricted subsample of married, full-time employed men and women are presented separately.

Free time is in many ways the mirror image of total work time. As might be expected from the finding of a very narrow sex difference in primary total work time, a similar pattern is found in the distribution of free time.

Across all countries, the average weekly hours of free time are roughly equiv-alent to the standard full-time weekly hours of (paid) work. Table 9.4 shows that Denmark and the Netherlands are the only countries where the mean weekly quantity of primary free time for all men and women exceeds 40 hours per week. At the other end of the scale, the average free time for Italian women, Swedish women, and men from the United States is closer to 30 hours per week. For the remainder, the mean weekly primary free time falls in the range 34–39 hours.[5]

The final column in Table 9.4 shows the difference between men's and women's mean hours of free time. Although men's hours of free time are greater than those of women in the same survey sample, this difference, on average, is not large. In Australia, Norway, and the United States, for those aged 20–59 years, women's average free time exceeds that of men, although only by less than an hour and a half per week. The Netherlands, Australia, and Norway all come within a fraction of an hour of complete parity between the sexes in average primary free time.

Table 9.4 Comparison of men's and women's mean primary free time

Survey	All men and all women			Married, employed full-time		
	Men	Women	Gender gap in free time (men–women)	Men	Women	Gender gap in free time men–women
Australia 1992	36:43	36:43	−0:00	31:49	29:26	2:22*
Canada 1992	39:13	35:56	3:16*	33:28	28:25	5:03*
Denmark 1987	42:20	41:04	1:11	37:33	36:13	1:21
Finland 1987	37:15	35:15	2:00*	33:44	31:13	2:30*
Italy 1980	37:38	31:23	6:14*	—	—	—
Netherlands 1985	41:48	41:39	0:08	38:27	38:02	0:25
Norway 1981	37:15	37:22	−0:06	34:44	31:10	3:34*
Sweden 1991	31:34	29:39	1:55	29:18	27:42	1:35*
UK 1985	37:04	35:52	1:11*	33:28	30:12	3:15*
United States 1985	33:02	34:25	−1:22	28:56	28:18	0:39
For pooled database	36:56	35:30	1:26*	32:54	30:13	2:41*

Note
* Difference between the men's and women's hours significant at the 0.05 level.

Italian men are exceptional, enjoying more than six and a half hours (or 21 percent) more free time than Italian women, but the more typical pattern in these seven countries is for the sex difference in mean free time to be less than half that of the Italians. On average, across all the data in the pooled sample, men only enjoy an extra 3.9 percent free time when compared with women.[6]

The gender gap in free time between married full-time employed men and women, shown in the final column of Table 9.4, is almost twice as large as for all men and women. Even in this case, however, men only have an extra 8.3 percent advantage. The gap is widest in Canada (just over five hours per week), moderate (3.5–1.5 hours per week) in a majority of countries and insignificant in Denmark, the Netherlands, and the United States. Even when restricting the analysis to respondents with many of the characteristics of dual-earner households, the gender difference in mean primary free time is a slim foundation on which to build the case for women's double burden. These findings are broadly consistent with those of Nock and Kingston (1989), who found that gender had only minor effects on leisure.

The small differences in total (paid and unpaid) work and free time are, however, partly the result of specialization. As the data makes clear, even in modern Western societies, specialization by gender is a prominent feature of social organization. One might speculate as to what would happen if men and women resembled each other, that is, were similar in all social characteristics except gender. This can be explored by multivariate form of analysis, which shows the effect of gender net of influences arising from specialization. In practice, this analysis is limited by the data available. As is typical with pooled data sets, the Multinational Time Budget Archive contains only a limited number of variables at a relatively high level of aggregation. For example, while there is some rudimentary information about educational attainment, there is no comparable information about income or the characteristics of spouses across all the surveys. A Multiple Classification Analysis (MCA) (Andrews *et al.* 1973) was employed to control for the nationality, age, marital, parental, and employment status of respondents, and their educational achievement.

The MCA results, shown in Table 9.5, are expressed as deviations from the grand mean. For example, being a citizen of the United States, independent of other influences, adds over six hours of total work to the grand mean for the whole sample, producing an adjusted mean of almost 56 hours per week. Employment and young children have the greatest impact on both total work and free time. Being employed and having young children reduces adult leisure time and increases total work time, independent of gender. Net of the influence of these variables across the whole pooled data set, on average, women would work for 5 hours 50 minutes per week total (paid plus unpaid work) more than men, and men would have 4 hours 52 minutes per week more free time than women. If men and women had similar employment profiles, and were identical in other important respects, then the predicted gender gap in total work time and in leisure time would become more substantial than what the raw unadjusted averages show. In practice, men and women have different and more specialized employment profiles and the actual gaps, even among full-time employed men and women, is never this large.

Table 9.5 Multiple classification analysis of time spent in primary total (paid and unpaid) work and free time

	Weekly hours total (paid + unpaid) work	Weekly hours free time
Grand mean	49.45	36.69
Deviation from grand mean		
Gender	**	**
Male	−3.07	2.03
Female	2.77	−1.83
Nationality	**	**
Australian	2.36	−1.18
Canadian	2.68	0.15
Danish	−2.16	7.21
Finnish	−1.74	0.13
Italian	—	—
Dutch	−2.05	2.64
Norwegian	−0.03	1
Sweden	−4.17	−0.67
United Kingdom	−0.69	−1.24
United States	6.38	−4.47
Age group	*	*
20–24 years	−0.45	−0.1
25–34 years	0.83	−0.52
35–44 years	0.87	−0.4
45–54 years	−0.66	0.34
55–59 years	−4.28	2.94
Marital status	**	**
Married, de facto	0.52	−0.98
Single, widowed, divorced	−1.33	2.49
Family status	*	*
No children, younger (<40 years)	−3.54	2.62
Youngest child <5 years	6.63	−4.42
Youngest child <17 years	0.28	−0.62
No children older (40+ years)	−2.25	1.65
Employment status	*	*
Full-time	4.81	−3.61
Part-time (<30 h/w)	0.1	1.54
Not employed	−13.84	9.59
Educational attainment	**	**
Did not complete high school	−1.74	0.25
Completed high school	−0.03	0.3
Qualification beyond high school	2.25	−0.39
Don't know	2.8	−6.79
Mulitple *R*-squared	0.123	0.109

Notes
* Significant at the 0.005 level.
** Significant at the 0.0005 level.

On the basis of the raw (unadjusted) quantity (the number of hours) of primary leisure time, men and women seem remarkably similar. However, this says nothing about any possible differences in the quality of leisure. It is to this issue that we now turn.

The quality of leisure

Combined activities

We now move on to consider the quality of leisure. As we noted earlier, we draw upon the Australian data because it is the only data set capable of supporting this level of detailed analysis. Other national data sets do not have sufficiently reliable detail about secondary activities, a fact indicated by a lower average number of episodes per day. Moreover, because the Australian survey collects information from all members of the household who are 15 years or older, it is possible to isolate men and women in dual-earner couples. The results of this separate analysis for dual-earners are not shown because they barely differ from the results shown in this section for all men and women.

The first of the three measures of the nature of leisure concentrates on the "purity" of leisure. From the total of 432,011 activity episodes in the Australian 1992 sample, 113,092, or 26 percent, are episodes where the respondent describes their "main" or primary activity as leisure. More than half of all primary leisure episodes are simple "pure leisure" with no other secondary activity. An additional one-third of primary leisure episodes consist of intense pure forms of leisure where a primary leisure activity is combined with a secondary leisure activity.

A better method for describing the incidence of particular dimensions of leisure activities is to explore the proportion of diary days that contain any record of that combination of activity. Table 9.6 is a frequency table showing the proportion of diaries in which the various leisure combinations appear.

As might be anticipated, some combinations of activities are prevalent while others are rarely found. Most diaries (91 percent) report simple, unaccompanied pure leisure activity. Nearly three-quarters of the diaries contain evidence of

Table 9.6 Frequency of combinations of leisure activities and other major activity groups

Primary activity	Secondary activity	Percent of diary days
Leisure	No activity	91.20
Leisure	Leisure	74.38
Leisure	Paid work	1.11
Leisure	Unpaid work	28.08
Leisure	With self-care	27.68

intense forms of leisure activity, where one leisure activity is combined with another leisure activity. Among the "leisure with leisure" category, 95 percent of these intense episodes involve passive leisure as the background activity, with leisure conversation (39 percent), listening to the radio (21 percent), television or video consumption (17 percent) the most common secondary activities.

At least one episode of primary leisure combined with secondary self-care activities is reported in 28 percent of the diaries. The most typical forms of this mixed activity involve eating (75 percent), drinking alcohol (7 percent), or smoking (7 percent) in combination with a primary leisure activity. In descending order, grooming or attending to personal hygiene, health care, sleep, and sexual activity are the background activities of primary leisure in the less frequently reported combinations. Activities are classified as belonging to self-care when the activity involves an element of attending to personal physiological needs.

A substantial proportion (28 percent) of diaries contain reports of primary leisure combined with unpaid work. In these cases, domestic responsibilities are the demands of care, which intrude upon the primary leisure activity and might be considered the prototypical form of contaminated leisure. The most frequent background activity of this type is childcare. Seventy-one percent of all episodes of this type include childcare responsibilities – while half consist of passive child-minding, the remainder require adults to interact directly with children.

The different quality of leisure experienced by men and women is summarized in Table 9.7. Despite the appearance of equality of aggregate leisure time, on the basis of two of three measures, the table shows that men, on average, enjoy a higher quality leisure than women. Let us examine each of these in turn.

Table 9.7 Gender differences in the quality of leisure measures

Measure of qualities	Mean for men	Mean for women	Significance
Combinations[a]			
Leisure with no other activity (hours:minutes per week)	24:22	21:04	***
Leisure with leisure (hours:minutes per week)	18:17	18:56	*
Leisure with unpaid work (hours:minutes per week)	8:14	9:45	***
Interrupted leisure			
Number of leisure episodes (per day)	6:34	7:37	***
Maximum length unbroken pure leisure (hours:minutes per day)	1:42	1:24	***

Notes

* Indicates *t*-test on the difference in the means, $P < 0.05$.
*** Indicates $P < 0.0005$.
a The other combinations (leisure with self-care and leisure with paid work) produce results that are less meaningful theoretically and are so infrequent as to be practically inconsequential.

Turning first to the issue of what accompanies primary leisure time, there is a clear patterning by gender. More than 61 percent of men's leisure is pure leisure, with no accompanying activity. On average, men spend more than 24 hours per week in pure leisure. By contrast, little more than half of women's leisure is pure leisure. Women, on average, spend 21 hours per week in pure leisure activities. The difference in mean hours of pure leisure is highly significant and cannot be attributed to sampling error. The obverse is also true, women experience a higher proportion of their leisure time contaminated by combination with unpaid work.

Interrupted leisure

In the context of roughly equivalent aggregate leisure times, the average number of leisure episodes offers a direct indicator of more harried leisure. By contrast, the average maximum length of episodes of pure leisure indicates leisure in its most relaxed and comfortable form.

On both these measures, the quality of men's leisure is higher than that of women. Women's leisure is significantly more harried than men's leisure, as indicated by a significantly higher number of leisure episodes. The interrupted quality of women's leisure is also captured by the significantly shorter duration of their maximal episode of pure leisure. Bearing in mind the likelihood that more of women's leisure episodes than men's will be contaminated with unpaid work, the cumulative effect of these differences between the genders is more profound than it may appear at first sight. In other words, women's leisure is more likely to be interrupted, to involve episodes of shorter duration, and to be associated with unpaid work.

Adult leisure

Adult leisure can be defined as time spent in a pure leisure activity or an intense leisure activity (leisure with leisure) without the presence of children. By contrast, family leisure represents "pure" and "intense" leisure spent in the company of children. Across the entire population (including households without children below the age of 15), more than four-fifths of all, otherwise unconstrained, leisure time is adult leisure time. However, overall, women have significantly lower average weekly hours of adult leisure (see Table 9.8).

Disaggregating this population according to the age of their youngest child shows a large gulf between those households with a child under the age of 10 and the rest of the population. The gulf between parents with young children and those with mature children or no children at all is much more profound than any difference between the genders.[7] More than 95 percent of all (pure and intense) leisure time among those with no children under 15 years of age is adult leisure. Among people whose youngest child is between 10 and 14 years of age, more than three-quarters of all pure and intense leisure is adult leisure. However, where youngest children are below the age of 10, the balance between adult and family leisure changes dramatically. Both parents spend less than half their pure

Table 9.8 Adult leisure by age of youngest child

Youngest child	Valid N	Proportion of leisure which is adult leisure (%)	Adult leisure (hours:minutes per week)		t-test for equality of means
			Male	Female	
Entire population	9,544	82.74	35:12	31:23	0.000
No children	6,948	95.69	42:47	39:31	0.000
10–14 years	727	75.74	25:20	24:52	0.768
5–9 years	717	44.81	9:47	9:01	0.476
2–4 years	552	43.23	5:32	5:23	0.995
<2 years	600	48.59	7:43	2:38	0.000

and intense leisure time exclusively in the company of adults. Put the other way around, the majority of their time is family leisure. Moreover, these proportions are stable until the youngest child reaches the age of 10.

Among those without children, the average weekly hours of adult leisure is the equivalent of a full-time workweek. For parents whose youngest child is in their early teens, this average falls by more than 10 hours per week. However, among parents of pre-teens, the mean weekly hours of adult leisure is less than a quarter of the hours available on average to those without children. The lowest level is found among the mothers whose youngest child is not yet 2 years of age, who average a meager 2 hours 38 minutes of adult leisure per week.

However, an analysis of the average weekly hours of adult leisure also reveals a relatively consistent pattern of gender difference. For each category of the age of youngest child, women's mean hours of adult leisure are lower than those of men. The gender gap in average weekly hours of adult leisure is statistically significant among the parents of very young children and for those without children under the age of 15. Fathers of children below the age of 2 years enjoy, on average, almost three times more weekly hours of adult leisure than the mothers of these children. The uneven distribution of this scarce resource is truly striking. Among those without children, in the sense described here, the mean weekly hours of adult leisure of both genders are more substantial but the difference of 3 hours 17 minutes per week is, nevertheless, notable. Among parents with a youngest child in age range of 2–14 years, gender differences are small.

These results are consistent with the finding that men experience children as an opportunity to play, while women are more likely to experience children as the occasion for unpaid work. When their youngest child is less than 2 years old, mothers devote an average of over 30 hours per week to primary, direct child care. The average for fathers is 8 hours per week. More than half (15 hours per week) of women's mean time spent in caring for these young children is spent on their physical care, in tasks such as carrying, comforting, feeding, changing, dressing, bathing, and tending to injuries and ailments. Almost a third of men's 8 hours of childcare is spent in playing with children. While women spend more hours than men playing with very young children, less than a sixth of their time spent in childcare involves playing with children. Weekly hours of primary childcare fall dramatically as the youngest child matures. However, the proportion of women's childcare devoted to play remains less than half that of men until the child reaches the age of 10.

From this analysis of adult leisure in relation to family leisure, two main points arise. Firstly, women are relatively disadvantaged by the distribution of adult leisure, although the major difference is between parents of young children and all other adults. When we consider family leisure, however, a more marked gender difference does emerge. Here, women are significantly disadvantaged by their uneven responsibility for the physical care of children. The data shows that fathers are mostly with their children in a context of play and have fewer direct care responsibilities than mothers. If there are benefits to be gained from the company of children, as many economists believe (Deaton and Muellbauer 1980), then it would seem that they fall disproportionately to men. In terms of gender equity, while the distribution of adult leisure may be an issue, the nature of the time spent with children remains the larger inequity.

Conclusion

This chapter has re-examined the idea that women have less free time than men. The belief that women suffer from a "double burden" or "second shift" has often been interpreted literally by sociologists, implying that women entering paid employment simply add these hours to their existing hours of housework and childcare. However, the analysis of time-use in ten OECD countries shows that, when paid and unpaid working time are added together, there is only a small difference in the average "total work time" of men and women. As might be expected on the basis of a relatively even distribution of total work time, the mean number of hours of primary leisure time of men and women is also remarkably similar.

How then can this finding of apparent gender equity in the objective circumstances of leisure be reconciled with the subjective impression of increased time pressure among women? We believe that the paradox is, in part, the result of a narrow concentration on the quantity of leisure time. Feminist scholars have claimed for some time that women have a distinctive experience of leisure that is difficult to disentangle from multiple and overlapping activities. However, their argument has largely remained unsubstantiated because of their insistence that only qualitative techniques can capture this experiential dimension of time. We have set out to demonstrate here that quantitative information gathered by mass survey techniques can be used to investigate the lived experience of time.

Furthermore, we show that this data lends support to the feminist claim of gender difference in relation to time. Measures based on comparing the sum of time spent in episodes of primary leisure disregard the constraining nature of women's unpaid family responsibilities and make the consequences invisible. Using our more sophisticated measures about the quality of leisure time, we show that men do have more high quality leisure than women.

Men have many more hours of pure leisure uncontaminated by combination with unpaid work. In addition, men's leisure is less likely to be interrupted than women's. The fragmentary character of women's leisure changes its quality. Fragmented leisure, snatched between work and self-care activities, is less relaxing than unbroken leisure. It is likely that this fragmented leisure will be experienced as more harried and therefore increase self-reported stress. Indeed, it may well be that the contemporary view of increased "time pressure" has more to do with this fragmentation than with any measurable reduction in primary leisure time.

The results of the more detailed analysis of leisure confirm that the social cleavage between parents and nonparents is as important as gender differences. The leisure of parents is oriented around family activities, especially when children are young. Nevertheless, women have less adult leisure than comparable men. Women are further disadvantaged by their disproportionate responsibility for the physical care of children. Women spend more time physically caring for children than playing with them. By contrast, the time fathers spend with their children is more likely to be in the context of play rather than care. In sum, a gender gap in leisure emerges.

The findings of this study remind us that throughout advanced societies, families still exhibit a pattern of specialization on the basis of gender. The large body of empirical evidence assembled in this chapter indicates that women continue to bear primary responsibility for family care. Unpaid work, especially housework and childcare, continues to be "women's work." Given the different value accorded to paid work and unpaid work in these societies, specialization by gender has social costs for women. Women pay a price in both earnings and the quality of leisure. When the characteristics of the leisure are considered, the apparent equity in leisure-time between men and women disappears.

We agree with Nancy Fraser that an important dimension of gender equity concerns the distribution of leisure time. To date, this issue has received elaborate theoretical treatment, on the basis of a priori suppositions and little effort has gone into testing them against empirical evidence. This chapter has shown that time-use surveys represent a rich source of information, capable of capturing not only the quantity of leisure time but also key aspects of its quality. The results of the analysis suggest that there continues to be a gender gap in leisure.

Notes

1 By contrast, some other theorists accept the "second shift" as a metaphorical concept because men never assume direct responsibility for domestic and family tasks. However, this apparent "equality" in the burden of all types of work masks a deep inequality in responsibility for domestic tasks that Rydenstam (1994) uncovers by event history analysis. This reminds us of the core issue at stake: do women's family responsibilities result in social disadvantage? If it can be shown that in most Western countries men get paid for 65–70 percent of all their primary work time while women get paid for only 30–35 percent of theirs, then the equality of "total" work time seems largely irrelevant.

2 Legislation about the confidentiality of official surveys precludes unrestricted access to the Australian Bureau of Statistics 1987 and 1992 Time Use Surveys.
3 Time-diary studies in the United States have, up to the time of writing have been limited to small samples (Robinson and Godbey 1997: 6, 68–74).
4 This idea is inspired by economists' experience with equivalence scales. As part of the process of determining the costs of children, economists have compared the expenditure of households with and without children. Obviously, households with young children have extra expenditure – they spend more on children's goods (baby food, diapers, pacifiers, children's clothing, specialized furniture, toys) than households without children. However, the simple assumption that the average cost of a child can be derived by subtracting the average cost of a couple from the average cost of a couple with a child produces anomalous results – in many instances the costs of children are negative (Douthitt and Fedyk 1988). Households with young children, for example, spend far less on restaurant meals. However, as Rothbarth pointed out, what this simple comparison inadvertently captures is the effect of income constraint. If the aim is to achieve an equivalent standard of living for each household type, then a proper procedure should ensure that the comparison is not contaminated by income constraints. He proposed that the best way to achieve this is to ensure that both types of household consumed a similar quantity of adult goods, typically operationalized as things like tobacco and alcohol.
5 Just what explains cross-national difference in the distribution of paid and unpaid total work by gender is the subject for another paper (see Bittman 1999).
6 Although the difference in means is statistically significant ($P < 0.0005$, with 46,931 df using a t-test), this is largely an artefact of the large sample size.
7 When considering the average proportion of (pure and intense) leisure that is adult leisure, the difference between the genders is small and is not statistically significant, but this masks some real gender differences in the absolute amounts of adult leisure.

References

Åas, D. (1982) "Designs for Large Scale Time Use Studies of the 24-hour Day" in Z. Staikov (ed.), *It's About Time, Proceedings of the International Research Group on Time Budgets and Social Activities*, Sofia: Bulgarian Sociological Association, pp.17–53.

Adam, B. (1995) *Timewatch*, Cambridge: Polity Press.

Andrews, F. M., Morgan, J., Sonquist, J., and Klem, L. (1973) *Multiple Classification Analysis: A Report on a Computer Program for Multiple Regression Using Categorical Analysis*, Ann Arbor: Institute for Social Research, University of Michigan.

Australian Bureau of Statistics (1993) *Time Use Survey Australia: User's Guide* Catalogue No. 4150.0 Canberra.

Baxter, J. and Bittman, M. (1995) "Measuring Time Spent in Housework: A Comparison of Two Approaches," *The Australian Journal of Social Research*, 1: 21–46.

Beck, U. and Beck-Gernsheim, E. (1995) *The Normal Chaos of Love*, Cambridge: Polity Press.

Becker, G. (1985) "Human Capital, Effort, and the Sexual Division of Labor," *Journal of Labor Economics*, 3: 33–58.

Berk, S. F. (1985) *The Gender Factory: The Apportionment of Work in American Households*, New York: Plenum.

Bittman, M. (1999) "Parenthood without Penalty: Time Use and Public Policy in Australia and Finland," *Feminist Economics*, 5: 27–42. See also Chapter 11 in this volume.

Bryant, W. and Zick, C. (1996) "Are We Investing Less in the Next Generation? Historical Trends in Time Spent Caring for Children," *Journal of Family and Economic Issues*, 17: 365–92.

Cheal, D. (1991) *Family and the State of Theory*, Toronto: University of Toronto Press.

Connell, R. W. (1987) *Gender and Power*, Cambridge: Polity Press.

Coverman, S. and Sheley, J. (1986) "Change in Men's Housework and Child-Care Time, 1966–1975," *Journal of Marriage and the Family*, 48: 413–22.

Davies, K. (1990) *Women and Time: The Weaving of the Strands of Everyday Life*, Aldershot: Avebury.

Deaton, A. and Muellbauer, J. (1980) *Economics and Consumer Behaviour*, Cambridge: Cambridge University Press.

Deem, R. (1988) "Feminism and Leisure Studies: Opening Up New Directions," in E. Wimbush and M. Talbot (eds), *Relative Freedoms*, Milton Keynes: Open University Press, pp. 1–17.

Douthitt, R. A. and Fedyk, J. (1988) "The Influence of Children on Family Life Cycle Spending Behavior: Theory and Application," *Journal of Consumer Affairs*, 22: 220–48.

England, P. (1982) "The Failure of Human Capital Theory to Explain Occupational Sex Segregation," *Journal of Human Resources*, 17: 358–70.

Esping-Anderson, G. (1990) *The Three Worlds of Welfare Capitalism*, Cambridge: Polity Press.

Forman, F. J. and Sowton, C. (eds) (1989) *Taking Our Time: Feminist Perspectives on Temporality*, Oxford: Pergamon.

Fraser, N. (1997) "After the Family Wage: A Postindustrial Thought Experiment," in B. Hobson and A. Berggren (eds), *Crossing Borders Gender and Citizenship in Transition*, Stockholm: Swedish Council for Planning and Coordination, pp. 21–55.

Frederick, J. A. (1995) *As Time Goes By ... Time Use of Canadians, General Social Survey*, Ottawa: Statistics Canada.

Gershuny, J. (1990) "The Multinational Longitudinal Time Budget Data Archive," Dublin: European Foundation for the Improvement of Living and Working Conditions.

Giddens, A. (1992) *The Transformation of Intimacy*, Cambridge: Polity Press.

Gilligan, C. (1982) *In a Different Voice: Psychological Theory and Women's Development*, Cambridge, MA: Harvard University Press.

Glucksman, M. (1998) "'What a Difference a Day Makes:' A Theoretical and Historical Exploration of Temporality and Gender," *Sociology*, 32: 239–58.

Goldschmidt-Clermont, L. and Pagnossin-Aligisakis, E. (1995) "Measures of Unrecorded Economic Activities in Fourteen Countries" Occasional Paper No. 20, New York: Human Development Report Office.

Hartmann, H. (1981) "The Family as the Locus of Gender, Class and Political Struggle: The Example of Housework," *Signs: Journal of Women in Culture and Society*, 6: 366–94.

Henderson, K. A. (1991) "The Contribution of Feminism to an Understanding of Leisure Constraints," *Journal of Leisure Research*, 23: 363–77.

Hill, C. and Stafford, F. P. (1985) "Parental Care of Children: Time Diary Estimates of Quantity, Predictability, and Variety," in F. T. Juster and F. P. Stafford (eds), *Time, Goods, and Well-being*, Ann Arbor: University of Michigan Press, pp. 415–37.

Hochschild, A. (1983) *The Managed Heart: Commercialization of Human Feeling*, Berkeley: University of California Press.

—— (1997) *The Time Bind*, New York: Henry Holt and Company.

—— and Machung, A. (1989) *The Second Shift*, New York: Viking.

Juster, F. Thomas (1985) "The Validity and Quality of Time Use Estimates Obtained from Recall Diaries," in F. T. Juster and F. P. Stafford (eds), *Time, Goods, and Well-being*, Ann Arbor: University of Michigan Press, pp. 63–92.

Kristeva, J. (1981) "Women's Time," *Signs: Journal of Women in Culture and Society*, 7: 16–35.

Landes, D. (1983) *Revolution in Time: Clocks and the Making of the Modern World*, Cambridge, MA: Belknap Press of Harvard University Press.

Larson, R. and Richards, M. (1994) *Divergent Realities: The Emotional Lives of Mothers, Fathers, and Adolescents*, New York: Basic Books.

Linder, S. (1970) *The Harried Leisure Class*, New York: Columbia University Press.

Lopata, H. (1971) *Occupation: Housewife*, Milton Keynes: Open University Press.

Meissner, M., Humphrey, E., Meis, S., and Scheu, W. (1975) "No Exit for Wives: Sexual Division of Labour and the Cumulation of Household Demands," *Canadian Review of Sociology and Anthropology*, 12: 424–39.

Morris, L. (1990) *The Workings of the Household*, Cambridge: Polity Press.

Niemi, I. (1993) "Systematic Error in Behavioural Measurement: Comparing Results from Interview and Time Budget Studies," *Social Indicators Research*, 30: 229–44.

Nock, S. L. and Kingston, P. W. (1989) "The Division of Leisure and Work," *Social Science Quarterly*, 70: 24–39.

Nowotny, H. (1994) *Time: the Modern and the Postmodern Experience*, Cambridge: Polity Press.

Oakley, A. (1974) *The Sociology of Housework*, London: Martin Robertson.

Oppenheimer, V. K. (1994) "Women's Rising Employment and the Future of the Family in Industrial Societies," *Population and Development Review*, 20: 293–342.

—— (1997) "Women's Employment and the Gain to Marriage: The Specialization and Trading Model," *Annual Review of Sociology*, 23: 431–53.

Pallié, B. (1993) "Estimating the Volume of Unpaid Activities in Canada, 1992: An Evaluation of Data from the General Social Survey," *General Social Survey Working Paper* No. 10, Ottawa: Statistics Canada.

Pateman, C. (1988) *The Sexual Contract*, Cambridge: Polity Press.

Robinson, J. P. (1985) "The Validity and Reliability of Diaries versus Alternative Time Use Measures," in F. T. Juster and F. P. Stafford (eds), *Time, Goods, and Well-Being*, Ann Arbor: University of Michigan Press, pp. 33–62.

—— and Gershuny, J. (1994) "Measuring Hours of Paid Work: Time-diary vs. Estimate Questions," *Bulletin of Labour Statistics*, 1: X1–XVII, Geneva: International Labour Organisation.

—— and Godbey, G. (1997) *Time for Life: The Surprising Ways Americans Use Their Time*, University Park, PA: Pennsylvania State University Press.

Rubin, L. B. (1995) *Families on the Fault Line: America's Working Class Speaks About the Family, the Economy, Race, and Ethnicity*, New York: HarperPerennial.

Rydenstam, K. (1994) "Who Takes Care of the Housework After Work," Paper presented at the XIIth World Congress of Sociology, Bielefeld, Germany.

Sainsbury, D. (1996) *Gender Equality Reforms and Welfare States*, Cambridge: Cambridge University Press.

Schor, J. B. (1991) *The Overworked American: The Unexpected Decline of Leisure*, New York: Basic Books.

Smith, D. (1979) "A Sociology for Women," in J. A. Sherman and E. T. Beck (eds), *Prism of Sex: Essays in the Sociology of Knowledge*, Madison: University of Wisconsin Press, pp. 135–87.

Szalai, A., Converse, P. E., Feldheim, P., Scheuch, E., and Stone, P. J. (1972) *The Use of Time: Daily Activities of Urban and Suburban Populations in Twelve Countries*, The Hague: Mouton.

Thompson, E. P. (1967) "Time, Work-Discipline and Industrial Capitalism," *Past and Present*, 38: 56–97.

Vickery, Clair (1977) "The Time-Poor: A New Look at Poverty," *Journal of Human Resources*, 12: 27–48.

Wimbush, E. and Talbot, M. (1988) *Relative Freedoms: Women and Leisure*, Milton Keynes: Open University Press.

Part V
International comparisons

10 A tale of dual-earner families in four countries

Shelley Pacholok and Anne H. Gauthier

Sue is a 34-year old, full-time insurance agent, and mother of 3-year old Alex. Her husband, John, also works full-time. During weekdays, Sue gets up at 6:15 a.m. and gets herself and Alex ready to start the day. She leaves home at 7:30 a.m., leaves Alex at daycare, and then commutes to work. She works at the insurance company from 8:30 a.m. to 4:30 p.m. At the end of her workday, Sue commutes back home, picks up Alex from daycare at 5:20 p.m., and finally reaches home just before 6 p.m. Her evening routine consists of preparing and eating dinner, playing with Alex from 7 p.m. to 8 p.m., getting Alex ready to go to bed at 8 p.m., and reading to him. By 9 p.m. she rapidly cleans the house, and finally gets some relaxation time at 9:30 p.m. before falling asleep at 11 p.m. In the interview, Sue reported that she felt rushed every day.[1]

Juggling family responsibilities and full-time work can be a real challenge. In the 1998 Canadian time-use survey (from which the above-mentioned case was drawn), 72 percent of full-time employed mothers whose youngest child was less than 5 years old said they felt rushed everyday, and 50 percent said that they would like to spend more time with family and friends.

The way families organize their time is influenced by numerous factors including spouses' characteristics, the demands and flexibilities of employers, and the support of governments in terms of family-friendly policies (Haas 1990; Baker 1997). How these elements play out in the day-to-day realities of families is less clear, however. In this chapter, we shed some light on the matter by examining the patterns of time use of dual-earner parents in four countries with very different systems of state support for families: Canada, Germany, Italy, and Sweden. As revealed in the chapter, the way dual-earner parents allocate their time varies substantially across these four countries, especially in terms of the gender division of paid and unpaid work.

The chapter is structured in six sections. The first section reviews the literature and highlights the fact that very few studies have been devoted to cross-national comparisons of family time. The second section discusses various theoretical perspectives related to parental time and the gender division of unpaid work. The emphasis here is on theories that link the macro-level characteristics of societies with expected micro-level behavior. In particular, we discuss the theoretical links between social policies and the gender division of paid and unpaid work. The third section expands on this theoretical discussion by introducing the four countries selected for this analysis and by providing an overview of the macro-level differences that may be expected to affect the organization of time in these countries. The fourth section presents our data and method, and the fifth section our results. The chapter concludes with a discussion of policies.

Review of the literature

There is a relatively large body of literature on the gender division of labor in families. It is briefly reviewed here in order to identify the micro-level determinants of time spent in housework and childcare, and to contrast this vast literature with the very limited one on the macro-level determinants. With regard to micro-level determinants, the literature indicates that one of the strongest predictors of time spent in housework and childcare is gender, with women spending more time in unpaid work than men (Hochschild 1989; Ferree 1990; Waltzer 1996). For men and women aged 25–45 years, this difference amounted to more than 2 hours per day in the mid-1980s (Gershuny and Robinson 1988). And although this gender gap has been reduced since the 1960s, women continue to bear the burden of the second shift (Hochschild 1989). The presence of children, and especially young children, are also known to increase time spent on housework and childcare, but again, the effect is larger on women's domestic labor than men's (Shelton 1992; Presser 1994; Perkins and DeMeis 1996; McFarlane *et al.* 2000).

The time availability of spouses is also known to affect their respective contributions to paid and unpaid work. Maternal employment affects time in unpaid labor with employed women spending less time on household labor than non-employed women (Vanek 1974; Fenstermaker Berk 1985; Rexroat and Shehan 1987; Bergen 1991; Kamo 1991; Brayfield 1992; Brines 1993; Acock and Demo 1994; Davies and Carrier 1999). However, the research also indicates that employed women still perform more household labor than men (Rexroat and Shehan 1987; Kamo 1991; Shelton and John 1993; Robinson and Godbey 1999). Men's paid work is consistently and negatively associated with their housework time (Shelton and John 1996).

The literature also suggests that earnings and education are key determinants of the gender division of housework. Most studies find that earnings have a significant impact on the division of household labor (Kamo 1988, 1994; Blair and Lichter 1991; Brayfield 1992; Shelton and John 1993; Presser 1994) and childcare (Presser 1986; Glass 1998). Most researchers find that the smaller the gap between husbands' and wives' earnings, the more equal is the division of household labor (Shelton and John 1996). Furthermore, many studies find that men's educational level is positively associated with their participation in housework (Kalleberg and Rosenfeld 1990; Brayfield 1992; Brines 1993; Haddad 1994; Presser 1994; South and Spitze 1994) and negatively associated with their partner's household labor time (Kamo 1991; Shelton and John 1993). On the other hand, women's educational level is generally negatively associated with their time spent performing household labor (Brines 1993; Shelton and John 1993; South and Spitze 1994; Strober and Chan 1998).

The literature on macro-level and institutional determinants of family time and the gender division of labor is much more limited. Two main topics have been examined. First, the works of Bittman (1999), Presser (1988, 1989, 1994) and Brayfield (1995) investigate how the number of hours worked per week, opportunities for flex-time and part-time work, work schedules, and parental leave benefits affect the division of labor. In general, results from these studies indicate that family-friendly policies serve to alleviate some of the second shift faced by working mothers. Second, some research examines the economic climate, employment opportunities, and gender wage equality as factors that may account for gender differences in paid and unpaid labor. Casper and O'Connell (1998) found that macroeconomic shifts, such as recessions, lead to reductions in paid work and income for men, which in turn increase fathers' involvement in childcare. However, others found that economic factors did not explain fathers' participation in domestic work (Coverman 1985; Coverman and Sheley, 1986; Glass 1998).

With the exception of Bittman (1999), these studies are restricted to single-country analysis. The cross-national literature on both the micro- and macro-level determinants of family time and gender division of labor is very limited. There is a small body of literature on the relationship between country-level attitudes towards gender equality and female labor force participation (see Haller Hoellinger 1994, 1999; Scott *et al.* 1996; Knudsen and Waerness 1999), and there is some literature on the impact of social policies on women's participation in paid work (especially after childbirth) (Gornick *et al.* 1997; Smith and Bachu 1999; Waldfogel *et al.* 2000). However, very little is known about the effect of welfare state policies on the gender division of unpaid work and childcare.

Our aim in this chapter is to add to this cross-national literature in order to increase our understanding of the relationships between macro-level institutions and social policies, on the one hand, and micro-level behavior one the other (i.e. individuals' time allocation). While most of the literature has focused on the gender division of housework, we also extend this literature by examining time spent on all three forms of work, namely paid work, housework, and childcare.

Theories

Four main theories have been suggested to explain the gender division of paid and unpaid work: (1) the resource-power perspective, (2) the socialization and gender-role perspective, (3) the time availability perspective, and (4) the welfare state perspective. We briefly review each of these theoretical frameworks here. Although these theories tend to be formulated and empirically tested in single-country studies, we reframe them in a cross-national perspective with the aim of theoretically linking macro-level institutions and policies and the micro-level allocation of time.

According to the resource-power perspective, resources such as income, education, and occupational status are thought to contribute to relationship power, making it possible for the spouse with the most power to engage in fewer unpleasant tasks such as housework (Huber and Spitze 1983; Brines 1993). According to this perspective, the smaller the gap between husbands' and wives' earnings, the more equal the division of labor.[2] From a cross-national perspective, countries with a relatively small earnings gap between men and women are expected to have a more equal gender division of paid and unpaid work than those countries with a larger wage gap.

The socialization/gender-role perspective suggests that husbands and wives perform household labor in differing amounts depending upon what they have learned and have come to believe about appropriate behavior for men and women. Scholars employing this perspective hypothesize that couples with more traditional attitudes will have a more unequal division of household labor than those with egalitarian attitudes. (Greenstein 1996).[3] Therefore, from a cross-national perspective, it is expected that couples in countries with very traditional gender attitudes will display a less egalitarian division of paid and unpaid work than in other countries.

The time availability/constraint framework perspective posits that the division of domestic labor is the result of rational considerations of who has the most time to do household tasks, in view of other time commitments.[4] The labor force status of spouses, the number of hours worked, the spouses' work schedule, and the number and age of children have all been posited to affect the time availability of spouses and therefore their respective contribution to paid and unpaid work – although the work elasticity of men and women may differ (Shelton and John 1996). Therefore, cross-national differences in the duration of the workweek, the prevalence of part-time work, and the opportunities to take time-off to look after children are all expected to affect the gender division of paid and unpaid work.

Finally, from a welfare state perspective, gender differences in time spent in paid and unpaid work are related to the availability of welfare and family policies that provide support for parents.[5] For example, these policies may influence the labor force participation of mothers, which in turn, is linked to the ways in which families organize their time. Similarly, the provision of parental leave, and the opportunities for parents to share such leave, is expected to influence the gender division of labor. Therefore, we anticipate that cross-national differences in family policies will be reflected in differences in the gender division of labor across countries, with the most supportive family policies being associated with more time devoted to childcare.

Overall, these various theoretical perspectives point to several factors that may be influencing family time and the gender division of labor including the characteristics of workplaces (e.g. flex-time, hours of work, wages), attitudes about gender roles, and opportunities and constraints resulting from governmental policies (e.g. childcare provision and subsidies, parental leave). These theoretical frameworks provide a foundation for the following hypotheses about cross-national differences in the gender division of labor. We expect that parents will have a more egalitarian division of labor in countries that (1) promote gender equality in the workforce (especially with regard to wages), (2) are highly supportive of working parents (as opposed to mothers only), and (3) endorse norms of gender equality. Further, we anticipate that (4) parents will devote more time to childcare in countries that encourage more nonwork hours (through parental leave schemes, shorter workweeks, longer annual vacations, and flex-time) than in countries that do not offer these opportunities.

The cross-national context

In order to examine the links between macro-level institutions and micro-level behavior, we strategically selected four countries that differ substantially in terms of their welfare and family policies. Canada, Germany, Italy, and Sweden belong to the four welfare state regimes identified in the literature (Esping-Anderson 1990; Ferrera 1996; Orloff 1996, 1997; Lewis 2000).

- Canada belongs to the so-called liberal model, characterized by limited state support for families. It has a high level of child poverty, a low percentage of publicly subsidized childcare places, and a relatively short maternity and parental leave.[6] From a cross-national perspective, Canada ranks among the countries providing low levels of support for working parents (Gornick *et al.* 1997).
- Germany belongs to the conservative, or corporatist, welfare state regime. It is a regime that has traditionally supported a very unequal division of labor between men and women by providing very limited childcare facilities, and allowing women to take long absences from work to care for their children.[7] Cross-nationally, Germany also stands out in view of its strong support for very traditional gender roles.[8]
- Italy belongs to the Southern European welfare state regime characterized by low levels of cash support for families and low to medium levels of support for working parents (Gauthier 2002). Very limited provision for childcare is available for very young children in Italy. On the other hand, a very high proportion of children of age 3 to school age are enrolled in publicly financed institutions.
- Sweden belongs to the social-democratic model. It is characterized by a high level of protection against contingencies such as unemployment and sickness, and by extensive and comprehensive state support for families. It has a low level of child poverty, and is also strongly supportive of gender equality (Singh 1997). Sweden ranks among the countries providing the highest level of support for working parents (Gornick *et al.* 1997). It has also a very high women-to-men wage ratio.

Table 10.1 summarizes the organization of work and the nature of state support for families in the four countries. We distinguish four areas: work and

Table 10.1 Key indicators of the context of work and the organization of time in four countries, 1990s

Areas	Indicators	Canada	Germany	Italy	Sweden
Work	Standard workweek (hours)[a]	40–48	36	36–38	40
	Actual annual hours of work[b]	1780	1557	1682	1613
	Legally mandated vacation days and average vacation days[c]	10	18 (30–35)	(42)	32
	Labor force participation of women[d]	70	63	46	75
	Labor force participation of women with children[e]	69	51	46	78
	% Part-time employment among women[f]	28	33	23	22
	% employees with flex-time[g]	23	33	19	32
Earnings	Ratio of men-to-women earnings[h]	65	74	83	91
Childcare	% of children aged 0–2 in publicly financed care[i]	5	10	6	48
	% of children aged 3 to school age in publicly financed care[j]	50	78	95	80

Parental leave				
Total duration of maternity and parental leave (no. of weeks)[k]	50	162	65	85
Parental leave cash benefits (% of wages)[l]	55	20	30	65
Father's right to parental leave[m]	Parents can share	Parents can share	Parents can share	Parents can share. Also 30 days reserved exclusively for fathers (non-transferable)
Flexibility in parental leave[n]	None	The parent taking leave can work up to 19 hours/week	May be taken until the child is 8 years old	May be taken until the child is 8 years old. May also be fragmented.
Number of days for child sickness[o]	0	25	0	120
Opportunities to reduce number of hours of work[p]	None	None	None	May reduce work hours by 25% until the child has finished first year of school
Index of support for working parents[q]	32.4	34.1	50.6	61.9
School				
Number of teaching hours per year (elementary school)[r]	950	760	748	624
Number of days of school per year[s]	199	219	204	178–190
School schedule[t]	8:45 a.m.–15:25 p.m. (with midday break)	8:00 a.m.–12:30 p.m. (no midday break)	8 a.m.–12:30 p.m. for 6 days or 8 a.m.–12:30 p.m. and 14:00–16:30 p.m. for 5 days	Flexi-pattern

(Table 10.1 continued)

Table 10.1 Continued

Notes and sources:

a Workweek: www.usis.usemb.se/human/1996/index.html – Data refers to year 1996.

b Annual work hours: www.ilo.org/public/english/employment/strat/kilm/table.htm – Data refers to year 1994–95.

c Vacation days: In Canada, workers are entitled to a minimum of two weeks of vacation per day (see: www.hronline.com/lib/quicklaw.php:provision=av). In Germany, the minimum is 18 days, but the average is 30–35 days. The figure for Italy refers to the average and not the mandated minimum. Source: www.timesizing.com/1vacatns.htm – Data refers to 2000–01.

d Labor force participation: OECD (2000). *Historical statistics 1970–1999.* (Paris: OECD).

e Labor force participation with children: Germany, Italy, and Sweden: OECD (2001), table 4.1, year 1999–2000. Canada: www.vifamily.ca/profiling/table37a.htm – data refers to 1996. For married or cohabiting women with children under 6, the labor force participation rate is 69 percent. It is 55 percent for lone-mothers with children under the age of 6.

f Part-time: OECD (2001), table E (appendix). Year 1999.

g Flex-time: OECD (2001), table 4.8 – Data refers to year 1994–95.

h Earnings: Germany, Italy, and Sweden: http://unstats.un.org/unsd/demographic/ww2000/table5g.htm – Data refers to year 1994/99. Canada: data from Statistics Canada (1996). *Earnings of Men and Women 1996* (Ottawa: Statistics Canada).

i Childcare: OECD (2001), table 4.7 – Data refers to year 1999–2000.

j See i above.

k Parental leave: OECD (2001), table 4.7 – Data refers to year 1999–2001.

l Cash benefits: Moss and Deven (1999). Note that these figures refer to parental leave cash benefits and not to maternity leave.

m Father's right to parental leave: Moss and Deven (1999).

n Flexibility: Moss and Deven (1999).

o Child sickness: Moss and Deven (1999).

p Opportunities for reduced hours: Moss and Deven (1999).

q Index of support: Gornick *et al.* (1997).

r Teaching hours: Germany, Italy, and Sweden: http://nces.ed.gov/pubs98/condition98/c98p38.pdf Year 1994. Canada: www.learning.gov.ab.ca/k12/ curriculum/instruct_time.pdf. Note that because education is an area of provincial jurisdiction, we restricted the data here to the Province of Alberta (the other provinces may have slightly different provisions. Data refers to primary education.

s Days of school: Germany, Italy, and Sweden: http://nces.ed.gov/pubs/esn/n35cc.html. Canada: www.learning.gov.ab.ca/k12/curriculum/instruct_time.pdf. Note that because education is an area of provincial jurisdiction, we restricted the data here to the Province of Alberta (the other provinces may have slightly different provisions. Data refers to primary education.

t Schedule: Germany, Italy, and Sweden: www.epsaweb.org/primary_education_in_sweden.htm. Canada: Information obtained from a specific school in Alberta (provisions may slightly vary across schools). Data refers to primary education.

earnings, childcare, parental leave, and school. In order to understand globally the organization of family time, it is indeed important to look not only at the work component, but also at how other institutions (such as schools) regulate families' time.[9]

The contrasts between the four countries are large. According to the data in Table 10.1, Canadians face the longest workweek, the highest annual number of hours of work and the shortest vacations.[10] Canadian parents also face the shortest parental leave, and have the lowest provision of childcare to help them combine work and family responsibilities. Germany appears at the other extreme in terms of workweek and annual hours of work,[11] in addition to offering the longest parental leave. However, this time availability in Germany comes at a certain cost in view of the low level of cash benefits paid during parental leave. Parents of school-age children in Germany also have to cope with the very short duration of school days (from 8 a.m. until 12:30 p.m.). This means having to arrange alternative childcare for the afternoons, or to work only on a part-time basis.

Sweden presents a very different situation for working parents, with a relatively long workweek and relative long work hours, but with extensive childcare facilities. The Swedish welfare state also provide parents with the opportunity to reduce their hours of work, spread their parental leave until the child's 8th birthday, and take time off because of children's sickness. Therefore, what distinguishes the Swedish situation from the other three is its greater flexibility in the organization of time.

Finally, Italy falls in an intermediate situation with a relatively short workweek, and extensive public provision for children aged 3 to school-age. Italy has the lowest female labor force participation rate, but a higher proportion of full-time working women than in Germany.

However, the reality in terms of time constraints and time opportunities is more complex than the simple picture portrayed here. For example, when deciding on the organization of time, families must not only consider whether or not they have the opportunity to take time off work, but also whether or not they can afford it, and whether or not there are childcare facilities available (and affordable) if they want to devote more time to paid work. We will obviously not be able to disentangle these various factors in the empirical section of this chapter. However, it is clear from these indicators that the societal organization of time does vary considerably across countries.

Data and methods

In this chapter, we use time-use surveys from Canada, Germany, Italy, and Sweden[12] to analyze cross-national differences in families' organization of time. The four surveys, carried out in the late 1980s and early 1990s, all used the diary method by which each respondent's time allocation was captured during a 24-hour period.[13] The surveys differ in terms of their mode of data collection (see Table 10.2), but the empirical literature suggests that these various modes of

Table 10.2 Time-use surveys

Country	Title of the survey	Year of the survey	Age range	No of cases[a]	Response rate[b]	Type of diary	Mode of data collection	Survey period
Canada[c]	Time-use (General Social Survey, Cycle 7)	1992	15+	8,996	77%	1-day diary	"Yesterday" diary, telephone interview	12 months (January to December)
Germany[d]	Time Budget Survey	1991/92	12+	25,812	Quota	2-day diary	"Fresh" self-completed diary and home visit	4 months (October 1991 and January, April, July 1992)
Italy[e]	L'Uso del Tempo in Italia (The use of time in Italy)	1988/89	0+	37,724	75%	2 or 3-day diary	"Fresh" self-completed diary	12 months (June 1988–May 1989)
Sweden[f]	Time-use survey	1990/91	20–69	7,140	75%	2-day diary	Home visit and "Fresh" self-completed diary (mailed back)	2 months (September 1990 and May 1991)

Sources: Fisher (2002) and country-specific information.

Notes

a Total number of complete diaries. The actual number of respondents is smaller.
b Response rate for the total sample.
c Canada: A time-use survey was also carried out in 1998. We used the 1992 survey since it was closer in time to the other surveys used in this chapter.
d Germany: A new time-use survey is currently in the field (2000/01).
e Italy: A new time-use survey is scheduled to take place in 2002/03.
f Sweden: A time-use survey was carried out in 2000/01. The data was not available at the time of writing this chapter.

data collection do not affect the comparability of the data (Robinson and Godbey 1999). Samples are all nationally representative. Response rates for the Canadian, Italian, and Swedish surveys were around 75 percent. The response rate is unknown in Germany as a quota sample was used.

For the purpose of this chapter, we focus on married or cohabiting couples with children. We also consider single adults and couples without children as benchmarks for analytical purposes. In order to exclude older childless couples, and older couples whose children may already have left home, we restrict the analysis to married or cohabiting individuals aged 25–49 years. In our analysis, we define full-time workers as those employed 30 or more hours per week, and part-time workers as those employed less than 30 hours per week. The full-time and part-time status was determined on the basis of data about the number of hours of work during the week prior to the survey. However, this information was not available in the Italian survey, thus only allowing us to distinguish employed from nonemployed individuals (for the purpose of this analysis, full-time in Italy, therefore, includes both full-time and part-time). Summary information in terms of number of cases, number of children, and weekly work hours is reported in Table 10A.1 in Appendix.

These four surveys were harmonized into a common set of background and time-use variables. For the purpose of this chapter, we distinguish three main categories of activities: paid work (including travel to and from work), housework, and childcare.

Method of analysis

Our method of analysis proceeds in two steps. First, we examine the cross-national differences in the labor force composition of parents. Although our interest is mainly in the pattern of time-use of dual-earner couples, it is important to stress that dual-earner couples represent a very different fraction of all couples with children in all countries (the likely result of cross-national differences in ideologies and in welfare state support for families). We then move to the analysis of patterns of time use. We examine how time spent on paid work, housework, and childcare varies with the presence and age of children in the four countries, and how it varies with the employment status of spouses. Results presented in the empirical section are based on data that has been weighted for both population sampling issues and the day of the week.[14]

Data limitations

Although diary data is considered in the literature to be more reliable than stylized data about how much time was devoted to a specific activity during a recall period of one week, or one month (Robinson and Godbey 1999), our data nevertheless has some limitations. First, we should stress that we are basing our analysis on the so-called primary activity, that is, the main activity that was reported on respondents' diaries. For the purpose of this chapter, we ignore secondary (or simultaneous) activities. This omission is likely to lead to an underestimation of time spent on some activities, especially childcare since the supervision of children is often carried out in parallel to some other activities, for example cleaning or cooking. Second, we should also stress that by adopting a life-cycle perspective, we are giving a longitudinal interpretation to cross-sectional data. This may result in biased conclusions if there is a selectivity process at work by which adults who decide to have children have different characteristics (and a different allocation of time) than adults who remain childless.

Third, we should also stress that although we are able to take into account the employment status of the husband and wife, our analysis is done on an individual basis and not on a couple basis. In other words, we are not matching the diaries of husbands and wives, and have to assume that there is a correspondence between the average time use of married women in dual-income couples and that of married men in dual-income couples. Only in Italy and Germany was data collected from more than one household member. We did not exploit this information here (i.e. we did not match husbands and wives).

Finally, in view of the very restricted cross-national literature on family time, we opted for a descriptive analysis in this chapter rather than a multivariate analysis. While this allowed us to estimate time devoted to specific activities while controlling for some factors (such as employment and family status), it prevented us from testing whether some of the intra- and inter-national differences were statistically significant. This is a shortcoming considering the fact that dual-earner families in the four countries do differ on key characteristics such as their average number of children and average weekly hours of work: characteristics that are known to influence the time availability of parents and their family responsibilities. Therefore, part of the cross-national differences that will be reported in the next section may be due to these differences.

Results

We begin our analysis by looking at the composition of the population by employment status. Here, we restrict our analysis to married (or common-law) individuals aged 25–49 years. Results in Table 10.3 show that among parents with children under the 5, dual-earners represented 35 percent of cases in Canada, 44 percent in Italy, 48 percent in Germany, and 56 percent in Sweden. Of these, a larger percentage of respondents were employed full-time (as opposed to part-time) in Canada and Sweden. The reverse was observed in Germany. Full-time earners also represent a larger percentage of cases when older children are present, as opposed to younger children.

What this data suggests is that a larger proportion of parents are able to combine full-time work and family responsibilities in Sweden, as compared to other countries, likely because of the more extensive provision of childcare facilities. Similarly, the greater availability of part-time work in Sweden and the possibility of reduced hours of work for parents also mean that a large proportion of parents are able to combine part-time work and family responsibilities. The

Table 10.3 Distribution of cases by employment and family status by country (%) (married or cohabiting individuals aged 25–49, weighted data)

Family status	Employment status[a]	Canada	Italy	Sweden	Germany
No child	FT/FT	47.9	50.3	69.2	54.3
	FT/PT	6.9	0.0	9.0	16.6
	FT/NE	28.7	40.5	13.5	19.3
	Other	16.4	9.3	8.2	9.8
	Total	100.0	100.0	100.0	100.0
Child <5	FT/FT	27.5	43.7	33.0	21.0
	FT/PT	7.1	0.0	23.0	27.2
	FT/NE	52.3	51.1	38.4	48.3
	Other	13.1	5.2	5.7	3.4
	Total	100.0	100.0	100.0	100.0
Child 5+	FT/FT	46.4	43.9	59.2	32.0
	FT/PT	9.7	0.0	20.5	26.8
	FT/NE	30.3	49.4	16.9	31.2
	Other	13.6	6.8	3.4	10.0
	Total	100.0	100.0	100.0	100.0

Note

a FT/FT: full-time dual-earners; FT/PT: husband is full-time employed, spouse is part-time employed; FT/NE: husband is full-time employed, spouse is not employed; "Other" includes cases for which the husband was not employed or employed part-time (in Canada, this category also includes cases for which the number of hours of work was unknown).

relationship between state support for families and employment status is complex, however. For example, the high percentage of part-time work in Germany is likely the result of the very short school schedule of children which, combined with limited childcare, means that mothers oftentimes have to opt for part-time work to suit their children's schedule. As for Canada and Italy, the large percentage of one-earner families likely reflects gender ideology (in Italy) and a lack of childcare facilities (in Canada).

It should be noted here that the distribution of cases in Table 10.3 is based on information about the main activity of the respondent during the week prior to the survey. In Canada, Germany, and Sweden, there was a separate category for being on maternity or parental leave. Respondents who answered that they were on maternity or parental leave were coded as being not employed in our analysis.[15]

The second part of our story is related to the organization of time after controlling for differences in the composition of the population by employment status. In other words, how do full-time dual-earner couples use their time? Results appear in Figure 10.1 and distinguish full-time dual-earners without children under 18, with children under 5, and with children aged 5 and over. Among full-time dual earners without children, men and women devote around 6–7 hours per day on paid work (weekly average),[16] and about 1–3 hours per day on housework. Surprisingly, the sum of paid and unpaid work is relatively equal across the four countries and between men and women. The only major

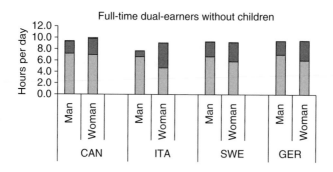

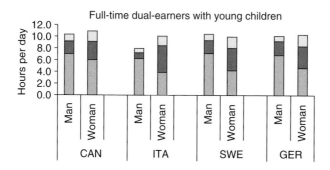

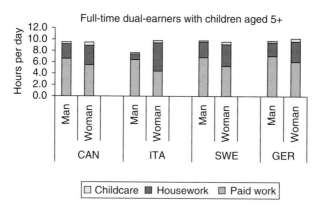

Figure 10.1 Allocation of time to paid work, housework, and childcare by full-time dual-earners by gender, family status, and country (weighted data).

difference is observed in Italy with men devoting a very small amount of time to housework, and women devoting a very large amount of time to it (Italian women also devote the smallest amount of time to paid work).

How does the birth of children alter this organization of time? In all four countries, the presence of young children under 5 years increases the total time devoted to paid and unpaid work, by about 1 hour per day. While 1 hour per day may seem very small, we again have to stress the fact that time devoted to child-care typically occurs in parallel to another activity, and is likely under-estimated in our analysis. In addition, with the exception of Italy, the total time spent on paid and unpaid work is surprisingly equal across genders. Women in Canada and Germany devote slightly more time to the combined paid and unpaid work activities, while the opposite is observed in Sweden. Furthermore, the presence of young children tends to enlarge the gap between men and women, especially in Italy.

What Figure 10.1 also shows is that while the arrival of children does not affect time devoted to paid work by men, it reduces it for women in all four countries. Even though mothers with young children are still working full-time (as in Figure 10.1), they are devoting less time to paid work than their childless counterparts. This reduction is around 1 hour per day and may reflect an agreed reduction in the workweek with the employer, or a reduction caused by absences from work (likely to take care of children). Such a scenario is possible in Sweden where parents have the right to reduce their hours of work by 25 percent until their child has completed the first year of school (Moss and Deven 1999). The reduction in hours of paid work following the transition to motherhood may also reflect the greater flexibility of the Swedish parental leave system which can be taken in fraction of days or whole days until the child is 8 years old. It may also result from mothers taking time off because of a child's sickness (up to 120 days per year are allowed) or because of problems with their childcare arrangements.

Figure 10.2 presents the same results activity by activity in order to further highlight the cross-national differences and the differences by family status. The data is again restricted to full-time dual-earners. The first thing to notice is that men in all four countries devote similar amounts of time to paid work, and that this time allocation is relatively insensitive to family status. However, and as pointed out earlier, women's allocation of time to paid work is reduced with the transition to motherhood, and slightly picks up again when the children are older (with the exception of Canada).

In Canada, Germany, and Sweden, men devote around 2 hours per day to housework, while Italian men devote only 1 hour per day to this activity. Moreover, time devoted to housework by men appears to be relatively insensitive to family status. In contrast, time devoted to housework by women does increase with the transition to motherhood. It is also slightly higher when children are 5 years old and over than when children are younger. Time devoted to childcare follows a different pattern and is higher when younger children are present than when older children are present. In all four countries, women devote substantially more time to childcare than men. However, the gender difference is much smaller when older children are present.

Finally, in Figure 10.3, we turn our focus to the variations in patterns of time-use by employment status. This time, we restrict the analysis to parents with children under the age of 5. Our objective here is to see the extent to which fathers alter their allocation of time according to their wife's employment status. For the purpose of this analysis, we only examine couples in which men are employed

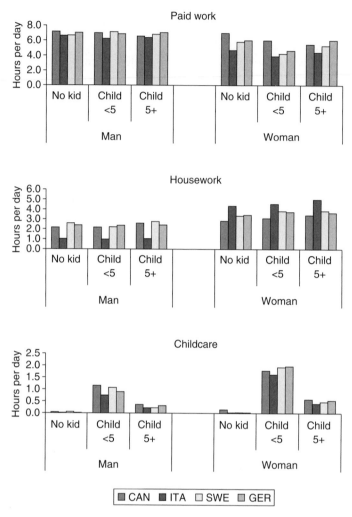

Figure 10.2 Allocation of time to paid work, housework, and childcare by full-time dual-earners by gender, family status, and country (weighted data).

full-time (i.e. only the employment status of mothers is allowed to vary). Results show that men's patterns of time-use are hardly affected by their wives' employment status. Fathers whose wives are employed full-time, part-time, or not employed devote surprisingly the same amount of time to paid work, housework, and childcare. In other words, fathers in dual-earner couples do not contribute more to housework and childcare than fathers in single-earner couples. What is also particularly interesting is the relative similarity across countries in men's allocation of time, with the notable exception of Italian men.

As for mothers, their allocation of time obviously varies with their employment status in that full-time employed mothers devote more time to paid work

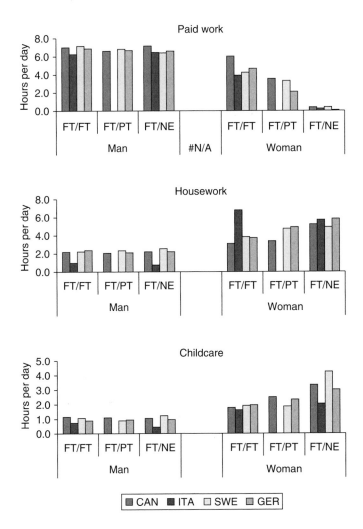

Figure 10.3 Allocation of time to paid work, housework, and childcare by parents with children under the age of 5 by gender, employment status, and country (weighted data).

than nonemployed mothers, and less time to housework and childcare. However, there is no perfect substitution. Full-time employed mothers devote more time to paid and unpaid work (combined) than nonemployed mothers. The difference is about 2 hours per day in Canada and Germany, only 1/2 hour per day in Sweden, and 4 hours per day in Italy. Italian mothers who are employed full-time are obviously confronted with an enormous double shift, much higher than their counterparts in the other countries.

The organization of care is a complex story: one that varies according to the demographic composition of the family (number and age of children), household structure (and the presence of nonbiological caregivers in the household), labor force status of the spouses, weekdays versus weekends, the time of the year (school versus nonschool months), and the macro-level organization of work and childcare. It was not possible here to examine the contribution of all these factors to the organization of care. Our focus on dual-earner parents nonetheless revealed some substantial differences in the organization of care – and more generally, in the total allocation of time to paid and unpaid work – in the four countries. In particular, dual-earner parents in Canada appeared to be the most egalitarian in their allocation of time. Both devote long hours to paid work, and both share relatively equally in unpaid work. This may be relatively surprising considering the limited state support for working parents in Canada, including the limited provision of public childcare and the relatively short duration of parental leave.

Dual-earner parents in Sweden, on the other hand, appeared to share paid and unpaid work in a much less gender equal way than what would be expected. Women, and not men, appear to take advantage of the flexible work and parental leave arrangement, and consequently devote relatively little time to paid work (even if employed full-time) and relatively more time to unpaid work. This result is in line with other studies showing that Swedish fathers take only a small proportion of parental leave days (about 10 percent of all days taken) (Haas and Hwang 1999).

Dual-earner parents in Germany share some characteristics with their Swedish counterparts with women largely reducing their hours of paid work when young children are present, and by devoting more hours to unpaid work. This may reflect the very low take-up rate of parental leave by fathers in Germany (less than 2 percent of fathers) (Pettinger 1999), and the relatively low provision of public childcare for very young children.

Finally, dual-earner parents in Italy have the most unequal gender division of paid and unpaid work, with women assuming a very large share of the total time devoted to unpaid work. Even when time devoted to paid and unpaid work is combined, Italian dual-earners still have the most unequal gender division of labor. On the other hand, and somewhat surprisingly, Italian mothers devote the least amount of time to childcare as compared to mothers in the other three countries (but devote the largest amount of time to housework). There are three possible explanations. First, it is possible that Italian mothers may be devoting as much time (or even more) to childcare than mothers in the other countries, but that they are less likely to report childcare as a primary activity. Second, it is also possible that somebody else in the household is looking after children, for example the grandmother, in view of the higher proportion of two- and three-generation households in Italy (Treas and Cohen 2001). Finally, Italy has an extensive system of pre-school institutions for children aged 3 and above (Meyers and Gornick 2001). Therefore, mothers may not need to devote as much time to their children as mothers in the other countries because their pre-school children are more likely to be at school during the day.[17]

While these findings may not directly test the relationship between the macro-level organization of work and care and the individuals' allocation of time, they nevertheless suggest that macro-level factors may affect the organization of time of dual-earners by providing both constraints and opportunities.

Conclusion

In examining the way that dual-earner couples organize their time in four countries, we have attempted to highlight the possible ways in which macro-level phenomena, such as institutions and state policies, are linked to micro-level behaviors, in this case the organization of time. Our further objective was to broaden the research on family time by including paid work, housework, and childcare. Our findings indicate that the organization of family time varies significantly by gender, presence and age of children, and employment status. In addition, there are considerable variations across countries.

Using the four theoretical frameworks discussed earlier, we can draw several conclusions about our findings. From a resource-power perspective, we expected that countries having a relatively small gender gap in earnings (such as Sweden) would also have a more egalitarian division of labor than those countries with a larger earnings gap. Our findings suggest otherwise. For example, in Canada, full-time dual-earner mothers with children under the age of 5 spend 1.6 hours more per day on unpaid work than men, as compared to 2.4 hours for Sweden. This is somewhat surprising given that Canada has the largest earnings gender gap with a ratio of 65 (male-to-female earnings). Sweden, on the other hand, has the smallest earnings gender gap with a ratio of 91.

Using a socialization/gender-role framework, we expected that, due to more traditional beliefs about gender relations, the division of labor between men and women in Italy and Germany would be relatively inequitable. Our findings do find some support for this perspective. While Italian men and women spend similar amounts of time in paid work when children are absent, the time gap widens considerably when children are present. Full-time employed mothers with children under the age of 5 spend 6.2 hours per day in unpaid work in Italy as compared to 1.7 for men. On the other hand, our results do not reflect the public opinion data on gender equality according to which Germany – and not Italy – displayed the most traditional attitudes (Kunzler *et al.* 1999).

According to the time availability/constraint perspective, we expected that parents in Sweden would spend more time with their children than couples in countries with fewer opportunities to reduce their time spent in paid work. This prediction was only partially supported by our findings. On the one hand, Swedish mothers and fathers do not spend more time on childcare than their counterparts in Canada, Germany, and Italy. On the other hand, and as mentioned in the methodological section of this chapter, time spent on childcare (as primary activity) captures only a fraction of total time devoted to, and spent with, children. In fact, full-time employed Swedish mothers devote more time to leisure than mothers in the other countries, and it is likely that a large fraction of this leisure is spent with children. Additional analyses on secondary activities and with whom activities were carried out would need to be done in order to shed more light on this issue.[18]

Finally, from a welfare state perspective, we were expecting parents in countries with a strong family policy to devote more time to their children because of greater opportunities for combining work and family responsibilities, but also because of the implicit importance attached to parenting. Of all four countries, Sweden has the most extensive support for families but, as seen earlier, Swedish parents do not devote more time to childcare than parents in the other three countries. Furthermore, Swedish parents do not have the most egalitarian division of unpaid work (Canadians do). On the other hand, the family policies in force in Sweden appear to be allowing a larger proportion of mothers to combine work and family responsibilities. Of the four countries analyzed here, Sweden displays the largest fraction of dual-earner couples.

In all four countries, especially when children are present, women spend substantially more time than men in both childcare and housework. The finding that gender is an important predictor of the organization of family time in all four countries is consistent with the literature. We found that the transition to parenthood brought a reallocation of time for both women and men, however, the transition effectively widened the gap spent in paid and unpaid work between women and men. We also found that the degree to which this occurred varied cross-nationally, with Canadian parents having the most egalitarian division of labor, followed by Sweden, Germany, and Italy.

These findings raise several important policy concerns and we conclude this chapter by turning to a discussion of the implications of our findings for welfare and family policy issues. Most feminists, progressive reform groups, and labor unions agree that paid maternity and/or parental leave policies are essential in order to promote gender equity (Baker 1997). However, it also appears that when benefits are "gender-neutral" – that is, available to both women and men – it is women who take advantage of these programs more often than men. For example, in countries with parental leave policies, mothers are far more likely to take parental leave than fathers, which has the unfortunate effect of reinforcing gender differences in child-rearing responsibilities (Presser 1989; Haas 1990; Baker 1997). Baker (1997) argues that this traditional division of labor is maintained (even in countries with generous parental leave benefits) because legislation is implemented within a gender-structured labor market where women do not enjoy the same opportunities as men. Therefore, social programs must also aim to improve women's labor market opportunities, especially in regard to pay equity. However, Presser (1989) notes that these programs alone will not resolve the gender-based inequalities that exist either at work or at home unless accessible, affordable, quality childcare is available to parents from all income groups. Finally, eliminating a gender-based division of labor will require ideological changes on the part of men and women that simultaneously encourage women's labor force participation and men's involvement in housework and childcare.

Appendix

Table 10A.1 Descriptive statistics

Survey	Employment and family status[a]	Women			Men		
		Number of cases[b]	Number of hours of work per week[c]	Number of children[d]	Number of cases[b]	Number of hours of work per week[c]	Number of children[d]
CAN92	FT/FT no kid	286	47.5	0.60	295	42.0	0.70
	FT/FT kid <5	149	47.4	1.79	139	39.6	1.84
	FT/FT kid ≥5	175	48.4	1.65	221	40.6	1.60
	FT/PT kid <5	39	47.5	1.94	24	21.1	2.02
	FT/NE kid <5	245	46.4	1.97	273	6.5	2.14
GER92	FT/FT no kid	567	n/a	0	626	n/a	0
	FT/FT kid <5	931	n/a	1.65	907	n/a	1.70
	FT/FT kid ≥5	1,169	n/a	1.56	1,321	n/a	1.55
	FT/PT kid <5	n/a	n/a	n/a	n/a	n/a	n/a
	FT/NE kid <5	1,155	n/a	1.84	1,026	n/a	2.00
ITA89	FT/FT no kid	278	42.2	0	294	39.4	0
	FT/FT kid <5	144	44.1	2.05	306	36.8	2.06
	FT/FT kid ≥5	271	44.1	1.28	454	38.0	1.31
	FT/PT kid <5	152	43.3	2.23	175	21.6	2.49
	FT/NE kid <5	320	42.5	2.09	204	22.4	2.14

(Table 10A.1 continued)

Table 10A.1 Continued

Survey	Women				Men			
	Employment and family status[a]	Number of cases[b]	Number of hours of work per week[c]	Number of children[d]		Number of cases[b]	Number of hours of work per week[c]	Number of children[d]
SWE91	FT/FT no kid	232	41.2	0		256	40.6	0
	FT/FT kid <5	330	44.1	1.85		327	42.0	1.89
	FT/FT kid ≥5	512	44.9	1.64		554	41.8	1.63
	FT/PT kid <5	644	42.9	1.97		606	16.4	1.97
	FT/NE kid <5	664	42.5	2.17		642	0	2.17

Notes

FT/FT no kid: dual-earner couple (full-time employed) without children.
FT/FT kid <5: dual-earner couple (full-time employed) with children under the age of 5 (see "note a" for exceptions).
FT/FT kid ≥5: dual-earner couple (full-time employed) without children under the age of 5, but with children 5–17 (see "note a" for exceptions).

a The category FT/FT kid <5 refers to children below the age of 5 in Canada and Italy, below the age of 6 in Germany, and below the age of 7 in Sweden.
b Number of cases used in the analysis (excludes diaries with more than 60 minutes of unclassified or missing time).
c Weekly number of hours of work (based on a retrospective question). These figures refer to hours worked in the week prior to the survey or to hours normally worked. Normally, women in the FT/NE category devote zero hours to paid work. However, results suggest otherwise in Sweden. This is probably linked to the fact that we classified mothers on maternity leave as being unemployed, but that these women may nevertheless have answered a positive number of hours normally worked.
d Number of children below the age of 18 (below 19 in Canada, Germany, and Sweden). Normally, we expect childless couples to have zero children. The 0.6 and 0.7 values observed in Canada is due to the fact that a category of living arrangement coded as "other" was classified as childless while in fact a fraction of such respondents appear to have had children in their household.

Acknowledgments

The authors wish to thank the Multinational Time Use Study and Statistics Sweden for having granted access to the data. The authors bear responsibility for all errors and omissions. This chapter has benefited from the financial support of the Social Sciences and Humanities Research Council of Canada (regular grant and Canada Research Chair program).

Notes

1 Real case drawn from the 1998 Canadian time-use survey. The names are however fictional.
2 For a more detailed discussion of this perspective see Kamo 1988; Brayfield 1992; Shelton and John 1993; Presser 1994.
3 For a more thorough discussion of the gender-role framework, see Huber and Spitze 1983; Greenstein 1996.
4 This framework is also referred to as demand/response capability (Coverman 1985), time availability (Perrucci et al. 1978; Hiller 1984), and the situational view (England and Farkas 1986).
5 More detailed discussions can be found in Esping-Andersen (1990); Sainsbury (1996); Korpi (2000); and Lewis (2000).
6 Since December 31, 2000, parental leave has been largely extended in Canada, from 25 to 50 weeks. See: www.hrdc-drhc.gc.ca/ae-ei/pubs/10-00.shtml. Also, the province of Québec differs substantially from the rest of Canada in offering a much larger support to working parents. In the context of this chapter, we ignore these provincial differences and focus on the Canadian average.
7 In some welfare state typologies, Germany is classified as belonging to the "modified male breadwinner" regime (see Walby 2001).
8 According to data from the International Social Science Programme (ISSP), 23 percent of respondents in West Germany were opposed to female labor force participation when dependent children were present (in 1994). In Italy, Canada, and Sweden the corresponding figures were 15, 6, and 3 percent, respectively (Kunzler et al. 1999).
9 The retail and banking sectors also regulate family time through their opening hours.
10 Cross-nationally, the United States tends to rank number one, not Canada.
11 The recent reduction of the workweek to 35 hours in France places it at a more extreme position than Germany. See: www.futurenet.org/5Millennium/5_35HourWork.html.
12 We excluded the United States from our analysis because there were no large-scale surveys carried out during our reference period. The 1985 survey was deemed too old for our analysis (and did not contain important variables such as the spouse's employment status), the 1992–94 survey was missing too many key variables for our analysis, and the sample for the 1998 survey was too small.
13 At the time of writing this chapter, data from the 1998 Canadian survey were available. However, data from more recent surveys for the other countries were not available (2001 German survey, 2002 Italian survey, and 2000 Swedish survey).
14 Data collection for the Canadian and Italian surveys was spread throughout the 12 months of the year, but not in the German and Swedish surveys.
15 Oftentimes, labor force surveys do not include such a category and parents on maternity or parental leave are instead coded as being employed, thus inflating the fraction of dual-earner families. This difference can be particularly large. For example, according to the OECD (2001), the employment rate of all mothers with children in Sweden was 87 percent in 1990, as opposed to 69 percent in the time-use survey.

16 This is the equivalent to 42–49 hours per week. While this figure may appear to be high, one should remember that the data takes into account any overtime, as well as time traveling to and from work (as well as coffee breaks).

17 Another possible factor is that the average number of children for dual-earners in Italy in our sample is slightly lower than in the other three countries (see Table 10A.1 in Appendix).

18 The harmonized version of the Multinational Time Study is currently restricted to primary activities and does not contain harmonized data with whom activities were carried out.

References

Acock, A. and Demo, D. (1994) *Family Diversity and Well Being*, Thousand Oaks, CA: Sage.

Baker, M. (1997) "Parental Benefit Policies and the Gendered Division of Labour," *Social Service Review*, (March): 52–71.

Bergen, E. (1991) "The Economic Context of Labor Allocation," *Journal of Family Issues*, 12: 140–57.

Bittman, M. (1999) "Parenthood Without Penalty: Time Use and Public Policy in Australia and Finland," *Feminist Economics*, 5(3): 27–42. See also Chapter 11 in this volume.

Blair, Sampson L. and Lichter, D. (1991) "Measuring the Division of Household Labor," *Journal of Family Issues*, 12(1): 91–113.

Brayfield, A. (1992) "Employment Resources and Housework in Canada," *Journal of Marriage and the Family*, 54: 19–30.

—— (1995) "Juggling Jobs and Kids: The Impact of Employment Schedules on Fathers' Caring for Children," *Journal of Marriage and the Family*, 57: 321–32.

Brines, J. (1993) "The Exchange Value of Housework," *Rational Society*, 5: 302–40.

Casper, L. and O'Connell, M. (1998) "Work, Income, the Economy, and Married Fathers As Child-Care Providers," *Demography*, 35: 243–50.

Coverman, S. (1985) "Explaining Husbands Participation in Domestic Labor," *The Sociological Quarterly*, 26: 81–97.

—— and Sheley, J. (1986) "Change in Men's Housework and Child-Care Time, 1965–1975," *Journal of Marriage and the Family*, 48: 413–22.

Davies, L. and Carrier, J. (1999) "The Importance of Power Relations for the Division of Household Labour," *Canadian Journal of Sociology*, 24(1): 35–51.

England, P. and Farkas, G. (1986) *Households, Employment, and Gender: A Social, Economic, and Demographic View*, New York: Aldine.

Esping-Andersen, G. (1990) *The Three Worlds of Welfare Capitalism*, Princeton, NJ: Princeton University Press.

Fenstermaker Berk, S. (1985) *The Gender Factory: The Apportionment of Work in American Households*, New York: Plenum.

Ferrera, M. M. (1996) "The Southern Welfare State in Social Europe," *Journal of European Social Policy*, 6(1): 17–37.

Ferree, M. M. (1990) "Beyond Separate Spheres: Feminism and Family Research," *Journal of Marriage and the Family*, 52(November): 866–84.

Fisher, K. (2002) Technical Details of Time Use Studies, Release 3, 30 June 2002. Institute for Social and Economic Research, University of Essex [http://www.iser.essex.ac.uk/mtus].

Gauthier, A. H. (2002) "Family Policies in Industrialized Countries: Is there Convergence?," *Population*, 57(3): 447–74.

Gershuny, J. and Robinson, J. P. (1988) "Historical Changes in the Household Division of Labor," *Demography*, 25(4): 537–52.

Glass, J. (1998) "Gender Liberation, Economic Squeeze, or Fear of Strangers: Why Fathers Provide Infant Care in Dual-Earner Families," *Journal of Marriage and the Family*, 60: 821–34.

Gornick, J., Meyers, M., and Ross, K. (1997) "Supporting the Employment of Mothers: Policy Variation across Fourteen Welfare States," *Journal of European Social Policy*, 7: 45–70.

Greenstein, T. (1996) "Husbands' Participation in Domestic Labor: Interactive Effects of Wives' and Husbands' Gender Ideologies," *Journal of Marriage and the Family*, 58(August): 585–95.

Haas, L. (1990) "Gender Equality and Social Policy: Implications of a Study of Parental Leave in Sweden," *Journal of Family Issues*, 11(4): 401–23.

Haas, L. and Hwang, P. (1999) "Parental Leave in Sweden," in P. Moss and F. Deven (eds), *Parental Leave: Progress or Pitfall? Research and Policy Issues in Europe*, Brussels: CBGS-Publications, pp. 45–68.

Haddad, T. (1994) "Men's Contribution to Family Work: a Re-Examination of 'Time Availability,'" *International Journal of Sociology of the Family*, 24: 87–111.

Haller, M. (1999) "Attitudes Toward Gender Roles in International Comparison: New Findings from Twenty Countries," in R. Nave-Herz and R. Richter (eds), *New Qualities in the Life Course, International Aspects*, Wuezburg: Ergon Verlag, pp. 45–68.

—— and Hoellinger, F. (1994) "Female Employment and the Change of Gender Roles: The Conflictual Relationship Between Participation and Attitudes in International Comparison," *International Sociology*, 9(March): 87–112.

Hiller, D. (1984) "Power Dependence and Division of Family Work," *Sex Roles*, 10: 1003–19.

Hochschild, A. (1989) *The Second Shift*, New York: Viking.

Huber, J. and Spitze, G. (1983) *Sex Stratification: Children, Housework, and Jobs*, New York: Academic Press.

Kalleberg, A. L. and Rosenfeld, R. A. (1990) "Work in the Family and in the Labor Market: A Cross-national, Reciprocal Analysis," *Journal of Marriage and the Family*, 52(May): 331–46.

Kamo, Y. (1988) "Determinants of Household Division of Labor: Resources, Power, and Ideology," *Journal of Family Issues*, 9: 177–200.

—— (1991) "A Nonlinear Effect of the Number of Children on the Division of Household Labor," *Sociological Perspectives*, 34: 205–18.

—— (1994) "Division of Household Work in the United States and Japan," *Journal of Family Issues*, 15: 348–78.

Knudsen, K. and Waerness, K. (1999) "Reactions to Global Processes of Change: Attitudes toward Gender Roles and Marriage in Modern Nations," *Comparative Social Research*, 18: 161–96.

Korpi, W. (2000) "Faces of Inequality: Gender, Class and Patterns of Inequalities in Different Types of Welfare States," *Social Politics: International Studies in Gender, State and Society*, 7(Summer): 127–91.

Kunzler, J., Schulze, H.-J., and van Heeken, S. (1999) "Welfare States and Normative Orientations Toward Women's Employment," *Comparative Social Research*, 18: 197–225.

Lewis, J. (2000) "Gender and Welfare Regimes," in G. Lewis, S. Geewirtz, and J. Clarke (eds), *Rethinking Social Policy*, Sage Publications.

McFarlane, S., Beaujot, R., and Haddad, T. (2000) "Time Constraints and Relative Resources as Determinants of the Sexual Division of Domestic Work," *Canadian Journal of Sociology*, 25(1): 61–82.

Meyers, M. K. and Gornick, J. (2001) "Cross-National Variation in ECEC Service Organization and Financing," in S. B. Kamerman (ed.), *Early Childhood Education and Care: International Perspectives*, New York: Columbia University, The Institute for Child and Family Policy, pp. 141–76.

Moss, P. and Deven, F. (eds) (1999) *Parental Leave: Progress or Pitfall? Research and Policy Issues in Europe*, Brussels: CBGS-Publications.

Orloff, A. (1996) "Gender in the Welfare State," *Annual Review of Sociology*, 22: 51–78.

—— (1997) "On Jane Lewis's Male Breadwinner Regime Typology," *Social Politics*, 4: 188–202.

Perkins, H. Wesley and DeMeis, D. (1996) "Gender and Family Effects on the 'Second-Shift' Domestic Activity of College-Educated Young Adults," *Gender and Society*, 10(1): 78–93.

Perrucci, C., Potter, H., and Rhoads, D. (1978) "Determinants of Male Family-Role Performance," *Psychology of Women Quarterly*, 3: 53–66.

Pettinger, R. (1999) "Parental Leave in Germany," in P. Moss and F. Deven (eds), *Parental Leave: Progress or Pitfall? Research and Policy Issues in Europe*, Brussels: CBGS-Publications, pp. 123–40.

Presser, H. (1986) "Shift Work among American Women and Child Care," *Journal of Marriage and the Family*, 48: 551–63.

—— (1988) "Shift Work and Child Care among Young Dual-Earner American Parents," *Journal of Marriage and the Family*, 50: 133–48.

—— (1989) "Can We Make Time for Children? The Economy, Work Schedules, and Child Care," *Demography*, 26: 523–43.

—— (1994) "Employment Schedules Among Dual-Earner Spouses and the Division of Household Labor by Gender," *American Sociological Review*, 59: 348–64.

Rexroat, C. and Shehan, C. (1987) "The Family Life Cycle and Spouses' Time in Housework," *Journal of Marriage and the Family*, 49: 737–50.

Robinson, J. P. and Godbey, G. (1999) *Time for Life: The Surprising Ways Americans Use Their Time*. 2nd edn, University Park, PA: The Pennsylvania State University Press.

Sainsbury, D. (1996) *Gender, Equality and Welfare States*, Cambridge: Cambridge University Press.

Scott, J., Alwin, D., and Braun, M. (1996) "Generational Changes in Gender Role Attitudes: Britain in a Cross-National Perspective," *Sociology*, 30: 471–92.

Shelton, B. A. (1992) *Women, Men, and Time: Gender Differences in Paid Work, Housework, and Leisure*, Westport, CT: Greenwood.

—— and John, D. (1993) "Does Marital Status Make a Difference?," *Journal of Family Issues*, 14: 401–20.

—— and —— (1996) "The Division of Household Labor," *Annual Review of Sociology*, 22: 299–322.

Singh, R. (1997) *Gender Autonomy in Western Europe: An Imprecise Revolution*, London: Macmillan.

Smith, K. E. and Bachu, A. (1999) "Women's Labor Force Attachment Patterns and Maternity Leave: A Review of the Literature," On-line: www.census.gov/population/www/documentation/twps0032/twps0032.html

South, S. J. and Spitze, G. (1994) "Housework in Marital and Non-Marital Households," *American Sociological Review*, 59(June): 327–47.

Strober, M. H. and Chan, A. M. K. (1998) "Husbands, Wives, and Housework: Graduates of Stanford and Tokyo Universities," *Feminist Economics*, 4(3): 97–127.

Treas, J. and Cohen, P. (2001) "Maternal Co-residence and Contact: Evidence from Cross-National Surveys," Paper presented at the IUSSP conference on the Allocation of Resources Across Generations. Taipei, December 2001.

Vanek, J. (1974) "Time Spent in Housework," *Scientific American*, 231(November): 116–20.

Walby, S. (2001) "From Gendered Welfare State to Gender Regimes: National Differences, Convergence or Restructuring?'" Paper presented to Gender and Society Group, Stockholm University. On-line: www.sociology.su.se/cgs/Walbypaper.doc

Waldfogel, J. Higuchi, Y., and Abe, M. (2000) "Family Leave Policies and Women's Retention After Childbirth: Evidence from the United States, Britain, and Japan," *Journal of Population Economics*, 12(4): 523–46.

Waltzer, S. (1996) "Thinking About the Baby: Gender and Divisions of Infant Care," *Social Problems*, 43(2): 219–34.

11 Parenthood without penalty

Time-use and public policy in Australia and Finland

Michael Bittman

After many decades of struggle throughout the "developed" world, unpaid domestic labor remains stubbornly segregated by gender. Despite demands for domestic equality, housework and childcare continue to be, in practice, primarily "women's work." A critical determinant of the distribution of unpaid work is responsibility for the care of young children, as the earliest works of second-wave feminism make clear (Firestone 1970). This chapter reviews evidence from time-use surveys in Australia and Finland to examine the prospects for the most frequently suggested solutions to adjusting the distribution of domestic labor between the genders: (1) renegotiation of domestic division of labor, (2) substituting market provision for unpaid labor, and (3) public provision of key services. This analysis shows the limits of private renegotiation, and suggests that institutions beyond the walls of the family home – the market and the state – are more effective levers, in the short term, for achieving greater gender equality in domestic labor.

Time-use surveys provide a remarkable window on the world of unpaid work. In this chapter, Australian data are used to represent the social policy regimes typically found in developed English-speaking countries.[1] Finland was chosen as a contrast country on both theoretical and methodological grounds. The proportion of Finnish women working full-time resembles that found in the United States or Canada but the level of public expenditures resembles other Scandinavian countries. Alone among Western nations, Finland represents an instance of a country that combines a high level of expenditure on the public provision of social services and a remarkably high proportion of the female population in full-time employment. While other Scandinavian countries, such as Sweden or Norway, spend a comparable proportion of GDP on social services and have high rates of female labor force participation, a relatively high proportion of this participation takes the form of part-time employment. In antipodal contrast to Australia, Finland offers a unique opportunity to observe what happens when patterns of employment similar to the United States are combined with high levels of public expenditure on social services. Fortunately, both the Central Statistical Office of Finland and the Australian Bureau of Statistics collected data on time-use in 1987. Only minor adjustments for local variations are required to make the Finnish survey comparable with the Australian survey.[2]

The problem

On average, the time that men devote to unpaid family responsibilities is half of that spent by women. Almost regardless of their position in the life course, men's weekly hours of unpaid work tend to be a fixed quantity.[3] The time women spend in unpaid work varies throughout the life course, expanding and contracting in accordance with their responsibility for others (spouse, children, or a frail relative). The largest shifts in women's time-use are associated with the care of young children (Bittman and Pixley 1997: 101–11).

A reduction in men's paid work hours generally results in greater leisure time, so that men literally can chose between (paid) work and leisure. The best predictors of the hours men apportion to leisure are the hours they must commit to paid work. For women, however, it is statistically more likely to be a choice between paid and unpaid work. In other words, the best predictor of the time women spend in paid work is how little or how much time they spend in childcare and other domestic responsibilities (Bittman 1992: 11, 70–2).

Taking all this information together, if one asks: "How do family responsibilities affect the life chances of men and women?" then the answer is that family responsibilities do not harm the careers of men but have adverse effects on the careers of women. The social disadvantages that flow from women's family responsibilities under current arrangements include:

- interrupted labor force attachment and downward social mobility – few women recapture the career trajectory they had before childbirth;
- lower lifetime earnings, and less employment security;
- increased exposure to the risk of poverty;
- increased dependency on a male "provider" and low marital bargaining power;
- restricted opportunities for public participation, since family responsibilities are organized around private homes.

Three possible solutions

The central policy question is: how can we best change this situation? There has been a lot of discussion about how employment could be reconfigured in a "family friendly way." However, this discussion only addresses one facet of the problem, focusing on what happens at the factory, the sales counter, or the office and neglecting what happens at home. Broadly, there are three means of reducing the undesirable effects of family responsibilities by redistributing unpaid work at home. Firstly, there could be a renegotiation of responsibilities within households leading to a more equitable division of labor between men and women. Secondly, the household could outsource some of their domestic labor to the market (thereby reducing the burden of unpaid work faced by women). For example, households could employ a nanny, purchase pre-cooked meals, pay someone else to walk the dog, etc. Thirdly, the state could absorb some of the responsibilities formerly performed by households. The clearest examples of this are government subsidized childcare centers, or state provided school lunches. Let us examine each of these alternatives in turn.

Social change through renegotiating the domestic division of labor

According to opinion polls, there has been a distinct change in men's and women's values concerning the sexual division of domestic labor. In Australia, as elsewhere in the English-speaking world, the large majority of both men and women believe that childcare, housework, and shopping should be shared equally between men and women (Bittman and Pixley 1997: 147–9). Researchers in this field of study talk about the diffusion of "egalitarian attitudes." However, actual behavior tells a different story. In Australia in 1992, the ratio of men's to women's average time spent in unpaid work was 34:66 (Bittman and Pixley 1997). The ratio is similarly unequal in all OECD countries on which there is information. When men's and women's average time in all forms of work, paid and unpaid (as primary activity), is considered the ratio is broadly equal (Bittman and Goodin 2000: 15–16).

A simple test of the rigidity of sex roles is the degree of segregation of domestic tasks. Segregation refers to the fact that a task is sex-stereotyped by being viewed as the exclusive responsibility of one sex, creating a division between "women's work" and "men's work." In 1992, Australian men continued to specialize in mowing the lawn and polishing the car, while women still did an overwhelming proportion of laundry, physical care of children, cleaning, and cooking. Perhaps more disappointingly, even when both partners are in full-time employment, that is, when the "breadwinning" role is shared, the sex segregation in unpaid work tasks does not diminish, with both men and women conforming to stereotype (Bittman and Pixley 1997: 113).

Summarizing briefly the history of the sexual division of labor in Australia 1974–92, change has taken an unexpected form (Bittman 1995). Although the gap between men's and women's average time spent in unpaid work has decreased, this has come about because of an unexpected sharp reduction in women's hours of unpaid work rather any large change in men's hours. The most dramatic change can be seen in the diminishing hours women spend in the kitchen, and in laundry, ironing, and clothes care. Women have also increased their activity in home maintenance and car care – both classical masculine areas of responsibility. In other words, women's hours of unpaid work are becoming more like men's hours. Let us call this the "masculinization of women's domestic labor." While men have increased the hours they devote to childcare their share of this responsibility has not grown because women's time spent in childcare has increased at the same rate. In the context of repeated moral panic about the neglect of children, the evidence shows that parents have been devoting an ever-increasing amount of time to primary face-to-face childcare despite falling family size (Bittman and Pixley 1997: 143–4; Robinson and Godbey 1997: 106). Naturally, time spent with children present but in the background and not the focus of activity may have declined. At the same time, contemporary child-rearing practices encourage more direct, and intense, interaction with children.

Why has change in the organization of domestic work taken the form of the masculinization of women's hours? After all, one might expect that, since men are as equally committed as women to the new values of domestic egalitarianism, these new attitudes would result in increased participation in unpaid work by men. How can individuals reconcile a strong commitment to egalitarian sharing of house-work, with the actual inequality in the division of domestic tasks (i.e. a ratio of 2:1)? Researchers so far have proposed two solutions to this paradox; "the theory of lagged adaptation" and something that might be called "pseudomutuality."

Jonathan Gershuny and his co-workers (Gershuny *et al.* 1994) assert that men need more or better socialization if they are to perform the more equitable roles of husband and father newly demanded of them. Due to a traditional upbringing, the theory goes, men lack domestic competence and appropriate role models. After a sufficient time, however, men will adapt.

However, longitudinal data do not support this hypothesis (Bittman and Matheson 1996). There is some evidence for a very small short-term lagged adap-tation (i.e. after 5 years men work out how to use the washing machine). But, the sons of women influenced by second-wave feminism are no more "housework ready" than the generation before them. Tracking individuals over time confirms that women's adaptations are far greater than those made by men, and that they are immediate. The changes in the pipeline appear, once again, to be chiefly in the behavior of women, with only marginal changes in men from the current or future generations. In the face of this evidence, it is hard to believe that short-ening men's hours of paid work, as some politicians are currently recommending in the Netherlands, will lead to a better distribution of work at home.

The alternative but phony solution to reconciling egalitarian values with unequal practice is "pseudomutuality." Pseudomutuality is a miscarried solution to the problem of a disjunction between belief in equality and actual inequality. Relationships can be mutual or nonmutual. Pseudomutuality occurs when the recognition of nonmutuality is forbidden or at least very painful. It consists of ways of denying nonmutuality or, conversely, of affirming mutuality where none exists. In a small-scale qualitative project researching 65 couples in Sydney, Australia, it emerged that this is a regular and relatively stable outcome. There are two chief mechanisms at work in the creation of pseudomutuality, namely: (1) misapprehension, and (2) discursive redefinition of equality. With the aid of these processes, men tend to inflate the size of their own contributions and diminish the significance of their partner's contributions. Women often colluded in these processes and usually found it difficult to raise these issues without, at the same time, raising the specter of termination of the relationship.

There exists an unexpected broad consensus about the need for equality in domestic division of labor. Men have increased their time spent in childcare but not at a faster rate than women. The accumulated findings of numerous studies, using a variety of methods, show that 25 years of exhortations and demands have not substantially increased the contribution made by men to the total unpaid work performed. The activities of individuals and governments over a quarter of century have not succeeded in renegotiating the domestic division of labor, except by making it more acceptable for women to spend less time. Equity between men and women is improving only because the time women spend in domestic labor is coming down, not because that of men is rising. The obvious question, then, is: how have women achieved this historic reduction? The answer appears to lie in the growth of domestic outsourcing services provided either privately through the market or publicly by the state.

Markets

Commodifying what was once produced in the home has been labeled "outsourcing." Continuing the tradition of the theory of economic progress (Clark 1940), the Australian business analyst and forecaster, Phillip Ruthven, provides a colorful description of the whole gamut of Western history in terms of outsourcing. "It is only by outsourcing of household activities that any industry can be created..." he claims. Ruthven summarizes this process saying:

- We outsourced the *growing* of things to create the agrarian age industries.
- We outsourced the *making* of things to create the industrial age of industries.
- We are now outsourcing the *doing* of things (services) to create the infotronics age" (Ruthven 1997: 2, emphasis in the original).

According to Ruthven, households in the agrarian or pre-industrial period "had to be or tried to be largely self-sufficient. They produced and consumed almost all the goods and services themselves, as household-unit economies." During the industrial period, households concentrated on working outside the home to acquire market goods, but most household services were provided on an "amateur" do-it-yourself basis. In contrast, the post-industrial age, is characterized by the growth of household service industries (Ruthven 1994: 1, 1997: 2).

Ruthven is not alone in predicting a significant increase in paid domestic work throughout the developed world. Many writers (Wrigley 1991: 318; Gorz 1994: 91; Hondagnue-Sotelo 1994: 50) have spoken about a "resurgence of domestic employment." Following the large decline in the percentage of the industrialized countries' labor force employed as paid domestic servants, until the 1970s all the efforts of researchers of paid domestic employment had been devoted to explaining why domestic service was characteristic of pre-modern societies (e.g. Coser 1973: 31).

Perhaps this association with feudalism, hierarchy, and servility explains the high level of unease, even alarm, surrounding the academic discussion of this issue, especially among feminists. Recent qualitative studies of domestic workers, in the genre of occupational studies, have tended to concentrate on the significance of paid domestic labor for dividing women, either by class or by race/ethnicity (Arat-Kroc 1989; Glenn 1992; Romero 1992). Work as a paid domestic servant in the homes of the wealthy, according to this view, is one of the few employment opportunities available to women of color and immigrant women. Paid domestic work becomes a "low skill," low-pay labor market ghetto, reproducing hierarchical relations of gender and race, from which there is little hope of escape.

Ironically, exploitation of women domestics is viewed by some feminists as the undesirable outcome of the very success of liberal feminism (Ostrander 1987; Meagher 1997). According to this line of reasoning, the growth in the demand for paid domestic service is seen as a consequence of the emergence of a category of highly paid women working in management and other formerly male-dominated professions. However, the very success of these women is predicated upon escaping the entanglements of home and transferring this burden to poorly paid domestic labor.

In Britain, the class nature of the "resurgence of domestic labor" has received more attention than racial or ethnic dimensions. The work of Nicky Gregson and Michelle Lowe (1994) has attracted significant interest. On the evidence of a rising number of advertisements, they conclude that there has been a boom in the demand for paid domestic workers, especially nannies and cleaners. Under a Thatcherite social policy regime which did little to redistribute wealth to the needy, the growing income disparity between double-income professional households and low-income households explains both the demand for paid domestic labor and the supply of individuals willing to perform it. All the English-speaking countries, including Australia and the United States, have experienced increasing dispersion of earnings over recent decades but the rate of this increase was faster in the United States and United Kingdom (Atkinson *et al.* 1995). The widening gap between rich and poor might be expected to increase demand for paid domestic services in all English-speaking countries, although this should be most visible in the United States and United Kingdom.

Household outsourcing can be studied through analysis of consumer expenditure surveys. My information is based on the analysis of three Household Expenditure Surveys (HES) conducted between 1984 and 1994 by the Australian Bureau of Statistics. HES is collected by means of an expenditure diary, and contains detailed information about expenditure on all items. Let us begin with an analysis of the most recent data (1993–94) about expenditure on the commercial goods and services which replace tasks entirely.

The first surprise is that the activity which is the source of so much hand-wringing self-reproach, i.e. cleaning, is the smallest item of expenditure. As can be seen in Figure 11.1, only 4 percent of households bought any cleaning services on the market in the two-week period covered by the survey. Importantly, in the face of increasing inequality of income, this proportion did not increase over the ten years of the study, even among the highest income groups – real expenditure between 1984 and 1994 remained constant (Bittman *et al.* 1999). Neither the level of expenditure nor the rate of change supports the proposition that there is a "boom" in outsourced cleaning.

Nine percent of households outsourced some gardening/lawn mowing, indicating that more than double the number of households outsourced the predominantly masculine activity of "yard work" than replaced even some portion of the

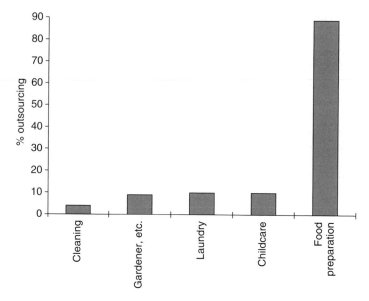

Figure 11.1 Proportion of Australian households outsourcing domestic tasks (in the last two weeks), 1993–94.

predominantly feminine activity of cleaning. Ten percent of households outsourced clothes care by making use of dry cleaning and laundry services.

While about 10 percent of all Australian households purchased some kind of childcare, a more meaningful statistic is that 30 percent of households with a child aged 0–12 years (the range used in the calculation of official childcare statistics) outsourced some childcare. Using expenditure to trace the outsourcing of childcare in Australia captures all formal childcare (both market and publicly provided care), since a cash contribution for childcare is required in all cases.[4] The expenditure survey records only outlays on institutional childcare, and does not distinguish between spending on privately run child care centers and spending publicly provided childcare centers. Childcare is obviously a significantly outsourced activity in Australia. It is also, as will be shown later, the fastest growing area of outsourcing.

All these varieties of outsourcing pale into insignificance in comparison with the outsourcing of meal preparation (meals out, food-to-go, and school lunches). In any two-week period, over 90 percent of households replace some meal preparation with restaurant meals or food-to-go. In an inversion of the pattern for practically all other activities, less than 10 percent of households shun market replacements for their home cooking. Over the decade, expenditure on outright replacement of home cooking (both sit-down meals out and take away) has increased steadily. Despite some concerns about low pay, lack of health insurance cover, and the attendant risks to public health, strangely, there is relatively little hand-wringing about women and immigrant workers in the restaurant industry, especially when compared with maids and nannies.

The greatest growth has come in the outsourcing of childcare. For a dual-income family with a child aged 3 years, expenditure on childcare grew faster than home cooking replacement. It has risen more steeply (24 percent growth) in the last five years than in the 5 years before (9 percent growth). The rate of increased use of outsourced childcare has been much faster than the rate of increase in female labor force participation. In the context of a discussion about substitution, it is noteworthy that parents' increasing use of childcare centers has been accompanied by increases in the time that both mothers and fathers spend in face-to-face activities with their children. It seems that the social investment of time in the care of children by both parents and their surrogates has grown, continuing a trend that has applied for most of the twentieth century.

The use of market services for gardening and lawn mowing is growing, but more weakly than food preparation and childcare. Laundry and clothes care have continued to move in the opposite direction to that of food and childcare, that is, from the market production to the household production. Perhaps this is because "Set and Forget" automatic washing machines and dryers make it possible to combine laundry with other activities, to schedule laundry in "downtime" for other major activities, and this eliminates the time costs of both travel and waiting.

How does the consumption of outsourced domestic services relate to social inequality? An analysis of expenditure patterns shows that the consumption of outsourced domestic goods and services increases as income increases. However, there is no case where these goods and services could be technically classed as luxury goods. Seventy percent of even the poorest households (in bottom 10 percent band of the income distribution) bought a meal out, food-to-go or a school lunch in the last two weeks. However, these low-income households in 1993–94 spent an average of less than US $5.00 per week,[5] while households in the highest 10 percent of the income range spent US $28.50 on meals out and food-to-go. As expected, among households with the lowest income outsourced food is more likely to be food-to-go than among those with the highest income.

The consumption of paid childcare among those with children aged 0–12 years increases regularly with increases in income. However, a high proportion of low-income groups have access to formal childcare in Australia and not that much lower than that of high-income groups (Bittman *et al.* 1999: 15). The predominant form of childcare service is institutional (expenditure on child minding center fees, creche fees, kindergarten or preschool fees). Less than 1.3 percent of Australian households with a child between the ages 0–12 years employ a nanny. Australians, it seems, typically do not use nannies and there has been no observable trend towards a change in this situation.

How can we reconcile these results with Gregson and Lowe's (1994) published results for Britain? There are two broad alternatives. Either things are very different in Australia, or using advertisements in *The Lady* is a poor way to measure demand, or both. In the case of childcare, the differences between the United Kingdom and Australia over the 1980s and early 1990s are likely to reflect the political differences (cabinet incumbency by parties with very different political programs), and the consequent differences in the balance of state and market provision. While Australia significantly expanded and subsidized institutional childcare places over this period, the United Kingdom did not.

Is there anything to suggest that the trend towards outsourced cleaning should be fundamentally different in the United Kingdom and Australia? It might be possible to argue that differences stem from different histories of class formation, so that Britain's aristocratic past is more conducive to paid domestic service than Australia's symbolic commitment to egalitarianism. Alternatively, the method-ological limitations of Gregson and Lowe's study may have misled them. However, the answer to these questions will remain unknown until there is a similar investigation of trends in domestic outsourcing in the United Kingdom based on a systematic analysis of expenditure survey data.

State

The major problem with relying on the growth of marketized domestic services to replace women's unpaid labor in the home is the issue of public goods. The present arrangements for rearing children inappropriately privatize the public goods aspect of children, penalizing women for becoming mothers (Folbre 1994). As might be expected, a solution for market failure to supply public goods is to rely on state provision.

In the age of dual-income families, one solution is to provide women with entitlements as individuals, rather than as wives or mothers, and to socialize the costs of children (Sainsbury 1996). This implies policies that encourage a strong attachment to the labor market and improve gender equality in earnings, espe-cially the lifetime earnings of mothers (Joshi 1991; Waldfogel 1997). Income from a living wage finances an acceptable standard of living during working life, and contributory superannuation can be used to ensure retirement incomes. Recognizing the public benefits means establishing institutions, such as parental leave and universal entitlement to childcare, which allow individuals and fami-lies to have children without being excessively penalized for this choice (Folbre 1994; England and Folbre 1999).

Many of these policy proposals have been introduced in Finland. Since both Australia and Finland conducted time-use surveys in 1987, there is the opportu-nity to compare the results of the naturally occurring experiment in social policy and directly study the effects on the distribution of family responsibilities.

As might be expected, men's "working hours" in Australia and Finland are roughly similar. Finnish women are more strongly attached to the labor market than their Australian counterparts. The most profound difference between the countries is the gender gap in average hours of paid work – the gap between Australian men's and women's hours is double that between the sexes in Finland (Bryson *et al.* 1994).

Conversely, as can be seen in Table 11.1, the average time spent in unpaid work by Australian women is significantly greater than that of either Finnish women or men from either country. Finnish women spend 22 percent less time than Australian women in unpaid work.

Table 11.1 Time spent in unpaid work (weighted population means – hours/week)

	Women	Men	Gender gap
Australia	33.02	15.40	17.62
Finland	25.78	15.17	10.61
National gap	7.24	0.23	7.01

It is equally clear that in absolute terms Finnish men do no more than their Australian counterparts (around 15 hours per week). Any progress towards sexual equality in Finland appears to have come from the reduction in time spent by women, and not as a result of an increased commitment of time by Finnish men. This pattern also holds true for the time parents say they spend in face-to-face childcare as a main activity. After controlling for confounding factors, Australian women's responsibility for childcare is consistently high through those years most crucial to career development. Compared to Australian women, the effects of childcare for Finnish women appear to be remarkably less burdensome. Indeed the Finnish women's pattern appears closer to that of men. Men follow the now familiar pattern of 3–4 times lower involvement, with Finnish men being involved the least.

In the relevant period, some 80 percent of parents of children under school age in Finland worked outside the home and so it is to be expected that the Finnish system of maternity/paternity leave and childcare is comparatively comprehensive (Huttunen and Tamminen 1989: 7). In addition to a child allowance system that provides parents with a modest sliding scale of benefits until their children are 17, the Finnish state provides maternity/paternity leave, nursing leave, reduced working hours, and compulsory education between the ages of 7 and 17 years.

At the time of the survey, expectant mothers in Finland were eligible for a government grant of 3 months maternity leave at full replacement of their previous pay. Up to 30 days of this grant could be taken before the baby's due date for arrival. All parents were granted a further seven and half months parental leave at 80 percent of previous earnings. Parents could divide this leave so that the father's share was up to but not exceeding six and a half months. In practice, only 5 percent of fathers took up this opportunity but most took 12 days off work after the birth of their child (Huttunen and Tamminen 1989).

In addition to leave, each new mother receives a maternity benefit to cover the basic clothing, bedding, and other equipment for the new baby. After the expiry of maternity/paternity leave, parents are entitled to nursing leave until their child reaches the age of 3. Parents taking nursing leave from their job forfeited their salary but were eligible for a cash benefit equivalent to the costs incurred by the state in the provision of municipal day care. Parents of children under 4 years of age and children just beginning school qualified for state compensated reduced working hours.

The 1973 Children's Day Care Act was aimed at ensuring the right to public support for day care for all children under 3 years of age. The Act prescribes the minimum staff qualifications and child/staff ratios according to the age of the children and the type of group and applies to both private day centers and their municipal counterparts. Additionally, family day care in Finland is run along lines familiar to Australians except that family day care staff must complete a minimum 250-hour course of instruction and are supervised by university trained overseers. By contrast, 63 percent of Australian children in 1987 were cared for exclusively under informal care arrangements, with relatively trivial financial support from the state. A high proportion of the remainder were in low quality care, whereas 78 percent of Finnish children received high quality state subsidized formal childcare.

Figure 11.2 shows the net effect of Finnish childcare policy. The generous maternity/paternity leave available during the child's first year, universal coverage, and reluctant fathers, combine to ensure that most Finnish children are cared for by their mothers for the first year of their life. Finnish women's childcare halves at the end of this period despite a significant benefit available to those who stay home to care for their own children. After the first 24 months of the child's life, Finnish mothers' time spent in direct childcare begins to resemble that of Finnish fathers, and continues to fall until children reach school age (7 years of age). Thereafter, there is an even closer convergence, all of which facilitates parents' speedy return to work.

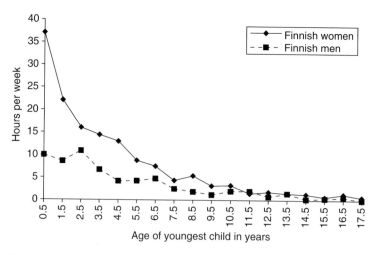

Figure 11.2 Parents' hours per week spent in face-to-face childcare, by the age of youngest child (1987).

Conclusion

In the current social context, family responsibilities are a significant cause of sexual disadvantage. The results of more than two decades of attempts to privately renegotiate the domestic division of labor have been disappointing. Women have generally been the ones leading the process of social adjustment. It is clear that institutions beyond the family – markets and the state – appear to be offering the greatest prospects for transcending the present inequalities. There may be a number of reasons for welcoming the process of outsourcing. The commodification of domestic labor need not arouse fear, provided that it is not part of a low-wage regime. Market substitutes for unpaid domestic work may reap the economic advantages of specialization and increasing scale. The comparison of Australia and Finland suggests that social policy can make a difference. Finnish social policies have not eradicated sexual inequality, but social policies can reduce its pernicious effects. The key policies seem to involve recognition of the value of publicly provided childcare that can enable women to have a continuing attachment to the labor market (bypassing the public good issue). The experience of Scandinavia shows that entitlements to generous parental leave, high quality childcare, and to family-friendly hours of paid work are all necessary components of an equitable solution to the difficulties of combining work and family in the twenty-first century.

Notes

1 Australian time-use data are among the highest quality data in the world (Australian Bureau of Statistics 1993), arguably superior to that of the United States or United Kingdom (which at the time of writing lacked large official time-use surveys) or Canada (which ignores simultaneous activities). The assumption that Australia is representative of the time-use patterns in other English-speaking countries is supported by broad comparisons of time-use in these countries (see Robinson and Godbey 1997; Bittman 1998; Bittman and Goodin 2000).

2 The Finnish data can readily be reclassified into the 57 activity areas used in the Australian Study. Since the Australian survey covered the city of Sydney only, the Finnish rural population has been excluded for the purposes of this comparison. Comparability was further increased by discarding the Finnish data on respondents between 10–14 years of age. The final data sets for our analysis comprise 1,611 cases for Australia and 8,820 cases for Finland.

3 The exceptions are sons living at home (whose weekly hours of unpaid work are a fraction of those of other adults) and the small category of men who outlive their spouses (whose weekly hours of unpaid work are similar to those of comparable women).

4 Of course, this statistic only tells us about the proportion of childcare outsourced through the market and the state. We know from specialized childcare surveys that the "informal childcare" provided without payment by relatives, friends, and neighbors, accounts for almost half of all childcare in Australia.

5 Using exchange rates current at the time of writing.

References

Arat-Kroc, S. (1989) "In the Privacy of Our Own Home: Foreign Domestic Workers as a Solution to the Crisis in the Domestic Sphere in Canada," *Studies in Political Economy* 28: 33–58.

Atkinson, A. B., Rainwater, L., and Smeeding, T. (1995) "Income Distribution in OECD Countries: Evidence from the Luxembourg Income Study," Social Policy Studies No. 18, Paris: OECD.

Bittman, M. (1992) *Juggling Time: How Australian Families Use Time*, Canberra: Australian Government Publishing Service.

—— (1995) "Changes at the Heart of Family Households: Family Responsibilities in Australia 1974–1992," *Family Matters*, 40: 10–15.

—— (1998) " Land of the Lost Long Weekend – Trends in Free Time Among Working Age Australians 1974–1992," *Loisir et Société/Society and Leisure*, 21: 353–78.

—— and Goodin, R. E. (2000) "An Equivalence Scale for Time," *Social Indicators Research*, 52(3): 291–311.

—— and Matheson, G. (1996) "All Else Confusion: What Time Use Surveys Show About Changes in Gender Equity," Social Policy Research Centre Discussion Paper No.72, Kensington: Social Policy Research Centre, University of New South Wales.

—— and Pixley, J. (1997) *The Double Life of the Family: Myth, Hope and Experience*, Sydney: Allen and Unwin.

——, Matheson, G., and Meagher, G. (1999) "The Changing Boundary Between Home and Market: Australian Trends in Outsourcing Domestic Labour," *Work, Employment and Society*, 13: 249–73.

Bryson, L., Bittman, M., and Donath, S. (1994) "Men's and Women's Welfare States: Tendencies to Convergence in Theory and Practice?" in D. Sainsbury (ed.), *Engendering Welfare States: Combining Insights of Feminist and Mainstream Research*, London: Sage, pp. 118–31.

Clark, C. (1940) *The Conditions of Economic Progress*, London: Macmillan.

Coser, L. (1973) "Servants: The Obsolescence of an Occupational Role," *Social Forces* 52(1): 31–40.

England, P. and Folbre, N. (1999) "The Costs of Caring," *Annals of American Political and Social Science*, 561: 39–51.

Firestone, S. (1970) *The Dialectic of Sex: The Case for Feminist Revolution*, New York: Morrow.

Folbre, N. (1994) "Children as Public Goods," *American Economic Review*, 84(2): 86–90.

Gershuny, J., Godwin, M., and Jones, S. (1994) "The Domestic Labour Revolution: A Process of Lagged Adaptation?," in M Andersen, F. Bechhofer, and J. Gershuny (eds), *The Social and Political Economy of the Household*, Oxford: Oxford University Press, pp. 151–97.

Glenn, E. N. (1992) "From Servitude to Service Work: Historical Continuities in the Racial Division of Paid Reproductive Labor," *Signs*, 18(1): 1–45.

Goldschmidt-Clermont, L. and Pagnossin-Aligisakis, E. (1995) "Measures of Unrecorded Economic Activities in Fourteen Countries," Occasional Paper No. 20. New York: United Nations Human Development Report Office.

Gorz, A. (1994) *Capitalism, Socialism, Ecology*, London: Verso.

Gregson, N. and Lowe, M. (1994) *Servicing the Middle Classes: Class, Gender and Waged Domestic Labour in Contemporary Britain*, London: Routledge.

Hondagnue-Soleto, P. (1994) "Regulating the Unregulated? Domestic Workers Networks," *Social Problems*, 41(1): 50–64.

Huttunen, E. and Tamminen, M. (1989) *Day Care as Growth Environment*, Helsinki: The National Board of Social Welfare in Finland.

Ironmonger, D. (1996) "Counting Output, Capital Input and Caring Labor: Estimating Gross Household Product," *Feminist Economics*, 2(3): 37–64.

Joshi, H. (1991) "Sex and Motherhood as Sources of Women's Economic Disadvantage," in D. Groves and M. McClean (eds), *Women's Issues in Social Policy*, London: Routledge.

Meagher, G. (1997) "Recreating 'Domestic service': Institutional Cultures and the Evolution of Paid Household Work," *Feminist Economics*, 3(2): 1–27.

Ostrander, S. (1987) "Women Using Other Women," *Contemporary Sociology*, 16(1): 51–3.

Robinson, J. P. and Gershuny, J. (1994) "Measuring Hours of Paid Work: Time-Diary vs Estimate Questions," *Bulletin of Labour Statistics*, 1: X1–XVII. Geneva: International Labour Organisation.

—— and Godbey, G. (1997) *Time for Life: The Surprising Ways Americans Use Their Time*, University Park, PA: Pennsylvania State University Press.

Romero, M. (1992) *Maid in the US*, London: Routledge.

Ruthven, P. (1994) *The New Age: What It Is, and the Implications for Business*, Melbourne: IBIS Business Information.

—— (1997) *Part 1 Business and Wealth Creation: An Historical and Future Perspective*, Melbourne: IBIS Business Information.

Sainsbury, D. (1996) *Gender Equality Reforms and Welfare State*, Cambridge: Cambridge University Press.

Waldfogel, J. (1997) "The Effects of Children on Women's Wages,"*American Sociological Review*, 62(2): 209–17.

Wrigley, J. (1991) "Feminists and Domestic Workers," *Feminist Studies*, 17(2): 317–29.

Note
Details of Australian time-use surveys

There are four large-scale time-use data sets in Australia. The first data set, produced by a survey conducted by the Cities Commission (1975), was designed to compare the lifestyle in a regional growth center (Albury/Wodonga) with metropolitan Melbourne. The Cities Commission survey collected data from only one respondent from each household in 1974. The other three data sets are based on official surveys conducted in 1987, 1992, and 1997 by the Australian Bureau of Statistics (ABS 1988, 1993, 1998). The 1987 survey was a pilot survey of the Sydney Statistical District only, whereas the other two were national in scope. The ABS surveys collected time-diaries on designated days at four separate periods over the calendar year (with the aim of capturing seasonal variation) from all household members over the age of 14 in randomly selected private dwellings. The diaries were formatted in five-minute time intervals, with space for respondents to record their main activity, "what else" they were doing at the same time, the location of the activity, others present during the activity, and (in 1997) who they did this [activity] for.

A team of coders classified the respondents' "own words" descriptions of their activities into a nesting 3-digit code. Most contemporary activity classifications are derived from a remarkable international collaboration under the directorship of Hungarian statistician Alexander Szalai, in which thirteen nations simultaneously conducted time-use surveys using a commonly agreed activity classification (Szalai *et al.* 1972). The Cities Commission survey adopted the Szalai activity classification and detailed concordances between activity classifications used in Australian surveys have been relied on ever since (ABS 1988, 1993, 1998; Bittman 1992).

Sample sizes and response rates for the various surveys are show in Table A1. Under Australian legislation respondents selected for official surveys can be required to participate. The ABS stringently enforces confidentiality and data security.

The mostly widely accepted benchmark for data quality is the average number of activity episodes recorded in each diary, with diaries containing over 20 episodes considered to have reached the threshold of acceptable quality (Juster 1985; Robinson 1985). The average number of episodes in each Australian survey is shown here.

Table N1 Australian time-use surveys, response rates

Households	1974	1987	1992	1997
Fully responding	1,492	681	3,013	3,321
Partly responding	119	130	889	850
Fully nonresponding	782	107	465	384
Total effective sample	2,393	918	4,367	4,555
Response rate (%)	62	88	89	92
Final sample of persons	1,492	1,611	7,045	7,281
Response rate for persons (%)	62	89	85	84
Final sample of diary days	1,492	3,181	13,937	14,315

Survey year	Average number of activity episodes per day
1974	27.9
1987	
Day 1	23.5
Day 2	22.3
1992	
Day 1	31.8
Day 2	30.2
1997	
Day 1	29.1
Day 2	27.5

References

Australian Bureau of Statistics (1988) *Time Use Pilot Survey, Sydney May–June 1987 Sydney*, Cat. no.4111.1, Sydney: ABS.

—— (1993) *Time Use Survey Australia: User's Guide* Cat. no.4150.0, Canberra: ABS.

—— (1998) *Time Use Survey Australia: User's Guide* Cat. no.4150.0, Canberra: ABS.

Bittman, M. (1992) *Juggling Time*, Canberra: Australian Government Publisher.

Cities Commission (1975) *Australians' Use of Time: A Contribution of Social Planning to Urban Development and Land Use Design*, Canberra.

Juster, F. T. (1985) "The Validity and Quality of Time Use Estimates Obtained from Recall Diaries," in F. T. Juster and F. P. Stafford (eds), *Time, Goods, and Well-Being*, Ann Arbor: University of Michigan Press.

Robinson, John P. (1985) "The Validity and Reliability of Diaries Versus Alternative Time Use Measures," in F. T. Juster and F. P. Stafford (eds), *Time, Goods, and Well-Being*, Ann Arbor: University of Michigan Press, pp. 33–62.

Szalai, A., Converse, P. E., Feldheim, P., Scheuch, E. K., and Stone, P. J. (1972) *The Use of Time: Daily Activities of Urban and Suburban Populations in Twelve Countries*, The Hague: Mouton.

Index